W9-CYX-927

A THIRD COLLECTION

Papers by
Bernard J.F. Lonergan, S.J.

Edited by
Frederick E. Crowe, S.J.

PAULIST PRESS ● GEOFFREY CHAPMAN
New York/Mahwah   London

Acknowledgement
The Publisher gratefully acknowledges the use of the following materials: "Christology Today: Methodological Reflections," which appeared in *Le Christ hier, aujourd'hui et demain* (proceedings of a Symposium on Christology held in 1975 at Laval University, Quebec), published by Laval University Press, 1976: "Aquinas Today: Tradition and Innovation," which appeared in *The Journal of Religion*, Vol. 55, 1975, pp. 165-180 reprinted in *Celebrating the Medieval Heritage*, Supplement to *The Journal of Religion*, Vol. 58, 1978, pp. S1-S17 is reprinted by permission of The University of Chicago Press; papers that appeared in Vol. 32 (1977) of the Catholic Theological Society of America's *Proceedings* and Vol. 51 (1977) of the American Catholic Philosophical Association's *Proceedings;* works of Bernard Lonergan that were published in the journal, *Lonergan Workshop;* "Mission and the Spirit" was originally published in *Concilium,* "Experience of the Spirit," in 1976 and is used with permission.

Copyright © 1985 by
Bernard J. F. Lonergan, S.J.

All rights reserved. No part of this book may be reproduced or transmitted in any form or by any means, electronic or mechanical, including photocopying, recording or by any information storage and retrieval system without permission in writing from the Publisher.

Library of Congress
Catalog Card Number: 84-61028

Paulist ISBN: 0-8091-2650-8 (paper)
          0-8091-0363-X (cloth)
Chapman ISBN: 0 225 66432 1

Published in Great Britain in 1985
by Geoffrey Chapman
a division of Cassell Ltd.
1 Vincent Square, London SW1P 2PN

Published by Paulist Press
997 Macarthur Boulevard
Mahwah, N.J. 07430

Printed and bound in the
United States of America

Contents

iii

Contents

PART THREE:
THEORY AND PRAXIS

Editor's Introduction

This volume of Bernard Lonergan's papers is in chronological sequence to *Collection* and *A Second Collection,* beginning therefore at 1974 where the latter left off and bringing us down to 1982. Further, the papers within the volume are likewise arranged in simple chronological order and, since they were all written in response to requests and the requests followed no recognizable pattern, there is no thematic order in the volume.

Publishers find that lack of unitary theme reprehensible—quite understandably, for they have to sell the works they print and need a topic on which to construct a sales pitch. Some readers too will find it reprehensible, for they buy a book expecting to read it as a book. So I draw their attention to the title, chosen by Lonergan years ago for the first volume of the series: it is a *collection,* very exactly that, and each item should be read as a unit and taken on its own merits. I especially recommend this to newcomers to Lonergan. ''Dialectic of Authority'' might provide them with ideas to ponder, and so might ''Christology Today'' and ''Pope John's Intention''; but, if they try to fit those chapters into a pattern, without some knowledge of the mind from which all three proceed, they are likely to feel somewhat confused.

Does that mean there is no overall unity in the collection? Those familiar with Lonergan will have little doubt on the matter. There is a unity, but it is the background unity of the mind that produced the papers, of the subjectivity that, from the base of a securely appropriated foundation, can move in many directions with surety and find ever new and continuously creative applications.

There are drawbacks to such a collection. An obvious one: cer-

1

tain passages are repeated, sometimes almost word for word. But it would have been unfair to readers to delete the repetitions and smooth out the remainder. Unfair to newcomers, if they take each chapter as a unit in the way I advise; but equally unfair to veteran Lonergan readers, who want to know exactly what Lonergan said and often find a sudden new and illuminating nuance in what to the untrained eye is merely repetitious.

Resisting the temptation to analyze these last writings of Lonergan, I conclude with a few scattered remarks on their editing. I acknowledge the omission of several papers many would wish included; but Fr. Lonergan did not agree to their inclusion and they are, after all, his papers and this is his collection. Most of those that are included had been published already, but there have been many editors with different ideas on what to do with his usage—not just in regard to spelling and punctuation, but in regard to his writing style too. My policy has been to revert regularly to the original typescript, to let Lonergan write in his own way, even if that means retaining minor flaws, like the misquotation (it seems) of a proverb. When we are reading a great creative thinker, we want his words not those of his editor; it may happen that a misquotation is relevant to the point he is making. My contributions are therefore almost entirely limited to spelling and punctuation, with the addition of a couple of subdivision headings and numbers. The footnotes have been brought into the form a volume requires, but I thought it would be a convenience to readers of previously published papers to retain the earlier numbering of the notes.

Part One

Tradition and Innovation

1

Dialectic of Authority

Authority is legitimate power. The dialectic will emerge from a reflection on power and legitimacy.

The source of power is cooperation. Cooperation is twofold. There is cooperation down the ages. There is cooperation at any given place and time.

Without cooperation down the ages human life today would not differ from that of the most primitive tribe. It would be not merely Preaurignacian, as the celebrated ethologist, Konrad Lorenz, has been repeating to students, but would resemble that of the isolated people recently discovered in the forest rain-country in the Philippines. Power today results from all the achievements of the past that have been accumulated, developed, integrated. Any present is powerful in the measure that past achievement lives on in it.

Besides the cooperation that extends down the ages, there is the cooperation that is going on here and now. The group can do so much that the individual cannot do. The group of groups is so much more efficient than the isolated group. Grouping groups is a device that can be reapplied again and again and, with each reapplication that results in an organic whole, power is multiplied.

As the source of power is cooperation, so the carrier of power is the community. By a community is not meant a number of people within a frontier. Community means people with a common field of experience, with a common or at least complementary way of understanding people and things, with common judgments and common aims. Without a common field of experience people are out of touch. Without a common way of understanding, they will misunderstand one another, grow suspicious, distrustful, hostile, violent.

Without common judgments they will live in different worlds, and without common aims they will work at cross-purposes. Such, then, is community, and as it is community that hands on the discoveries and inventions of the past and, as well, cooperates in the present, so it is community that is the carrier of power.

The exercise of power is twofold. For men live in two worlds. From infancy they live in a world of immediacy, a world revealed by sense and alive with feeling. Gradually they move into a world mediated by meaning and motivated by values. In this adult world the raw materials are indeed the world of immediacy. But by speech one asks when and where, what and why, what for and how often. Answers cumulatively extrapolate from what is near to what is ever further away, from the present to one's own and to others' memories of the past and anticipations of the future, from what is or was actual to the possible, the probable, the fictitious, the ideal, the normative.

As exercised within the world mediated by meaning and motivated by values, power resides in the word of authority. It is that word that brings the achievements of the past into the present; it is that word that organizes and directs the whole hierarchy of cooperating groups in the present; it is that word that distributes the fruits of cooperation among the cooperating members; it is that word that bans from social intercourse those that would disrupt the cooperating society. In brief, the word of authority is the current actuality of the power generated by past development and contemporary cooperation.

To a great extent the word of authority resides in the sum total of current institutions. By this sum total I mean all ways of cooperating that at any time are commonly understood and commonly accepted. Example defines roles and points to tasks. Custom fixes requisite qualifications and links consequents to antecedents. So in the home and in the educational hierarchy, in the learned professions, in industry and commerce, in politics and finance, in church and state there develops a vast and intricate web of interconnections that set the lines along which cooperation occurs and uncooperativeness is sanctioned.

I have employed the word, institution, in its broadest sense. It is the product of use and wont. It is the sum of the ways of cooperating that commonly are understood and commonly are accepted. It changes slowly, for a new common understanding and a new common consent are not easily developed. Nonetheless, it is within the matrix of use and wont that power comes to be entrusted to individuals within community. There is the spontaneous articulation of the kinship group. There is the need of leaders in times of stress. There is the advantage of arbitrators in disputes. There is the role of judges in settling whether injustice has been done and, if so, what satisfaction is to be made. By way of safeguard rules of due process are devised both with regard to the selection of officials and with regard to the manner in which their office is to be fulfilled. Such rules may remain unwritten. The officials may act only in the name of some subgroup in the community. But eventually there are rules that are enacted as laws, and there are officials that act in the name of the whole community.

So we come to a distinction between authority and authorities. The authorities are the officials to whom certain offices have been entrusted and certain powers delegated. But authority belongs to the community that has a common field of experience, common and complementary ways of understanding, common judgments and common aims. It is the community that is the carrier of a common world mediated by meaning and motivated by values. It is the validity of those meanings and values that gives authority its aura and prestige.

A rhetorical and juridical concept of culture assumed that one and only one set of meanings and values was valid for all mankind. Travel and research have dissipated that illusion. There are many differentiations of human consciousness: linguistic, religious, literary, systematic, scientific, scholarly, introspective. With each differentiation there is a shift of horizon, a transformation of available meanings, a transvaluation of values. So it is that from an empirical point of view culture has come to be conceived as the set of meanings and values that inform a common way of life.

Such meanings and values may be authentic or unauthentic. They are authentic in the measure that cumulatively they are the result of the transcendental precepts, Be attentive, Be intelligent, Be reasonable, Be responsible. They are unauthentic in the measure that they are the product of cumulative inattention, obtuseness, unreasonableness, irresponsibility.

Authenticity makes power legitimate. It confers on power the aura and prestige of authority. Unauthenticity leaves power naked. It reveals power as mere power. Similarly, authenticity legitimates authorities, and unauthenticity destroys their authority and reveals them as merely powerful. Legitimated by authenticity authority and authorities have a hold on the consciences of those subject to authority and authorities. But when they lack the legitimating by authenticity, authority and authorities invite the consciences of subjects to repudiate their claims to rule. However, subjects may be authentic or unauthentic. Insofar as they are authentic, they will accept the claims of legitimate authority and legitimate authorities, and they will resist the claims of illegitimate authority and illegitimate authorities. On the other hand, insofar as they are unauthentic, they will resist legitimate claims, and they will support illegitimate claims.

Dialectic has to do with the concrete, the dynamic, and the contradictory. Cooperation, power, and authority have to do with the concrete and the dynamic. Authenticity and unauthenticity add a pair of contradictories. The resulting dialectic is extremely complicated. Authenticity and unauthenticity are found in three different carriers: (1) in the community, (2) in the individuals that are authorities, and (3) in the individuals that are subject to authority. Again, unauthenticity is realized by any single act of inattention, obtuseness, unreasonableness, irresponsibility. But authenticity is reached only by long and sustained fidelity to the transcendental precepts. It exists only as a cumulative product. Moreover, authenticity in man or woman is ever precarious: our attentiveness is ever apt to be a withdrawal from inattention; our acts of understanding a correction of our oversights; our reasonableness a victory over silliness; our responsibility a repentance for our sins. To be ever attentive, intelligent, reasonable, responsible is to live totally in the world mediated by meaning and motivated by values. But man also lives in a world of immediacy and, while the world of immediacy can be incorporated in the world mediated by meaning and motivated by values, still that incorporation never is secure. Finally, what is authentic for a lesser differentiation of consciousness will be found unauthentic by the standards of a greater differentiation. So there is a sin of backwardness, of the cultures, the authorities, the individuals that fail to live on the level of their times.

The complexity of the dialectic of authority underscores what experience has long made quite plain. Inquiry into the legitimacy of authority or authorities is complex, lengthy, tedious, and often inconclusive.

A more effective approach is to adopt a more synthetic viewpoint. The fruit of authenticity is progress. For authenticity results from a long-sustained exercise of attentiveness, intelligence, reasonableness, responsibility. But long-sustained attentiveness notes just what is going on. Intelligence repeatedly grasps how things can be better. Reasonableness is open to change. Responsibility weighs in the balance short- and long-term advantages and disadvantages, benefits and defects. The longer these four are exercised, the more certain and the greater will be the progress made.

The fruit of unauthenticity is decline. Unauthentic subjects get themselves unauthentic authorities. Unauthentic authorities favor some groups over others. Favoritism breeds suspicion, distrust, dissension, opposition, hatred, violence. Community loses its common aims and begins to operate at cross-purposes. It loses its common judgments so that different groups inhabit different worlds. Common understanding is replaced by mutual incomprehension. The common field of experience is divided into hostile territories.

The breakdown of community entails the breakdown of cooperation. Different groups advocate different policies. Different policies entail different plans, and the different groups deploy all their resources for the implementation of the plans that accord with their policies. There may be a seesaw battle between them with the resultant incoherence and confusion. Or one side may gain the upper hand and then exploitation of the other follows.

Just as sustained authenticity results in increasing responsibility and order, increasing reasonableness and cohesion, increasing intelligence and objective intelligibility, increasing knowledge and mastery of the situation, so sustained unauthenticity has the opposite effects. But the remedy for the opposite effects lies beyond any normal human procedure. There is no use appealing to the sense of responsibility of irresponsible people, to the reasonableness of people that are unreasonable, to the intelligence of people that have chosen to be obtuse, to the attention of people that attend only to their grievances. Again, the objective situation brought about by sustained unauthenticity is not an intelligible situation. It is the product of inattention, obtuseness, unreasonableness, irresponsibility. It is an objective surd, the realization of the irrational. A natural situation yields fruits a hundredfold to the sustained application of intelligence. But an irrational situation is just stony ground, and to apply intelligence to it yields nothing.

However, beyond progress and decline there is redemption. Its principle is self-sacrificing love. To fall in love is to go beyond attention, intelligence, reasonableness, responsibility. It is to set up a new principle that has, indeed, its causes, conditions, occasions, but, as long as it lasts, provides the mainspring of one's desire and fear, hope and despair, joy and sorrow. In the measure that the community becomes a community of love and so capable of making real and great sacrifices, in that measure it can wipe out the grievances and correct the objective absurdities that its unauthenticity has brought about.

I speak of redemption from within the Christian tradition, in which Christ suffering, dying and rising again is at once the motive and the model of self-sacrificing love. But if one is willing to attend to the ideal types propounded by Arnold Toynbee in his *A Study of History,* a more general statement is possible. In that study, of course, Toynbee thought he was contributing to empirical science. Since then, however, he has recanted. But, I believe, his work remains a contribution not to knowledge of reality, not to hypotheses about reality, but to the ideal types that are intelligible sets of concepts and often prove useful to have to hand when it comes to describing reality or to forming hypotheses about it.

Relevant to present purposes would be Toynbee's creative minority, his dominant minority, his internal and external proletariat, and his universal religion within which a new civilization arises from the disorder and conflicts of the old. The creative minority are the representatives of progress. They are the leaders that gain the adhesion of the masses by successfully meeting the challenge of each successive situation. The dominant minority are the representatives of decline. They inherit the power of the creative minority, but they are unable to solve the problems that continuously multiply. The internal proletariat is constituted by the increasingly disaffected and disillusioned masses. The external proletariat are the less developed foreign peoples that are beginning to discover the weaknesses of their envied neighbor. In modern dress the internal and external proletariats would have to be related to John Kenneth Galbraith's multinational corporations. Religion, finally, in an era of crisis has to think less of issuing commands and decrees and more of fostering the self-sacrificing love that alone is capable of providing the solution to the evils of decline and of reinstating the beneficent progress that is entailed by sustained authenticity.

I have placed the legitimacy of authority in its authenticity. But besides the legitimacy of authority, there also is the assertion of that legitimacy, its legitimation. Legitimation is manifold. It occurs on any of the many differentiations of consciousness. In early human society it is a matter of myth and ritual. In the ancient high civilizations it became a matter of law. Among the loquacious and literary Greeks law was reinforced first by rhetoric and later by logic. Historians discovered that different laws obtained at different times and places. Systematizers sought to draw up codes that would express the eternal verities for all times and places. Philosophers sought principles that would underpin this or that system. But if the legitimacy of authority lies in its authenticity, none of these solutions is adequate.

By this I do not mean to deny what already I have affirmed. Besides authority there also are needed authorities. If there are to be authorities, then over and above their authenticity there is needed some external criterion by which their position can be publicly recognized. But while this external criterion is a necessary condition, it is not a sufficient condition. The sufficient condition must include authenticity. The external criterion need not be accompanied by authenticity. For in human beings authenticity always is precarious. Commonly, indeed, it is no more than a withdrawal from unauthenticity.

Such then is the dialectic of authority. It was well expressed by Barbara Barclay Carter in her preface to her translation of Don Luigi Sturzo's *Church and State* when she wrote:

> . . . in every form of social life and in human society as a whole two currents are invariably present, the *'organisational'* and the *'mystical'* or ideal, the one tending to conservation, to practical constructions that perpetuate an established order, the other to renewal, with sharpened awareness of present deficiencies and impellent awareness towards a better future. The distinction between them is never absolute, for they are made up of human individuals and reflect the complexity of human minds;

their action is an interweaving, the one eventually consolidating something of what the other conceives, yet they come together only to part anew; the conflict they manifest is the conflict between the ideal and its always only partial realisation, between the letter that kills and the spirit that quickens, and while the Church is essentially the expression of the mystical current in the face of the State . . . in the Church as in the State the two forces are perennially working.[1]

Previously published in Frederick J. Adelmann (ed.), *Authority* (Boston College Studies in Philosophy, Vol. III, Boston College and M. Nijhoff, The Hague, 1974), pp. 24–30.

Note

1. Luigi Sturzo, *Church and State,* tr. by Barbara Barclay Carter (London: Geoffrey Bles, 1939), p. 6.

2

Method: Trend and Variations

A scientific method will use crafts, skills, techniques: crafts to fashion its tools and instruments, skills to make the best use of them, techniques to obtain intended results. But in an essential respect a scientific method differs from craft, from skill, from technique. Each of these heads for a goal that is known in advance, that can be specified clearly and precisely, that will be reached if only one uses the means and performs the operations proper to the craft, the skill, the technique. But the goal of scientific method is never known in advance, for that goal is discovery, discovery of what as yet is not known, discovery often enough of what was not expected.

There is, then, a paradox inherent in the very notion of a scientific method, and it is just a part of this paradox that normally scientific development is a jump ahead of scientific method. Performance comes first. Once performance occurs, especially when successful performance occurs, there follows reflection. Only as a series of diverse reflections are pieced together, do there begin to emerge and take shape the prescriptions of a scientific method.

What holds for the origins of method, also holds for learning method. One may attain, it is true, a book knowledge, a merely notional apprehension, of method by reading a handbook on the subject. But a real apprehension, an intimate familiarity of what method means, and supposes, and implies, comes to most of us only through the long apprenticeship of studies at a university and work in a graduate school. Information is accumulated from books, understanding is advanced by lectures, the way to get things done comes to light in seminars. Slowly, gradually, for the most part inadvertently, there

are formed the habits, without formulating the precepts, of working
methodically.

Always there is very much to method that is too obvious to be
said, too routine to be listed, too familiar to be formulated. But however essential this massive underpinning of information in one's personal memory-bank, of cards in one's files, of accumulated insights
in one's outlook, of systematic investigation and subtle wrinkles in
one's procedures, still the light and meaning of it all reside in a central and irreplaceable experience. That experience may be had in
various ways. It may come in one's research when, as it were, the
darkness of a long and tedious tunnel yields to daylight and sun-
shine. It may happen when one studies and reflects on a work in
which great learning is, not a heap of odds and ends, but a relentless
procession of ordered fact overturning settled views and offering an
entrancing alternative. It may be just the denouement of a plot, conceived by the leader of a seminar, that week by week assembles the
data that upset anticipation and gradually establish the existence and
finally the breathtaking solution of a problem that had been ignored.
But whether one does so on one's own or under the guidance of another, in either case one finds out for oneself what is meant by discovery. It is that discovery of discovery that brings to light the end
of method, the goal to which all the tricks of the trade are directed,
the achievement without which all the tricks are merely tricks.

But if it is in the breakthrough that is revealed the living force
and lasting significance of method, it remains that the breakthrough
is the fruit of the tree of method, and without the roots of the tree and
the trunk and the branches and the blossoms there would be no fruit.
As science itself, so scientific achievement is the work of a scientific
community. It is within the scientific community that its members
are formed, it is on the past achievements of the community that its
current members build, it is through contemporary collaboration that
problems are given clearer outlines and the data for solutions are assembled and, if in this or that generation some individual has the
happy combination of acumen and industry and luck to achieve a
breakthrough, who would know about it were the scientific community not there to witness the event and to testify to its startling
quality?

The relevant scientific community not only witnesses and attests. It also is a judge. I once gave a talk to a group of psychiatrists

on a topic on which I had written a book, *Insight*. At the end there was a question period and in the course of it one of the doctors rose and remarked: "Our patients have plenty of insights. The trouble is they are wrong!" With the doctor, naturally, I was in total agreement. Besides sound ideas, there are merely bright ideas. Insights and ideas are very common. They are at most a dime a dozen. What counts is not the single insight. It is not the accumulation of insights. It is only the accumulation that point by point, all along the line, fits the data. It is the necessity of that fit that entitles the scientific community to judge the validity of a would-be breakthrough, for it is in the scientific community that there reside (1) awareness of what had already been achieved, (2) awareness of the further data still awaiting a satisfactory explanation, (3) awareness of the contribution actually made by the new view, (4) the grounded presentiment, the intelligent surmise, of new avenues for further exploration which now have come within man's reach, and (5), when the decision is a hard one, the additional exploration of virgin territory and the established anticipation of still further advance. As Dr. Kuhn has taught us in his *The Structure of Scientific Revolutions,*[1] in the scientific community, as elsewhere, nothing succeeds like success.

I have been setting forth a broad sketch, but to a broad sketch there must be added some details. Among them I would note the contrast of method with its elder sister, logic. Method is progressive and cumulative. It is progressive: week after week the New Method Laundry turns out perfectly laundered shirts, but scientific method does not keep repeating the same result; it keeps turning out ever new and fresh results. Again, method is cumulative; the new results are not just juxtaposed to the old; they grow out of it; they correct and qualify and complement what went before to yield a fuller and yet a single view.

In contrast, logic is static. Its conclusions, even before they are drawn, already are implicit in their premises and, were they not, then the concluding would be fallacious. Still, if logic is static, it is not useless. Its goal is an ever to be repeated ideal of clarity, coherence, rigor. At each step in its advance scientific thinking has to clarify its obscurities, iron out its inconsistencies, weed out its *non sequitur*'s. Again, as clarity, coherence, rigor are attained, there also is brought to light the need to move on. The greater the clarity, the coherence, the rigor, all the more evident becomes the contrast between the accepted view and the awkward outstanding data. So logic passes the torch over to method, and it is method's task to desert an established and logically ordered resting-place, to bring to birth a new viewpoint, to gain the adherence of at least a few followers, and by dint of clearing up the anomalies, which have blocked general acceptance, to win gradually the allegiance of an ever larger proportion of the scientific community.

I have been contrasting the static character of logic with the dynamism proper to method. In its most elementary form this contrast is that, what for logic are just propositions, for method are answers to questions. Just as propositions have their logical retinue of presuppositions and implications, so answers have not only their limited adequacy but also a larger inadequacy, by which they give rise to further questions. For a time answers to the further questions give rise to still further questions but, if they are restricted to a single topic, the flow of further questions will eventually dry up. There results a nest of interwoven questions and answers, and it is that nest that gives the context of any of the questions or answers on the topic. Next, topics are allied, and so lesser contexts merge to form larger ones bearing on a common theme. In turn, themes are related, to link larger contexts into still greater unities, and this process continues until there is reached what has come to be named variously, by Husserl one's horizon, by Heidegger one's world, by the analysts one's blik.

Now one's horizon, world, blik has interesting properties. There are objects that already have their place within it. There are others that can be fitted into it with a little effort or ingenuity. There are still others that do not belong to it, that can be accommodated within it only by altering or extending existing structures. The first class of objects are familiar; to advert to them is otiose; to discuss them is boring. But questions about the second class are relevant; to discuss them is interesting; to assimilate answers to them is to enlarge and enrich one's mental store. Finally, objects in the third class are just alien. About them one knows little and cares less. Talk about them is met with incomprehension. Books about them get no more than a passing glance. To have to study them only confirms the proverb that knowledge makes a bloody entrance.

These distinctions are relevant not only to describing a state of affairs but also to sketching the course of a development. As trees grow in the direction in which they catch the most sunlight, so generally there is a law of effect. Development goes forward where it succeeds. So one's horizon, world, blik tends to extend and expand where extension and expansion are already under way; and it tends to remain contracted and stunted where the beginnings of growth and organization have been haphazard, and repeated efforts have met with diminishing returns.

The key point here is context. To learn is not just the sensation of seeing or hearing or touching or the like. To learn is to perceive, and to perceive is to complete that hypothetical entity, the raw datum, with memories, associations, a structure, and one's emotive and expressive reactions. It is this difference between sensation and perception that underlies the range of strange phenomena called ocular illusions. The same difference enabled R. G. Collingwood in *The Principles of Art*[2] to urge convincingly that the artist paints a scene so as to be able to see it properly. It has Paul Achtemeier, in *An Introduction to the New Hermeneutic,*[3] correlating one's world with one's command of language: not only can one describe what one really sees, but also one really sees what one can describe. It led a chairman of a department of chemistry to remark to me a dozen years ago that theoretical developments in chemistry during the previous five years had enlarged enormously the field, not of knowledge, but of data. I would not upset the adage, Seeing is believing. But there is also some truth in the inverse statement, Believing helps you to see it.

It remains that believing can be too helpful. It can help one to see what is not there. What the investigator needs, what the methodologist recommends, is a mind well stocked with questions. The more precise and detailed the questions are, the better. So Collingwood could urge the archeologist never to dig a trench without first formulating just what questions he hoped to be able to settle or at least advance by the digging. If this advice of Collingwood's was not a little inspired by the aimless digging of amateurs, who not only discovered nothing but also destroyed the evidence that might ground future discovery, nonetheless it does contain the essential truth. The investigator needs a well-stocked mind, else he will see but not perceive; but the mind needs to be well-stocked more with questions than with answers, else it will be closed and unable to learn.

I have been speaking of one's horizon, world, blik, of the basis it provides for further learning and discovery, and no less of its limitations and the way they hem one in, so that one sees without perceiving, or again one perceives but lacks the background needed to understand. But it is not only one's horizon, world, blik that is broad or narrow, deep or shallow, ready to develop here and hemmed in there. Object and subject are correlative. The broadening, deepening, developing of the horizon, world, blik is also the broadening, deepening, developing of the subject, the self, the ego. The development that is the constitution of one's world is also the constitution of one's self. So for Heidegger man's being-in-the-world is an existential; his concern with this being of the self is concern with an ontology; and the psychiatrists back him up with their studies and speculations on the selves that fail to become. There is the frequently repeated remark of Freud's: Where the id was, the ego is to be. *Wo es war, soll ich werden.* There is Erich Neumann's use of Jung's archetypes to trace the origins and history of consciousness.⁴ There is Gerhard Adler's *The Living Symbol, A Case Study in the Process of Individuation,*⁵ depicting the transition from what Jung names the ego to what he names the self. There are the multiple personalities of unintegrated egos, and the schizoid personalities that are the concern of R.D. Laing in *The Divided Self.*⁶

I have been indicating elements in a dynamic and dialectical account of subject and horizon, self and world, ego and blik. The account is dynamic: it regards not just diverse states of affairs but the processes that bring them about. The account is dialectical for it speaks both of development and of limitation, of enrichment but also of failure or distortion or stunted growth. Such a dynamic and dialectical account is relevant to a method of religious studies in two ways. For, first, it is relevant to anticipations about the object. Just as we live in worlds as we know them, so too other people, distant from us in place or time, in class or culture, live in worlds as they know them. We must not expect them to live in our world. Again, as we are correlative to the world as we know it, so too are they. We must not expect them to be like us. Indeed, as it does not demean our own humanity that we are correlative to the world as we know it, so we must not think them to be less human than ourselves because they are correlative to their world as they know it. Nor is this respect for others, no matter how different from ourselves, a minor point in method. It is simply a matter of elementary intelligence. It is a matter of intelligence making us open to others, having enough in common with them really to inquire into their differences, to find the grounds of such difference, and so to come to understand them as they were.

But the dynamic and dialectical account is relevant not only to correct anticipations about the object of religious studies but also to confronting the student of religion with what a natural scientist would call his personal equation. Not only the people under investigation but also the investigators are human beings. They too live in a world as they know it. They too are correlative to their respective worlds. They too have begun their development from a heritage that rarely, if ever, is free from all distortion and aberration. But it is only as they become aware of all bias in themselves, only as they sedulously guard against all its manifestations, only then can they be genuinely open to others and really effective in coming to know them in truth and justice.

It remains the high privilege of method to raise the stature of individuals by making them members of a scientific community and so compensating for the weakness of any by the presence, the aid, the challenge of others. So the gifts of each become the leaven of the whole mass and, while this leavening process works its effects insensibly at any time, still over time it is not difficult to document its cumulative impact.

In illustration it will be most convenient to refer to Talcott Parsons' account of "The Theoretical Development of the Sociology of Religion."[7] The initial stage of the development was rationalist, evolutionary, positivist. Religion was regarded as superstition. It was explained either by biological or psychological factors beyond rational control, or else as a primitive pseudoscience resulting from a lack of accumulated knowledge, from limitations of technique, from an absence of sustained observation. Working independently as it would seem, Vilfredo Pareto disassociated religion from pseudoscience to connect it with sentiments; Bronislaw Malinowski associated rational knowledge and technique with the areas where they worked to acknowledge an englobing sphere of uncertainty and ignorance where magical practices took care at least of emotional needs; Emile Durkheim found objects to be sacred, not because of their inherent properties, but because of their symbolic function, a function he interpreted as expressing and reinforcing the sentiments most essential to the institutional integration of society; Max Weber finally on the basis of vast comparative studies was led to distinguish between problems of empirical causation (How did Caesar die? He was assassinated!) and, on the other hand, problems of meaning (Why do people die? What sense is there to it?); in the light of this distinction he maintained that the differences between Calvinist, Hebraic, Indian, and Chinese religion arise, not from differences in their social structures and social needs, but from different ways of handling problems of meaning.

As Parsons concludes, when we look back from the position of Weber to the nineteenth-century views of men like Tylor and Spencer, we find the latter hopelessly naive. Yet the shift was brought about, not by an appeal to any dogmatic religion or doctrinal theology, but by an ever closer and fuller examination of the appropriate data. Moreover, to this development one must add Parsons' own contribution, with the collaboration of Robert Bellah, which in the cybernetics of the social action system derives motion from energy and direction from information, places maximum energy at the bottom level and highest directional control at the top, has energy work upwards to move the whole system, and information to work downwards to direct the whole system, and finally finds religion itself the source of a principal directional control.[8]

The development in the sociology of religion, sketched by Parsons, is not some isolated freak, some accident or chance but, I should say, the normal product of method in an ongoing scientific community. For a time, often for a long time, fanciful guesses, wrongheaded opinions, mistaken philosophies can blend with science and deceive the academic world. But sooner or later they are exposed and, once exposed, forgotten. Forgotten, like the Euclidean structure of space exorcised by Einstein and Minkowski, like the necessity that ruled physical process up to quantum theory, like the iron laws of economics trumpeted on political platforms up to the depression of the early thirties.

It was suggested that I speak on *Method: Trend and Variations.* I spoke mostly of the trend, not indeed of some outward, historical trend that engulfs us and carries us along in its course, but of the inner trend by which our grasp of method begins, develops, takes command. Method begins with an apprenticeship, with doing what others have done, or advise, or demand. Method becomes meaningful in its own good time: when we discover for ourselves what a discovery is; and when we realize that the individual's achievement is a breakthrough because it occurs in a scientific community that needs it, witnesses it, attests it, judges it, embraces it, and sooner or later goes way beyond it. Method takes command when one assigns logic its subsidiary role, when one grasps how questions combine with answers, how they are woven together into contexts, how contexts merge into the horizons of subjects, how horizons can be open to and subjects can be eager for further development along certain lines yet, along others, subjects can be strangely inattentive, complacently obtuse, pompously irrational.

So much for the basic trend. It includes the variations for they, I think, stem from the resistance. One is told that the scientist is content to describe. But does that mean that he does not perceive? Or is perception identified with sensation? One is told that science is value-free. Does that mean that the scientist is impartial, that he has no axe to grind? Or does it mean that the psychologist reaches a scientific explanation when he can reproduce the process in a robot or at least in a rat? Can one be religious and nonetheless do scientific work in the field of religious studies? Can one be objective about one's own religion, about another's?

Such questions are basic. They admit practical solutions up to a point. But the full solution is to be had only on the level of a philosophic methodology, and not even there is a consensus to be expected. For ultimate issues rest on ultimate options, and ultimate options are existential. By them men and women deliberately decide—when they do not inadvertently drift into—the kind of men and women they are to be. Being a scientist is just an aspect of being human, nor has any method been found that makes one authentically scientific without heading one into being authentically human.

A lecture to the Southwestern Regional Joint Meeting of the societies affiliated with The Council on the Study of Religion, Austin College, Sherman, Texas, March 15, 1974. Previously unpublished.

Notes

1. Thomas S. Kuhn, *The Structure of Scientific Revolutions* (2nd ed., Chicago: University of Chicago Press, 1970; first published, 1960).

2. R. G. Collingwood, *The Principles of Art* (Oxford: Clarendon Press, 1938; reprinted 1945, 1955).

3. Paul J. Achtemeier, *An Introduction to the New Hermeneutic* (Philadelphia: Westminster Press, 1969).

4. Erich Neumann, *The Origins and History of Consciousness,* tr. by R. F. C. Hull (Princeton, N.J.: Princeton University Press, 1970. Bollingen Series, 42).

5. Gerhard Adler, *The Living Symbol: A Case Study in the Process of Individuation* (New York: Pantheon Books, 1961. Bollingen Series, 63).

6. R. D. Laing, *The Divided Self: An Existential Study in Sanity and Madness* (London: Penguin, 1967; first published, 1960, as *The Divided Self: A Study of Sanity and Madness*).

7. Talcott Parsons, Ch. 6 in his book *Essays in Sociological Theory, Pure and Applied* (revised ed., New York: Free Press, 1966; 1st ed., 1949, revised 1958), pp. 197–210.

8. Robert Bellah, *Beyond Belief: Essays on Religion in a Post-Traditional World* (New York: Harper & Row, 1970). pp. 9–12.

3

Mission and the Spirit

As man's being is being-in-the-world, his self-understanding has to be not only of himself but also of his world. So biblical writers not only employed Babylonian cosmology but also reinterpreted it. In similar vein Arabic philosophers remodelled Ptolemy's heavens, and in turn Aquinas reformulated their views on the order of the universe. Today with evolution naming the shape of things, Karl Rahner has written on "Christology within an Evolutionary View of the World."[1]

Rahner prudently omitted from his account the long series of discontinuities reaching from subatomic particles to mankind. But the omission only makes the more prominent the greatest discontinuity of all, the transition from the natural to the supernatural. Indeed, for Rahner this transition is especially arduous, for he is committed to the anthropological turn and, on that view, nature gives way to spirit, the supernatural at its root is divine self-communication in love, and the obediential potency of a formal ontology has to be translated into terms of consciousness.

I have been using Rahner to state the question I wish to discuss. It reads: What in terms of human consciousness is the transition from the natural to the supernatural? With that question alone am I at present concerned. No doubt, related questions abound. But in this paper I beg to leave them in abeyance.

1. VERTICAL FINALITY

By "finality" I would name not the end itself but relation to the end, and I would distinguish absolute finality, horizontal finality, and vertical finality.

Absolute finality is to God. For every end is an instance of the good, and every instance of the good has its ground and goal in absolute goodness.

Horizontal finality is to the proportionate end, the end that results from what a thing is, what follows from it, and what it may exact.

Vertical finality is to an end higher than the proportionate end. It supposes a hierarchy of entities and ends. It supposes a subordination of the lower to the higher. Such subordination may be merely instrumental, or participative, or both, inasmuch as the lower merely serves the higher, or enters into its being and functioning, or under one aspect serves and under another participates.[2]

The classicist view of the universe acknowledged hierarchy and the instrumental type of vertical finality. An evolutionary view adds the participative type: subatomic particles somehow enter into the elements of the periodic table; chemical elements enter into chemical compounds, compounds into cells, cells in myriad combinations and configurations into the constitution of plant and animal life.

Still one does not reach the evolutionary view simply by acknowledging hierarchy and the instrumental and participative types of vertical finality. An evolutionary view is a view of the universe. It can be fully grasped only by attending to the cause of the universe. For it is only as an instrument operating beyond its own proportion that the lower, as long as it is lower, can bring about and participate in the constitution of the higher; and it is only the cause of the whole universe that from lower species can bring about the emergence of successive higher species.

2. PROBABILITY AND PROVIDENCE

A theologian, if he thinks of evolution, turns to divine providence. A contemporary scientist that does so thinks of probabilities. Darwin's accumulations of chance variations have gained respectability as probabilities of emergence. His survival of the fittest becomes probabilities of survival. What holds for living things, also holds in inanimate nature. Quantum theory has ended the long reign of mechanist determinism and has enthroned statistical law.

An evolutionary view of the universe, at a first approximation, would be a conditioned sequence of assemblies. Each assembly would be an environment with its constituent species. It would function on the basis of classical law, and consequently it would continue to function until the disruption of its interdependent factors resulted from internal deterioration or external interference.

From any assembly to the next there would be a cumulative sequence of elements, where each element had its probability of emergence from the probability of survival of previously realized assemblies and elements.

In some such fashion, from a minimal beginning, schedules of probabilities of elements would link the emergence of successive assemblies of interdependent and mutually supporting factors. Granted very large numbers and very long intervals of time, Bernoulli's theorem of large numbers or, better, the De Moivre-Laplace limit theorem would make all but certain some close approximation to each step in the process.

When men operate on the small scale and can take all eventualities into account, they plan. When relevant factors are too numerous, combinations of agents too complicated, sufficiently accurate enumerations and measurements too difficult, then they have recourse to statistical science. But the omniscient and omnipotent cause of the whole universe does not operate blindly. He plans where men turn to probabilities. Nor does there come into existence, outside his planning, any agent that could interfere with his comprehensive design.[3]

3. THE SUPERNATURAL

Contemporary English usage commonly associates the supernatural with the spooky. But the term has a far older meaning, to which we have already adverted in speaking of vertical finality. For in a hierarchy of beings, any higher order is beyond the proportion of lower orders and so is relatively supernatural to them. But the infinite absolutely transcends the finite. It follows that the divine order is beyond the proportion of any possible creature and so is absolutely supernatural.

Our inquiry is with the absolutely supernatural. It regards man's vertical finality to God. It regards such vertical finality in the strictest sense, so that man is not merely subordinate to God but also somehow enters into the divine life and participates in it. When Rahner writes on Christology within an evolutionary perspective, he very explicitly means that there is a threefold personal self-communication of divinity to humanity, first, when in Christ the Word becomes flesh, secondly, when through Christ men become temples of the Spirit and adoptive sons of the Father, thirdly, when in a final consummation the blessed know the Father as they are known by him.

This threefold personal self-communication of divinity is the end. On this end much has been written. It need not be recalled here, for our concern is not with the end but with finality to it, with that finality as evolutionary, with that evolutionary finality as it enters into human consciousness.

Vertical finality is to its end, not as inevitable, but as a possibility. Its ends can be attained. They need not be attained. They may or may not be attained.

Vertical finality is multivalent. There need not be just one end beyond a given proper proportion. Indeed, the lower a being is in a hierarchic scale, the more numerous are the higher ends beyond its proper reach.

Vertical finality is obscure. When it has been realized in full, it can be known. When it is in process, what has been attained can be known, but what has not, remains obscure. When the process has not yet begun, obscurity prevails and questions abound. Is it somehow intimated? Is the intimation fleeting? Does it touch our deepest aspirations? Might it awaken such striving and groaning as would announce a new and higher birth?

Vertical finality to God himself is not merely obscure but shrouded in mystery. In this life we can know God, not as he is in himself, but only by deficient analogy. God himself remains mystery. Since potency is known by its act, and relation by its term, it follows that vertical finality to God himself can be known only in the measure that God is known, that it can be revealed only in the measure that God himself has been revealed, that it can be intimated perhaps but hardly in a manner that is unambiguous since vertical finality is multivalent and obscure, and intimations are not apt to make clear which of many possibilities lies in store.

Vertical finality enters into evolutionary perspective. It does so inasmuch as emergence, unfolding, development, maturity follow the analogy of evolutionary process. Such process is to be understood in accord with emergent probabilities and under divine planning and action. By the analogy of that process is meant, not some basis for *a priori* prediction, but only a basis for *a posteriori* interpretation. Here as elsewhere, things are known insofar as they are in act.

4. THE HUMAN SUBJECT

In a celebrated passage Aristotle granted that his ideal of the theoretic life was too high for man and that, if one lived it, one would do so not as a man but as having something divine present within one. Nonetheless he went on to urge us to dismiss those that would have us resign ourselves to our mortal lot. He pressed us to strive to the utmost to make ourselves immortal and to live out what was finest in us. For that finest, though slight in bulk, still surpassed by far all else in power and in value.[4]

It is not hard to discern in this passage an acknowledgment of vertical finality in its multivalence and in its obscurity. In its multivalence, for there is in man a finest; it surpasses all else in power and in value; it is to be let go all the way. In its obscurity, for what is the divine in man, and what would be going all the way?

One has only to shift, however, from the corpus of Aristotelian writings to that of the Christian tradition, to recognize in Aristotle's position a sign of things to come. So Christian humanists have spoken of a *praeparatio evangelica* in the Gentile world and, more bluntly, St. Paul said to the Athenians: "What you worship but do not know—this is what I now proclaim" (*Acts 17:23*).

If in the Greek patristic tradition *theoria* became the name of contemplative prayer, if medieval theologians derived from Aristotle's principles an argument that man naturally desired to know God by his essence, it still remains that Aristotle's thought offered rather

stony ground for the objectification of the life of the spirit. For the
priority accorded the object gave metaphysics a dominant role. Psychology had to think in terms of potencies, or faculties, that were not
among the data of consciousness. Worse, since psychology envisaged plant as well as animal and human life, the relation of operation
to object was conceived, not precisely as intentionality, but vaguely
as causality.[5] Further, the priority of objects entailed a priority of intellect over will, since will was conceived as rational appetite; and
on the priority of intellect over will, there somehow followed a
priority of speculative over practical intellect.

Intentionality analysis yields a contrasting picture of the subject. Along with the rest of modern science, it eschews dependence
on metaphysics. For metaphysicians do not agree. A critically constructed metaphysics presupposes a theory of objectivity, an epistemology. An epistemology has to distinguish between knowing, as
illustrated by any cognitional operation, and adult human knowing,
which is constituted by a set of cognitional operations that satisfy a
normative pattern. It follows that the single cognitional operation is
neither a merely immanent psychological event nor yet a properly
objective cognitional attainment. It has the intermediate status of an
intentional act: as given, it refers to some other; but the precise nature and validity of that reference remain to be determined; and
such determination is reached through the further intentional operations needed to complete the pattern constitutive of full objectivity.
In a word, phenomenology brackets reality to study acts in their intentionality. In the very measure that it prescinds from questions of
objectivity, it all the more efficaciously prepares the way for a convincing epistemology.

Intentionality analysis, like the rest of modern science, begins
from the given. Unlike the rest of modern science, which dilates
upon electrons and viruses, it can remain with the given, with human
intentional operations dynamically related in their self-assembling
pattern.

In its broad lines this dynamism rests on operators that promote
activity from one level to the next. The operators are *a priori,* and
they alone are *a priori.* Their content is ever an anticipation of the
next level of operations and thereby is not to be found in the contents
of the previous level.

Such operators are questions for intelligence: with respect to data they ask why, and what, and what for, and how, and how often. Such also are questions for reflection: with respect to the guesses, inventions, discoveries of human understanding they ask: Is that so? Are you sure? Such thirdly are questions for deliberation: they ask whether suggested courses of action are feasible, worthwhile, truly good or only apparently good.

Three types of operator yield four levels of operation. Each lower level is an instance of vertical finality, and that finality is already realized as the higher levels function. The lower level, accordingly, prepares for the higher and is sublated by it.

We experience to have the materials for understanding; and understanding, so far from cramping experience, organizes it, enlarges its range, refines its content, and directs it to a higher goal. We understand and formulate to be able to judge, but judgment calls for ever fuller experience and better understanding; and that demand has us clarifying and expanding and applying our distinctions between astronomy and astrology, chemistry and alchemy, history and legend, philosophy and myth, fact and fiction. We experience and understand and judge to become moral: to become moral practically, for our decisions affect things; to become moral interpersonally, for our decisions affect other persons; to become moral existentially, for by our decisions we constitute what we are to be.

Such vertical finality is another name for self-transcendence. By experience we attend to the other; by understanding we gradually construct our world; by judgment we discern its independence of ourselves; by deliberate and responsible freedom we move beyond merely self-regarding norms and make ourselves moral beings.

The disinterestedness of morality is fully compatible with the passionateness of being. For that passionateness has a dimension of its own: it underpins and accompanies and reaches beyond the subject as experientially, intelligently, rationally, morally conscious.

Its underpinning is the quasi-operator that presides over the transition from the neural to the psychic. It ushers into consciousness not only the demands of unconscious vitality but also the exigences of vertical finality. It obtrudes deficiency needs. In the self-actualizing subject[6] it shapes the images that release insight; it recalls evidence that is being overlooked; it may embarrass wakefulness, as it disturbs sleep, with the spectre, the shock, the shame of misdeeds. As it channels into consciousness the feedback of our aberrations and our unfulfilled strivings, so for the Jungians it manifests its archetypes through symbols to preside over the genesis of the ego and to guide the individuation process from the ego to the self.[7]

As it underpins, so too it accompanies the subject's conscious and intentional operations. There it is the mass and momentum of our lives, the color and tone and power of feeling, that fleshes out and gives substance to what otherwise would be no more than a Shakespearian "pale cast of thought."

As it underpins and accompanies, so too it overarches conscious intentionality. There it is the topmost quasi-operator that by intersubjectivity prepares, by solidarity entices, by falling in love establishes us as members of community. Within each individual vertical finality heads for self-transcendence. In an aggregate of self-transcending individuals there is the significant coincidental manifold in which can emerge a new creation. Possibility yields to fact and fact bears witness to its originality and power in the fidelity that makes families, in the loyalty that makes peoples, in the faith that makes religions.

But here we meet the ambiguity of man's vertical finality. It is natural to man to love with the domestic love that unites parents with each other and with their children, with the civil love that can face death for the sake of one's fellowmen, with the all-embracing love that loves God above all.[8] But in fact man lives under the reign of sin, and his redemption lies not in what is possible to nature but in what is effected by the grace of Christ.

Before advancing to that high theme, let us remark that an intentionality analysis can provide an apt vehicle for the self-objectification of the human subject. Let us note too that the old questions of priority, of intellectualism and voluntarism and the like, are removed and in their stead comes what at once is simple and clear. Lower levels of operation are prior as presupposed by the higher, as preparing materials for them, as providing them with an underfooting and, in that sense, with foundations. But the higher have a priority of their own. They sublate the lower, preserving them indeed in their proper perfection and significance, but also using them, endowing them with a new and fuller and higher significance, and so promoting them to ends beyond their proper scope.

Further, when so understood, priorities lose their rigidities.

One might accord metaphysical necessity to such adages as *ignoti nulla cupido* and *nihil amatum nisi praecognitum.* But while they assert the priority of knowledge as one ascends from the lower to the higher, they tend to overlook the inverse priority by which the higher sublates the lower. It is in the latter fashion that orthopraxy has a value beyond orthodoxy. And surely the priority of the lower sets no rule that God must observe when he floods our inmost hearts with his love through the Holy Spirit he has given us (*Rom. 5:5*).

5. MISSION OF THE SON AND GIFT OF THE SPIRIT

The divine secret, kept in silence for long ages but now disclosed (*Rom. 16:25*), has been conceived as the self-communication of divinity in love. It resides in the sending of the Son, in the gift of the Spirit, in the hope of being united with the Father. Our question has been how to apprehend this economy of grace and salvation in an evolutionary perspective and, more precisely, how it enters into the consciousness of man.

First, I think, there is an awareness of a need for redemption. Human progress is a fact. There is a wheel that, as it turns, moves forward. Situations give rise to insights; insights to new courses of action; new courses of action to changed situations; changed situations to still further insights, further action, further change in situations. But such progress is only a first approximation to fact, for it is marred and distorted by sin. There is the egoism of individuals, the securer egoism of groups, the overconfident shortsightedness of common sense. So the intelligence of progress is twisted into the objectification of irrational bias. Worse, to simpleminded sins of greed there is added the higher organization of sophistry. One must attend to the facts. One must deal with them as in fact they are and, as they are irrational, obviously the mere dictates of reason are never going to work. So rationalization enters the inner citadel. There is opened a gap between the essential freedom all men have and the effective freedom that in fact they exercise. Impotent in his situation and impotent in his soul, man needs and may seek redemption, deliverance, salvation. But when it comes, it comes as the charity that dissolves the hostility and the divisions of past injustice and present hatred; it comes as the hope that withstands psychological, economic, political, social, cultural determinisms; it comes with the faith that can liberate reason from the rationalizations that blinded it.[9]

Secondly, the new order (*II Cor. 5:17*) comes in the visible mission of the Son. In him is presented: (1) the absolutely supernatural object, for he is God; (2) the object for us, for he is man; (3) for us as to be redeemed, for he dies to rise again. As visible, he is the sacrament of man's encounter with God. As dying and rising, he shows the way to the new creation. As himself God, already he is Emmanuel, God with us.

Thirdly, besides the visible mission of the Son there is the invisible mission of the Spirit. Besides *fides ex auditu,* there is *fides ex infusione.*[10] The former mounts up the successive levels of experiencing, understanding, judging, deliberating. The latter descends from the gift of God's love through religious conversion to moral, and through religious and moral to intellectual conversion.[11]

These three are cumulative. Revulsion from the objective reign of sin and from the subject's own moral impotence heightens vertical finality. Without the visible mission of the Word, the gift of the Spirit is a being-in-love without a proper object; it remains simply an orientation to mystery that awaits its interpretation. Without the visible mission of the Spirit, the Word enters into his own, but his own receive him not.

Such Christian origins are exemplary. As the Father sent the Son, so the Son sent the disciples on a mission to continue to the end of time. As the Father and the Son sent the Spirit to the disciples, so they continue to bestow the Spirit on the ever oncoming members of Christ. So the self-communication of the Son and the Spirit proceeds through history by a communication that at once is cognitive, constitutive, and redemptive: it is cognitive, for it discloses in whom we are to believe; it is constitutive, for it crystallizes the inner gift of the love of God into overt Christian fellowship; it is redemptive, for it liberates human liberty from thraldom to sin, and it guides those it liberates to the kingdom of the Father.

Experience of grace, then, is as large as the Christian experience of life. It is experience of man's capacity for self-transcendence, of his unrestricted openness to the intelligible, the true, the good. It is experience of a twofold frustration of that capacity: the objective frustration of life in a world distorted by sin; the subjective frustration of one's incapacity to break with one's own evil ways. It is experience of a transformation one did not bring about but rather underwent, as divine providence let evil take its course and vertical finality be heightened, as it let one's circumstances shift, one's dispositions change, new encounters occur, and—so gently and quietly—one's heart be touched. It is the experience of a new community, in which faith and hope and charity dissolve rationalizations, break determinisms, and reconcile the estranged and the alienated, and there is reaped the harvest of the Spirit that is ". . . love, joy, peace, patience, kindness, goodness, fidelity, gentleness, and self-control" (*Gal. 5:22*).

Previously published in Peter Huizing and William Bassett (eds.), *Experience of the Spirit: To Edward Schillebeeckx on his sixtieth birthday* (*Concilium*, Vol. IX, no. 10, 1976), pp. 69–78.—Here and elsewhere in the volume, biblical quotations are from *The New English Bible*.

Notes

1. Karl Rahner, *Theological Investigations,* Vol. V (*Later Writings*), tr. by Karl-H. Kruger (London: Darton, Longman & Todd; Baltimore: Helicon Press, 1966), pp. 157–192.

2. On vertical finality see my papers, "Finality, Love, Marriage" and "The Natural Desire to See God," *Collection: Papers by Bernard Lonergan, S.J.,* ed. by F. E. Crowe (New York: Herder and Herder, 1967), pp. 16–53, 84–95.

3. On statistical inquiry see my book, *Insight: A Study of Human Understanding* (London: Longmans, Green and Co.; New York: Philosophical Library, 1957), pp. 53 ff.; on emergent probability, *ibid.,* pp. 121 ff., 259 ff. On Aristotle and Aquinas on world order, see my *Grace and Freedom: Operative Grace in the Thought of St. Thomas Aquinas,* ed. by J. Patout Burns (London: Darton, Longman & Todd; New York: Herder and Herder, 1971), Ch. 4; on the origins of the notion of the supernatural, *ibid.,* pp. 13–19.

4. Aristotle, *Nicomachean Ethics,* X, 7, 1177b 26—1178a 2.

5. St. Thomas Aquinas, *In II de Anima,* lect. 6, no. 305 (Marietti edition).

6. On deficiency and growth motivation, see Abraham H. Maslow, *Toward a Psychology of Being* (Princeton: Van Nostrand, 1962), Ch. 3.

7. E. Neumann, *The Origins and History of Consciousness*, 1970; G. Adler, *The Living Symbol*, 1961.

8. Aquinas holds that apart from corrupt nature man naturally loves God above all: *Summa Theologiae*, I–II, q. 109, a. 3 c. and ad lm.

9. This paragraph summarizes what I wrote in *Insight*, pp. 214–242, 619–633, 688–703, 718–730.

10. *Sum. Theol.*, II–II, q. 6, a. 1.

11. Bernard J. F. Lonergan, S.J., *Method in Theology* (London: Darton, Longman & Todd; New York: Herder and Herder, 1972), pp. 122, 243.

4

Aquinas Today:
Tradition and Innovation

From the year 1879, when Pope Leo XIII issued his encyclical, *Aeterni Patris,* up to the second Vatican council, the influence of St. Thomas Aquinas was dominant in Roman Catholic schools of philosophy and theology. Since the beginning of the council Aquinas has abruptly gone out of fashion. Particularly in the period from 1920 to 1940 studies of his writings and of his thought poured forth in books and articles. [1] Since the council what had been a torrent has become a trickle.

No doubt the intervention of church authorities had not a little to do with the former dominance of Thomism. Again no doubt enthusiasm for medieval thought was discouraged both by Pope John's watchword, *aggiornamento,* and by the tendency in conciliar debates to use the word, Scholastic, as a term of reproach. But if one wishes to enter into the theological issues involved, one must turn one's thoughts, I suggest, to the ongoing interplay in human history of tradition and innovation.

The innovations I envisage are the successive large-scale developments in medieval and modern culture. They are specializations: in theology, in philosophy, in science, in scholarship. They have occurred at different times. Each was preceded by earlier stages in which their later separate tasks were undifferentiated parts in previous larger wholes. In each case their emergence generated identity crises in their former hosts and demanded the discovery and the development of new methods and procedures.

In this process, extending over centuries, Aquinas was a great representative of the medieval theological tradition of *lectio* and *quaestio*, of the reading that expanded into commentaries and of the questioning that grew into elaborate *summa*'s. But he also was a great innovator, winning for Aristotle a place of esteem within theological inquiry and a recognition for usefulness. Moreover, he carried through a distinction between natural and supernatural, and by it he prepared the way for the independent study of nature: for a philosophy that was not just a tool for theology; for a science that against Aristotle vindicated its own autonomy; for a scholarship that took the history of religion out of the competence of theologians to hand it over to scholars.

When I venture to speak to you on "Aquinas Today," it is to explore the ongoing relevance of Aquinas through these subsequent transformations of western culture and to leave you with the question whether the current lull in Thomist studies portends the end of Thomism or is perhaps just a pause for reflection, a Toynbean withdrawal preparing a new and more effective return.

My discussion falls into four parts. First, "Specialization" outlines different types of transformation a learned tradition may undergo. Secondly, "Aristotle Today" notes postmedieval limitations on Aristotle's acceptability. Thirdly, "Aristotle in Aquinas" inspects Aquinas' involvement in these limitations. Fourthly and finally, there is found as a remainder, "Aquinas Today."

1. SPECIALIZATION

I have been using the word, specialization, in one of its less usual meanings. Most commonly, it is thought to be a concentration on one field to the neglect of all others, of an increasing contraction of attention in that one field so that, as people say, one comes to know more and more about less and less. But what I have had in mind is something at once more general and more radical. It is more general, for it lumps the sciences together in a single category to contrast them with other fields of human activity. It is more radical, for it results in a differentiation of outlook, mentality, horizon; it sets up barriers to mutual communication; it has people living, so to speak, in different worlds.

An account of this type or aspect of specialization comes in two parts. There is a generic part that outlines the notion and implications of 'horizon.' There is a specific part that emerges when specialization passes a critical point and, as it were, ushers one into a new world. I shall speak of each of these in turn.

Etymologically horizon is what bounds or limits. The boundary or limit that concerns us here is the boundary to a person's interest and knowledge. What lies beyond that boundary, he neither knows nor cares. What lies within it, to some extent he knows and to some extent he cares.

The boundary is a variable. It varies in extent as some individuals or groups are found to know more than others. It varies in intensity as interest grows or slackens. It varies in selectivity as interest centers now in one area and now in another.

Such variations in extent, intensity, selectivity help fill out what we mean by relevance. The relevant in an absolute sense is what is known, what is of interest, what may be selected for attention and consideration. Again, as horizons change, there occur shifts in what is known, what is of interest, what merits selection, and so histories come to be rewritten, geniuses are pulled out of the shadows of the past into the light of day, and doctrines once obscure and forgotten take on a fresh lustre and acquire a new vitality and power.

In any individual his actual horizon is the fruit of his past development, and his past development in the main is his participation in the earlier developments of others and only on rare occasions the product of his own originality and creativity.

Moreover, such development admits categorization to yield a differentiation of horizons. It may pertain to the *prelinguistic* development to which the infant is confined; to the *commonsense* development of intelligence that specializes in the concrete and immediate; to the *religious* development that orientates man to God and in the universe; to the *scientific* development that unifies and relates, constructs and extrapolates, serializes and generalizes, to discover and reveal the cosmos; to the *scholarly* development that enters into the common sense of another place and time to understand its language, interpret its meanings, narrate its deeds and achievements; to the *philosophic* development that, in what now may seem its final phase, reflects on all of these, assigns each its proper competence, and relates each to the others.

In all of these spheres development initially is grafted upon natural endowment or previous attainment, and there it functions in a symbiosis so intimate and so complete that distinction seems superfluous and even arbitrary. But as advance continues in collaborating groups and cumulative achievement there begin to emerge in each sphere its proper procedures. On distinct procedures follow characteristic products, varying styles of growth and inner organization, functional separateness and disparate goals. Earlier the distinction of one sphere from another seemed fanciful. Later it has become a manifest fact, and the thought of any overall synthesis appears no more than a nostalgic dream.

I am urging, then, a source of radical cultural differences not to be identified simply with the diversity of traditions, the varieties of religious experience, the proliferation of languages, the conflicts of philosophies. It is a differentiation that is concealed in its early stages by its symbiosis with preceding achievement, and this concealment is permanent in the minds of those that advance no further. But the same differentiation for those that reach its later stages is all the more striking and strange, for the new enterprise detaches itself from its original host and proceeds, in the main, to expand and to function on its own.

Let me illustrate the matter for it is very much to our purpose. Infants (*in-fantes*) are those that do not speak, and Jean Piaget has observed and recorded the development of his own three children during the first twenty-four months of their lives. It was a cumulative process that may be recalled by mentioning the key notions of assimilation and adjustment, combination and group. It revealed that, if the human infant acquired slowly and laboriously what came to the animal cub spontaneously or at least rapidly, still the great advantage was on the side of the infant. The infant was slow because of its enormously greater plasticity, and it took longer because it learned immeasurably more.

Among other things the infant learned to speak, to match speech with action, to place an organism at the beck and call of meanings and values mediated by conventional signs. In the first instance such meanings and values are the fruits of the basic and homeliest developments of intelligence—common sense. As a procedure, a mode of development, it is common to mankind. But as a content, it is endlessly diversified; each village grows its own variety to mould the local 'ordinary' language, to make a man from the next village a stranger because his speech and his ways are different, and a man from another country not merely strange but foreign. Finally, however much the mastery of language begins in infancy, nonetheless so far apart are the earlier development of the infant and the later common sense embedded in ordinary language that a neurotic's departures from common sense can be described as infantile regression.

The proliferation of languages is also a proliferation of thought-forms and traditions, of literatures and histories. In this fashion there is constituted the field to be explored by scholarship. Basically the scholar is the man that adds to his native common sense some mastery of the common sense of other places and times. He is the linguist that translates, the exegete that interpets, the historian that reconstructs and narrates. Such basic scholarship, however, can be enlisted in the service of quite different goals. There is the classical scholarship that promotes the aims of a particular culture and provides the proper instrument for the education and the acculturation of its young. There is the quite different modern scholarship, universalist in outlook, affine to science in its aims, esoteric in its achievement of a group of professional specialists. Such a group was foreshadowed by the Maurists in France and by the Bollandists in the Low Countries. It was realized by the university seminars emulating the example set by Leopold von Ranke in Berlin. There has been built up an ongoing, cumulative tradition that developed new skills and techniques; new standards have been set; and competence to meet these standards is to be acquired only by serving a long and exacting apprenticeship. The outcome is specialization. Exegetical and historical works have ceased to be composed principally for the general public. Their primary audience has become an in-group of professors and graduate students. From being the servant of a particular though multinational culture, scholarship has become a distinct, self-sufficient, autonomous specialty.

A parallel result has followed on specialization in the sciences, and there it admits a more precise contrast. Eddington's two tables have become symbolic. There is the table apprehended by common sense: it is continuous, solid, heavy, with its own distinctive color, dimensions, contours. But the same table as envisaged by science is mostly empty space with here and there—though without exactly determinable position and momentum—what now is a wave and now a particle. What holds for the table, holds for everything. A few centuries ago scientific discovery could be communicated to the whole educated public and there be understood and discussed competently. But now there are two worlds. A different, technical language is needed to speak of the scientist's world. Only a new and distinct social group masters that language. Specialist journals report to the initiated new advances and discoveries. Specialist books are written to set forth their achievements and their aims. Specialist methods are developed to reach their distinctive goals, and specialist criteria are employed to test their success.

Science is the clear-cut paradigm of specialization. It offers its own distinct apprehension of the cosmos. That apprehension can be reached only through distinctive methods and techniques. It can be communicated only through a specially evolved language. It can be shared only by an ongoing, collaborating group of initiates.

Still parallel characteristics are to be noted in each of the endless varieties of common sense and of common sense's ordinary languages. They reappear in a new form when one contrasts the expertise of the scholar in his chosen field and his quite different skill, or perhaps his surprising gaucherie, in his everyday affairs. A completely new dimension is revealed when one departs from the observable religions of mankind and seeks to trace the path of the mystics into that region of which, one is told, those that speak do not know and those that know do not speak. There remain the philosophers, a group apart if ever there was one, yet seemingly unsure of their function. Some identify their cause with that of common sense or ordinary language. Others assume the role of spokesmen for science. Still others switch their reflective concern to the hermeneutics of existence and the originality of *Geschichte*. Greeks of old sought to be universalist and autonomous by discoursing on being. A few moderns take their cue from the differentiation of horizons by specialization and, through an appeal to authentic subjectivity, seek to distinguish and evaluate the various orientations of the polymorphic consciousness of man.

2. ARISTOTLE TODAY:
SCIENCE AND SCHOLARSHIP

Thought that was quite brilliant and investigation that was quite thorough in fourth-century Athens, today easily enough is out of date. The generic reason lies in the transforming specializations we have just considered. But there has to be added a more specific concern with science, with scholarship and, by repercussion, with that chameleon, philosophy.

There is no doubt that the knowledge available to modern scientists extends way beyond Aristotelian anticipations. But more important than the mere extent of scientific knowledge is the underlying conception of science itself. For it is change in the very notion of science that accounts not only for the new abundance of information but on a deeper level for the repercussion of scientific development on the notion and function of philosophy.

For Aristotle the sciences were not autonomous disciplines. Together with philosophy they formed a single block, a viewpoint still extant when Newton entitled his masterpiece, *Philosophiae Naturalis Principia Mathematica*. The sciences were distinguished from philosophy in the same manner as they were distinguished from one another—by their objects and, indeed, by their objects as they happened to be conceived. Moreover, since the object of metaphysics was the most general and fundamental of all—being as being—it followed that the principles of metaphysics held for all objects and that the basic terms of metaphysics supplied the core element in the basic terms of the sciences.

Against this crippling negation of autonomy the modern sciences struggled for centuries.[2] A first complaint was that science had to be concerned not with words but with things. It had some justification. It is true that in the *Posterior Analytics* Aristotle's premise is that scientific knowledge is about things: it is knowledge of the cause, knowledge that it is the cause, knowledge that the effect cannot be other than it is.[3] It remains that this premise is just a springboard. From scientific knowledge Aristotle proceeded at once to scientific syllogism, and to his theory of science as argument or proof of a special kind he devoted the substance of the work. So scientific knowledge comes to be conceived as a matter of essential predication,[4] and this conception is embedded in a linguistic matrix in which syllogisms work through middle terms,[5] categories are semantically elementary predicates,[6] and substances are the first subjects of predicates.[7] There is, in fact, quite a linguistic turn to Aristotelian thought.

A second point in the anti-Aristotelian campaign regarded controls. In the Aristotelian *Organon* categories were listed. Valid reasoning was explored. Its scientific variant was expounded. Topics were treated abundantly. Interpretation was outlined. Fallacies were exposed. Refining on this achievement the Scholastics introduced the formal disputation, in which assertions were to be proved syllogistically, objections were presented against the major premise or the minor, and answers commonly came in the form of distinctions. Distinctions acquired a bad name. They enabled a disputant to add his afterthoughts, and while such thoughts could be brilliant, they also could be the convenient inventions of the moment over which there was no effective control. To close this door to uncontrolled speculation the Royal Society in England had a rule: questions were not considered unless they could be settled by an appeal to observation or experiment. Science was to be not just science but empirical science.

The stand against verbalism and the exigence for empirical controls gradually brought about three effects. First was a shift from an excessively rigorous to a practically attainable ideal of science. Secondly, there was dropped Aristotle's concern with essences and essential predicates, and in their place came empirically grounded conceptual systems. Thirdly, the sciences were divided not by material and formal objects but by fields and methods. On each of these three a few words must be said.

First, Aristotelian science was to be causal, necessary, true. Modern science still speaks of causes, but it does not think of end, agent, matter, form; it thinks of correlation or concomitance. Again, up to this century scientists spoke of the necessary laws of nature and even of the iron laws of economics. But the reflections of logicians, the discoveries of mathematicians, the relegation of Newtonian mechanics to a limiting case, and Heisenberg's indeterminacy principle have made necessity in science a marginal notion. The laws of empirical science are not statements of what could not be other than it is. They merely state what could be the case and in fact happens to be so.

By the requirement and criterion of verifiability empirical science reveals its object to be not necessity but verifiable possibility. Finally, Aristotelian science wanted to be a Thucydidean possession for all time; science had to be true. But modern science claims no more for its positive achievements than probability. The ideal has ceased to be definitive achievement; it has become ongoing advance.

The second consequence was a shift from essences to systems. In the *Posterior Analytics* scientific knowledge was conceived in terms of scientific syllogisms. In such syllogisms the predicate pertained to the subject universally, necessarily, eternally.[8] But the modern shift from concepts and words to things is also a shift from the predicates of subjects to empirically established laws. Such laws are links, connections, relations; of their nature they imply terms that are linked, connected, related. Such terms may be conceived materially or formally. Conceived materially, they denote, at least in part, what could be known apart from the law. But conceived formally, they denote simply and solely what is implied by the law. For example, Newton conceived 'mass' as quantity of matter, and both 'quantity' and 'matter' had long been conceived independently of empirically established laws. But from the later viewpoint of the hypotheticodeductive system, one thinks of 'mass' simply as 'm,' that is, as the factor that recurs in a number of mechanical laws. When all the basic terms of mechanics are conceived in this fashion, there results a 'system,' that is a closed circle of basic terms and relations, where the terms fix the relations, the relations fix the terms, while both terms and relations are fixed by empirically established laws.[9]

The third consequence secured the autonomy of the sciences. As long as they were divided in terms of material and formal objects, they formed a single block under philosophic hegemony. The material objects were the subjects of essential predicates; the formal objects were the essential predicates on which scientific conclusions could rest. The material objects could be arranged in a hierarchy in accord with their generality, and thereby what was accepted in the more general science would automatically be transferable to the less general. This could cause no harm where the more general contained all the truth and nothing but the truth. But where such perfection was lacking, issues would be clouded, originality stifled, growth obstructed. Against such interference from argument came the appeal to observation and experiment, and by that recurrent appeal the con-

stitution of distinct sciences became the result of a distinction of
fields and of methods.

In a contemporary estimate of the Aristotelian corpus there are
to be noted not only a very notable divergence of the modern from
the ancient notion of science but also the emergence in very recent
centuries of a new scholarship. Its ideal has been the interpretative
reconstruction of the constructions of mankind. Its ramifications and
extent can be indicated only by the German name, *Geisteswissen-
schaften,* which Wilhelm Dilthey succeeded in distinguishing radically from the *Naturwissenschaften.* Its reality is witnessed by the
whole range of cultural studies and, for theologians, by the enormous bibliographies that confront them in the fields of biblical, patristic, medieval, and modern erudition. Its analysis has not yet
reached commonly accepted results. In my opinion the key element
is the acquisition of the common sense of another place and time,
and the closest Aristotelian equivalent to common sense is *phronēsis,* [10] the practical wisdom which Aquinas examined at considerable
length in his *Summa Theologiae.* [11]

3. ARISTOTLE TODAY: PHILOSOPHY

Our investigation now enters upon a more complex and delicate
phase. The role of philosophy in Thomist theology traditionally has
been conceived as that of a handmaid to a queen. Essential to that
role is the ability of philosophy to mediate between theology and its
auxiliary disciplines. But it is precisely this mediating role that is im-
pugned when a philosophy is attacked and attacked successfully because it has denied the sciences their autonomy. Accordingly a
notable and serious modification of Aristotelian philosophy seems
needed, if it is to continue to fulfill this mediating function in a contemporary Thomism.

It remains that a notable modification is one thing and a total rejection is quite another. In the history of thought there is no lack of
examples of a later position going quite beyond without completely
rejecting its predecessor. In arithmetic there is the transition from
Roman to Arabic numerals and then from decimal to binary notation;
in geometry the transition from Euclid's unformulated assumptions
to a contemporary exact formulation; in physics the transitions from

Newton's mechanics to Einstein's relativity and from Maxwell's electromagnetics to Heisenberg's indeterminacy; finally, in philosophy there is the whole category of advances that Hegel named sublation.

No doubt these instances are disparate. But they do illustrate two important points. First, totally unanticipated later developments can go quite beyond earlier attainment and yet maintain the continuity that is the secret of a tradition that admits innovation. Secondly, such an advance, when explicit and deliberate, in no way necessitates confusion between earlier and later contexts and procedures.

The transition we envisage is from logic to method. Aristotle himself would not admit the strict application of his own *Posterior Analytics* outside the field of mathematics.[12] Modern science places its reliance, not on any principles or laws it has discovered and may revise, but upon empirical method. Modern scholarship operates on similar lines in its very different field: it is a matter of growing familiarity with the data, advancing comprehension of their meaning and significance, and complete submission to the demand for revision when contrary data or a fuller comprehension come to light. My own study, *Verbum: Word and Idea in Aquinas,*[13] would show the continuity of such ideas of method with the Aristotelian and Thomist tradition, while my larger work, *Insight,*[14] sets forth a generalized empirical method that operates principally on the data of consciousness to work out a cognitional theory, an epistemology, and a metaphysics. First it asks what one is doing when one is knowing. Next, why is doing that knowing? Thirdly, what does one know when one does it?

A shift from logic to method is a change rather in structure than in content. Both logic and method start from principles, from what is first in an ordered set (*primum in aliquo ordine*). But the order of logic differs from the order of method. For logic what is first is premises. Among premises come first the most universal: they regard being, and so metaphysics is the first of the sciences. Because metaphysics is first, psychology has to be a faculty psychology: its basic terms are modifications of metaphysical terms, and so it has much to say of potencies and habits, which are not among the immediate data of consciousness, and it relates acts to objects not by intentionality but by efficient and final causality. Again, because metaphysics is first, a primacy goes to speculative intellect which concerns itself with metaphysics.

Method reverses such priorities. Its principles are not logical propositions but concrete realities, namely, sensitively, intellectually, rationally, morally conscious subjects. Among investigations the key place goes to the self-appropriation of the subject, to his discovery and acknowledgment of human authenticity and unauthenticity, to his option for authenticity and, thereby, for a philosophic foundation less showy but far more effective than an appeal to demonstrations. There follows the replacement of a faculty psychology by an intentionality analysis. Finally, as intentionality analysis distinguishes successive levels of conscious operations by the type of questions they answer, as it has questions for intelligence (what? why? how? what for?) precede questions for reflection (is that so? are you certain?) and both precede questions for deliberation (is it good? is it truly good?), so also it acknowledges the sublation of the earlier by the later. By sublation the later goes beyond the earlier, sets up a higher objective, introduces new operations, but so far from setting aside or interfering with the earlier preserves them in their integrity, refines their performance, extends their relevance, enriches their significance. On this showing speculative intellect loses its primacy. The key position now pertains to the deliberating subject, and his deliberations are existential, for they determine what he is to be; they are interpersonal, for they determine his relations with others; they are practical, for they make this earth a better or a worse place in which we are to live.

I have been describing a shift in priorities, and I must add that it does not of itself imply a change in content. The shift from abstract premises to concrete subjects is not privation but enrichment. A basis in cognitional theory is not a negation of metaphysics but the establishment of a critically structured metaphysics. To replace faculty psychology by intentionality analysis is to set aside a jejune and ambiguous scheme in favor of a wealth of ordered fact. To deprive speculative intellect of its pride of place and to acknowledge the primacy of conscience not only is a recognition of fact but also quiets the opponents of intellectualism without diminishing the power of intellect.

Further, the shift from logic to method includes an acknowledgment of the autonomy of science and of scholarship. But the autonomy recognized is under the control of method. Such controlled autonomy ensures both openness to current views and alertness to spot needed revisions. It grounds sharp distinctions between the results of scientific work and the extrascientific opinions of scientists, between scholarly conclusions and nonscholarly pronouncements. If it permits modern science and scholarship to correct what in the Aristotelian corpus might be mistaken for philosophy, it thereby puts on a rational basis what otherwise tended to be, initially the haphazard result of a long-sustained war of attrition, but later the wholesale desertion of a venerable and still valuable tradition.

Finally, there is an important difference between method in the sciences and method in philosophy. Empirical method leaves the sciences open to radical revision, because its appeal is to the data of sense but its basic terms and relations denote not the data of sense but constructs derived from empirically established laws. In contrast, the basic terms and relations of an empirically established cognitional theory are not just constructs but also data of immediate consciousness. Its basic terms denote conscious events. Its basic relations denote stages in conscious process. Hence, to introduce new basic terms and new basic relations and thereby establish a radical revision would be, not merely the revision of a theory, but the creation of a new type of consciousness.

4. ARISTOTLE IN AQUINAS

My title was: "Aquinas Today". But so far I have been speaking of "Aristotle Today." I have been stressing not his excellence but a defect. In his *Posterior Analytics* he conceived scientific knowledge in terms of scientific syllogism, and I have been urging that contemporary science, contemporary scholarship and at least one contemporary philosophy would counsel a shift from logic to method.

I now must add five observations. Three of them are theoretical. Two of them are factual. But the five together will help us make the turn from "Aristotle Today" to "Aristotle in Aquinas."

The first of the theoretical observations is that method, so far from excluding logic, includes it. It adds to logic such nonlogical operations as observing, describing, comparing, stumbling on problems, discovering solutions, devising tests, checking results. But integral to such nonlogical operations there are within method itself the properly logical operations of defining terms, formulating hypotheses, working out presuppositions, and inferring conclusions.

The second of the theoretical observations is that inferences can be explanatory without their premises being necessarily true. Fourteenth-century theologians were very accurate logicians and they rightly contended that what necessarily is true would be true in every possible world. But modern scientists are content with explanations that hold in this world. Indeed, they are content to claim that the explanations they offer are the best available at the present time.

The third of the theoretical observations is that sustained advance, ongoing development, continued progress is not a matter of deducing conclusions that follow necessarily from premises that are both true and necessary. In that case results are certain and enduring; but they are reached in a single leap and, once they are reached, the life of mind settles down into a routine. Sustained advance is a succession of fresh insights, of increasingly accurate hypotheses, of the emergence of quite new theories, of an ever greater command of data in precision, in variety, in extent, and of a constant openness to still further ideas.

Needless to say, such sustained advance is not the work of one person. It is not the work of several persons each working independently and in isolation from the others. It is the work of specialization bringing to birth its own distinct apprehension of the cosmos. That apprehension can be reached only through distinctive methods and techniques. It can be communicated only through a specially evolved language. It can be shared only by an ongoing, collaborating group of initiates, who preserve what has been achieved by the continuity of a tradition and keep it alive by the tension their innovations create.

On three theoretical there follow two factual observations. The first is that Aristotle in his own writings left necessary premises and conclusions to the mathematicians. His own rule was to seek in each subject no greater exactitude than the matter permitted. In his eyes it was just as silly to ask a politician for demonstrations as to accept plausible reasons from a mathematician. [15]

Our second factual observation is very brief. It is that the theology of Aquinas was not more influenced by the *Posterior Ana-*

lytics than was the philosophy of Aristotle. It is true that Aquinas quoted the *Analytics* much more than Aristotle did. But it also is true that he was not thereby caught in the implications of that work. For the implications depend upon essential predication, and Aquinas consistently denied that we knew either the essence of God or the substance of material objects.

The fact is that Aquinas regarded himself not as a philosopher or as a scientist but as a teacher. He was forever exemplifying the first sentence of the *Posterior Analytics* that all teaching and learning rests on previously acquired knowledge. In the *Contra Gentiles* he set forth his objectives as the communication of Christian truth. Such truth he divided into two sections. Truth that was both professed by faith and concluded by reason he would present with the demonstrative or the probable reasons he had found in the books of philosophers and saints. But there was further truth that exceeded the reach of human reason; arguments against it he would refute; but for it he could adduce only probable reasons and the testimony of authorities.[16] Again, the Prologue to his *Summa Theologiae* explains that it was written for beginners who found existing writings more a hindrance than a help. Either such writings needlessly multiplied questions, headings, arguments; or they followed the order of books they were commenting and neglected the order in which things can be taught; or their frequent repetitions both confused and wearied students. Accordingly, he proposed to present Christian teaching as briefly and clearly as the matter permitted.

If we bear in mind that Aquinas was a teacher, we also must remember that he taught in the medieval period when theology became a specialty. Then first there arose a collaborative, ongoing, cumulative process of reflection and formulation that topically ordered and explanatorily developed the Christian tradition as a whole. Its inspiration was the search of faith for understanding, and in this effort Anselm of Canterbury was the pioneer. In contrast, its implementation was a spontaneous growth. The traditional combination of *lectio* and *quaestio,* of reading that learnt from the past and of questioning that assimilated what it read, gave rise to a two-pronged advance. On the side of reading there was the succession from glossaries to commentaries and from *catenae* to such ordered catalogues of traditional views as Peter Lombard's *Four Books of Sentences.* On the side of questioning there emerged a technique that collected the incoherences, real or apparent, in traditional views and worked methodically towards their reconciliation. The juxtaposition and commonly the fusion of these two developments had the double effect of bringing tradition to life by the questioning and of making questioning significant by basing it on traditional materials.

Now the teaching career of Aquinas began a century and a half after the death of Anselm and a century after the death of Peter Lombard. On the intellectual vigor and academic diligence of the intervening period I can offer only soundings. Anselm may perhaps be regarded as brilliant as Aquinas; both of them wrote on the intricate relations of grace and free choice; but Anselm's work seems no more than a well-intentioned exercise in logic when compared with the wide information and the theoretical mastery exhibited by Aquinas. Nor was this theoretical mastery, as romantics might imagine, just the product of Aquinas' genius. Artur Landgraf studied at length the work of Aquinas' predecessors on grace and Dom Lottin has studied their thought on human liberty; and without these previous developments Aquinas would not have had even the categories in which he expressed his thought.

Aquinas, then, was not simply an innovator. He carried on the work begun by his predecessors. He did so within the academic framework they had developed. As they commented on the religious and philosophic heirlooms of tradition, so did he. As they solved series of questions, so did he. As they included Aristotle among their authorities, so did he. Yet it was just this seemingly incidental use of Aristotle that provided the vehicle for his perhaps greatest innovation.

For he quoted Aristotle from a mastery of the text, from a penetration of its grounds and implications, from a grasp of its significance for teaching Christian truth in his day. That significance was threefold. First there was the need for a coherent theological *Begrifflichkeit:* just as diverse statements in the Christian tradition needed to be reconciled, so too the many reconciliations devised by theologians needed the overall reconciliation that was to be obtained only by underpinning theological invention by a comprehensive system of thought. Secondly, there was the need for a unified apprehension of things: the search of faith for understanding could not be a merely partial understanding; it had to be coupled with an understanding of nature; else divine grace would be perfecting an unknown nature, and divine faith would be illuminating an unknown reason. Thirdly, there was the problem of the University of Paris. There had been translated the brilliant studies of Aristotle by Arabic thinkers; there had emerged Parisian Averroists; there had to be performed an apologetic task if an alien faith was not to obtain by its books a hegemony that it had failed to obtain by its arms.

5. AQUINAS TODAY

Though a singularly traditional thinker, Aquinas also was a great innovator. Other Christians before him had used the writings of philosophers in their theological work, but as the medieval period was the first in which theology became a full-fledged specialization (in the very strong sense in which I have been using the term), so Aquinas was the first to think through a theology with philosophic aid. How novel his procedure was, may be estimated from the virulence of the controversy between Augustinians and Aristotelians that followed his death. But how sound was his innovation, is confirmed by the lasting esteem in which subsequently he has been held.

I began by mentioning that today there is a lull in Thomist thinking and writing, and part at least of the reason would seem to lie in the specializations that have arisen since the days not only of Aristotle but also of Aquinas himself. But it remains that the motives Aquinas had in baptizing Aristotle are not less operative today than in the middle ages. As then, so today there can be needed an apologetic clarification of issues. As then, so today systematic thinking in theology stands in need of a broad and coherent basis. As then, so today an account of man's salvation cannot get along without an adequate understanding of man himself. R. P. Claude Geffré, O. P., has made the point at some length: we are living in a new age of theology.[17]

Whether or not this new age is to be thought discontinuous with its past will depend, I believe, on one's understanding both of the past and of the present. In any case my own studies have led me to expect a rather notable continuity. While I cannot on the present occasion justify this opinion, I do feel bound to indicate a few illustrations of what I have in mind.

First there is the continuity from the implicit to the explicit. I have argued explicitly for a method in theology. But the medieval specialization was implicitly methodical. Its commentaries and books of sentences sought to do what today is achieved in research, interpretation, and history. Its questions and *summa*'s did the work now carried on in dogmatics and systematics. Then as now theology operated methodically, but method now is talked about and then it was not.

Secondly, there is continuity in the shift from the Aristotelian ideal of science to the modern reality, for it involves a change more in structure than in content. Where before the metaphysical was primary, now the experiential is primary. Where Aquinas spoke of forms, we can experience insights. Where he transposed from Augustinian *veritas* to his own *esse*, we can advert with Newman to the unconditional character of assent. Where he discoursed at length on virtues as operative habits, we can think with the Greeks of *aretē* as excellence and develop the moral feelings that promote it. Where he conceived the grace of justification as a supernatural habit, we can note his doctrine that that grace makes us choose what is right where before we chose what was wrong, and so can give it the more familiar name of conversion. For him theology was not only science but—something better—wisdom; and this we can retain in terms of the successive sublations observed in intentionality analysis, where the curiosity of sense is taken over by the inquiry of intelligence, where inquiry is taken over by rational reflection, where reflection prepares the way for responsible deliberation, where all are sublimated by being-in-love—in love with one's family, in love with the human community, in love with God and his universe.

Thirdly, there is continuity by analogy. The world of Aquinas was very different from our own. His was a world of Babylonian and Ptolemaic ancestry, with this earth as its center, with its fixed species sustained by the benign influence of the heavenly spheres, with its short history of less than ten thousand years. How completely and intimately the thought of Aquinas was embedded in that world barely appears in summary accounts of his doctrine or in selected readings recommended to students. But it is a matter of manifest importance once one begins to read him extensively, to compare successive phases in his thought, to penetrate to the fine texture of his development.

For us his world was static and our own is dynamic. It is a

world in process. Its age is in numbers we do not comprehend. Its story is the slow interplay of classical and statistical laws, the formation of the galaxies and nebulae, of suns and planetary systems, the emergence of elements and compounds, the slow ascent of countless species of living things and their ecosystems.

But if scientific specialization differentiates our world from that of Aquinas, theology changes difference into analogy. As Aquinas conceived his world as coming from God and returning to him, so too can we. As Aquinas conceived man as the end of the material universe, so much more clearly and distinctly can we. Finally, as Aquinas, so we too can place the meaning and significance of the visible universe as bringing to birth the elect—the recipients to whom God gives himself in love, in the threefold giving that is the gift of the Holy Spirit to those that love *(Rom. 5:5)*, the gift of the divine Word made flesh and dwelling amongst us *(John 1:14)*, the final gift of union with the Father who is originating love *(I John 4:8, 16)*.

A lecture in the series, A Colloquy on Medieval Religious Thought, University of Chicago, Nov. 8, 1974. Previously published in *The Journal of Religion,* Vol. LV (1975), pp. 165–180, and in *Celebrating the Medieval Heritage: A Colloquy on the Thought of Aquinas and Bonaventure* (Supplement to *The Journal of Religion,* Vol. LVIII, 1978), pp. S1–S17.

Notes

1. Vernon Bourke, *Thomistic Bibliography, 1920–1940* (Saint Louis: Modern Schoolman, 1945).

2. Herbert Butterfield, *The Origins of Modern Science, 1300–1800* (revised ed. New York: Free Press, 1965; first published, 1949).

3. Aristotle, *Posterior Analytics,* I, 2, 71b 9–16.

4. *Ibid.,* Chs. 4–8.

5. *Prior Analytics,* II, 19, 66a 28.

6. *Categories,* 4, 1b 25–2a 4.

7. *Ibid.,*5, 2a 11.

8. *Posterior Analytics,* I, 4, 6, 8.

9. For similar presentations see Robert Bruce Lindsay and Henry Margenau, *Foundations of Physics* (New York: John Wiley & Sons, 1936), pp. 91, 213. Note how this duplicates the Aristotelian distinction between

"first in itself" and "first for us." Now there is a first "first for us" expressed in ordinary language as "hot" and "cold" and the "first in itself" that is the variable of the state named temperature. But there is also a second "first for us" of thermometer readings which also are named temperatures.

10. Aristotle, *Nicomachean Ethics*, VI, 5.

11. *Sum. Theol.*, II–II, 47–56.

12. Sir David Ross [W. D. Ross], *Aristotle's Prior and Posterior Analytics* (Oxford: Clarendon Press, 1949), p. 14.

13. B. Lonergan, *Verbum: Word and Idea in Aquinas*, ed. by David B. Burrell (Notre Dame: University of Notre Dame Press, 1967; first published in five articles, "The Concept of *Verbum* in the Writings of St. Thomas Aquinas," *Theological Studies*, 1946–1949).

14. *Insight*, 1957.

15. *Nicomachean Ethics*, I, 3, 1094b 23–27.

16. *Contra Gentiles*, I, 9.

17. Claude Geffré, *Un nouvel âge de la théologie* (Paris: Cerf, 1972).

5

Prolegomena to the Study
of the Emerging Religious
Consciousness of Our Time

The topic calls for clarification. I shall begin from brief comments on the terms in the title, and proceed to a few tentative statements on the substantial issue.

1. INTRODUCTION

"Prolegomena to the Study." What perhaps is desired is a framework within which the several contributions might come together. There cannot be expected any synthesis, for the contributions are as yet not available. At most there is possible a set of suggestions that might facilitate reflections.

"Consciousness." In loose usage 'consciousness' is equivalent to 'awareness,' 'knowledge.' More properly, 'consciousness' is an awareness of oneself or of some aspect of oneself. One is aware that the window is open, but conscious that one is about to sneeze.

"Emerging Consciousness." Different lines of inquiry lead to different accounts of the genesis of consciousness. Clinical psychologists relate the emergence of consciousness to the unconscious. So Jolande Jacobi has enumerated the points on which Freud and Jung initially agreed with regard to the 'ego' and the 'complex.'[1] She went on to describe Jung's later position which distinguished the col-

lective unconscious from the personal unconscious and resolved complexes into their collective and personal components. The collective components came to be named archetypes and were pronounced nonpathological. The personal components were viewed as modifications of the archetypes arising in personal history and providing a source for deviance.[2] Speculation on the archetypes led Erich Neumann to a genetic history of the emergence of the ego,[3] and Gerhard Adler has given us a complementary case history on the maturation process in which consciousness centered on the ego shifts to consciousness centered on the self.[4]

In contrast with clinical psychology, the social psychologist, George Herbert Mead, has stressed the social origin of one's awareness of self.[5] Personalists have urged that the notions of 'I' and 'you' emerge as differentiations of a prior 'we' or 'us.' And when the Marxist seeks to arouse the class consciousness of the workers, he is concerned less with the individuality of the workers and far more with their socioeconomic reality.

"Emerging Religious Consciousness." When one speaks of the religious consciousness emerging in our time, one is not thinking of the transmission of an already developed religion from parents to children or from proselytes to converts. Rather one's thoughts are about innovation. Settled religious belief or practise has been modified in some unexpected manner or measure. Concern with religion has been intensified or on the contrary has been relaxed. Interest in religion has increased where it had been slight, or vanished where it had been strong.

Moreover, inasmuch as changes in many individuals occur within the same period, one is led to suspect some *common* condition or cause or occasion, and so to look for some sociocultural factor in the genesis of the new religious consciousness. It remains, however, that a change in religious attitudes can be authentic only if it includes some inward ground for religious commitment, and so while outward factors have their role, an inward factor is also to be sought.

The Coalescence of Outer and Inner Factors. To distinguish two factors invites the question, How do they come together? An answer is to be had by reverting to the distinction already drawn between the two meanings of 'consciousness' and by going on to add a third.

This addition may be effected most expeditiously by noting three meanings of the word, experience, and by relating these meanings to the meanings of the word, consciousness.

As 'consciousness,' so too 'experience' can be used as a synonym for 'knowledge.' In this fashion we speak of a man of experience, and we mean a man that has long been engaged in some trade or profession, some art or craft, and has come to possess a full and balanced knowledge of the ins and outs of his way of life.

But there is also a rather technical use of the word, experience; it arises in certain analyses of the various components that together make up human knowing; it would denote an infrastructure within human knowing, and it would contrast the infrastructure with a suprastructure.

For example, any scientist will distinguish sharply between his hypothesis and the data to which he appeals. To the data the hypothesis adds a suprastructure of context, problem, discovery, formulation. But the data, as appealed to, are not yet the infrastructure. For, as appealed to, the data are named; and the naming involves its own suprastructure of a technical language and of the scientific knowledge that had to be acquired to use that language accurately. Moreover, this suprastructure supposes an ordinary language, through which one advances to a grasp of scientific terminology, and a commonsense style of knowledge, through which one advances to scientific knowledge. So finally one comes to the infrastructure. It is pure experience, the experience underpinning and distinct from every suprastructure. As outer experience it is sensation as distinct from perception. As inner experience it is consciousness as distinct from self-knowledge, consciousness as distinct from any introspective process in which one inquires about inquiring, and seeks to understand what happens when one understands, and endeavors to formulate what goes on when one is formulating, and so on for all the inner activities of which all of us are *conscious* and so few of us have any exact *knowledge*.

I say that all of us are conscious of these activities, for our sensing and feeling, our inquiring and understanding, our formulating and checking, our deliberating and deciding, are not unconscious but conscious.

I say that so few have any exact knowledge of these operations, for while they are conscious, still that consciousness is not knowledge but only the infrastructure in a potential knowledge that few get around to actuating by adding its appropriate suprastructure.

To conclude this subsection, let us note a possibility. It may be that inner religious and outer sociocultural factors come together to constitute a new religious consciousness inasmuch as (1) the inner religious factor resembles an infrastructure while (2) the outer sociocultural factor makes possible, or begins to countenance, or expresses, or interprets the religious experience.

Further Illustrations of Consciousness as Infrastructure. My book, *Insight,*[6] is an account of human understanding. As a book, it is an outer sociocultural factor providing expression and interpretation of events named insights. But at the same time it is inviting the reader to self-discovery, to performing in and for himself the illustrative insights set forth in successive chapters, to adverting to what happens in himself when the insights occur and, no less, to what is missing when they do not occur, until eventually as is hoped he will be as familiar with his own intelligence in act as he is with his ocular vision.

What can be done for insights, can also be done for feelings. Feelings simply as felt pertain to an infrastructure. But as merely felt, so far from being integrated into an equable flow of consciousness, they may become a source of disturbance, upset, inner turmoil. Then a cure or part of a cure would seem to be had from the client-centered therapist who provides the patient with an ambiance in which he is at ease, can permit feelings to emerge without being engulfed by them, come to distinguish them from other inner events, differentiate among them, add recognition, bestow names, gradually manage to encapsulate within a suprastructure of knowledge and language, of assurance and confidence, what had been an occasion for disorientation, dismay, disorganization.

I have been distinguishing between an infrastructure of insights as discoveries or of feelings as felt and, on the other hand, a suprastructure of insights as formulated in hypotheses or of feelings as integrated in conscious living. Perhaps I may add a few random indications that depth psychologists are not unaware of the existence and relevance of some such distinction.

In a study of Jung's psychology Raymond Hostie adduces evidence for his opinion that "Jung refuses to use 'consciousness' in

the strict sense of the word unless he is concerned with contents
which the subject relates consciously and explicitly to his own ego.
In (= Out of..?) his own words, therefore, consciousness equals reflective consciousness.''[7]

Karen Horney appeals to

> . . . the fact that there is no strict alternative between con-
> scious and unconscious, but that there are, as H. S. Sullivan has
> pointed out in a lecture, several levels of consciousness. Not
> only is the repressed impulse still effective—one of the basic
> discoveries of Freud—but also in a deeper level of conscious-
> ness the individual knows about its presence. . . . For the sake
> of saving repetitive explanations I shall use the term ''register''
> when I mean that we know what is going on within us without
> our being aware of it.[8]

In similar vein Wilhelm Stekel wrote:

> Our thinking is a polyphony. There are always several thoughts
> working simultaneously, one of which is the bearer of the lead-
> ing voice. The other thoughts represent the medium and low
> voices. . . . In this framework the whole material with which
> we deal in analysis is capable of becoming conscious. It is to be
> found predominately in the lower voices. It is covered up by
> other voices. To quote Klages, the thing in question is not so
> much a thing that is not thought as one that is not recognized.[9]

Application of the Foregoing. If consciousness has many meanings,
so too will religious consciousness have many. There follows at
once a basic clarification of what might be meant by ''emerging religious consciousness,'' namely, the transition from lesser to greater
luminousness, intensity, clarity, fulness.

For those that have lived their lives in the religion in which they
were born and brought up, the emergence of religious consciousness
is a relatively straightforward process of coming to assimilate the
available religious meanings, make their own the available religious
ideals, participate with their fellows in the customary rituals.

But, as already remarked, our concern is with an emerging religious consciousness that has a component of novelty. Such novelty
may be in response to social change. It may be released by cultural
difference. It may remodel any of the previously existing forms of

religious belief and practise, or scatter into idiosyncratic particular-
isms, or move (enthusiastically or reluctantly) towards ecumenism
or universalism.

On each of these something is to be said, first, on the social factor of alienation, next on the cultural factor of what may be named
the second enlightenment, and finally on certain distinctive features
of emerging religious consciousness in our time.

2. SOCIAL ALIENATION

Ours is a time of very large establishments. They are conspicuous in finance, industry, commerce. They have kept growing on all
levels of government with its numerous, far-reaching, and intricate
departments. They have extended into the intermediate zone in
which private initiative has yielded to public concern for general
utilities, for health, for education, for the level of employment, for
care of orphans, the sick, the aged. They are found when the adherents of a religion are numerous, their organization elaborate, their
transactions extensive.

The numerous tasks to be performed in a large establishment
generate the type of organization named bureaucracy. Policies determine goals. Procedures effect the division of labor. Standards settle acceptable performance. To spell out policies calls not only for
broad vision but also for the detailed knowledge of the man of experience. An efficient division of labor demands intimate knowledge
of the tasks to be performed and of the ability of employees to perform them; and to these must be added the long process of trial and
error or, alternatively, the enormous ingenuity that fits the many
parts into a smoothly functioning whole. Standards finally have to be
set not merely for the end-product but also for each of its distinct
stages; nor is it enough to set them without providing suitably exacting controls.

The more precise the policies, the more efficient the procedures, the more exigent the standards and their controls, then the
closer will be the approximation to the ideal bureaucracy. The cus-
tomer will be supplied with the very product or service that was intended for him or her or, on a further level of sophistication, with the
very variety of products or services intended for them. It is the glory

of the market system—underlined by the ineptitude of totalitarian bureaucracy—that it strives to meet demand and that it strives to adapt to changes in effective demand.

It remains that the large establishment and its bureaucratic organization is a fourfold source of that conjunction of dissatisfaction and hopelessness that is named alienation and foments revolutions.

For policies, procedures, standards are all expressed in general terms. Generalities never reach the full determinateness of concrete reality. But what is good has to be good in every respect, for the presence of any defect makes it bad. My point is very ancient, for over two millennia ago Aristotle pronounced equity to be virtue and defined it as a correction of the law where the law is defective owing to its universality.[10] Like laws, the policies, procedures, standards of a bureaucracy are universal. But unlike laws, they are not tolerant of equitable correction.

For such correction would have to be the work of those immediately concerned, or else it would have to be referred to those higher in authority. But to grant discretionary power to those immediately concerned would run counter to the purposes of bureaucracy: it would disperse initiative, interfere with the precise location of responsibility, cast doubt on the reliability of the product or the quality of the service. On the other hand, when the chain of command is from above downwards, any flow of information from below upwards tends to be sluggish, for it is apt to go unrewarded; unwelcome, for it adds to the work of those above; ineffective, for those above are unfamiliar with the situation below, less perceptive of the difficulties that are arising, with little insight into the solutions that are possible, and unsure of their own ability, if need be, to convince those still higher up.

Such rigidity is no great problem in a stationary society. But modern society is on the move. For the large establishment the line of least resistance is a judicious combination of apparent change and real stagnation. The product or service remains essentially the same, but the decor is piquantly novel and the advertising a fresh variation on the hard or soft sell.

There is a deeper level to the problem. As science advances by a process of trial and error, so too commerce, industry, finance enjoy no quicker or surer way to greater wisdom. As science can operate and apparently flourish for long periods despite its mistaken assumptions, so too can operations in other fields where perceptive attention to data and openness to fresh viewpoints are less developed. For we readily perceive what we expect. Conversely, we may sense what we cannot as yet formulate, but sensation remains mere infrastructure until a relevant suprastructure has been developed.

It is true, of course, that the recondite constructions of theoretical science demand an exactitude that would be out of place in the conduct of human affairs. But this does not completely invalidate my point. A new scientific discovery announces, not a change in nature, but a defect in earlier science. In contrast, a change in human affairs is a change in the way people feel and think and act. It is apprehended not by the natural scientist changing his theories but by the journalist reporting what is occurring and by the psychological or sociological historian noting what had been going forward. Is, for instance, the maximization of profit a socially desirable economic maxim? Some say yes and some say no, but one may also distinguish. What was desirable in individual entrepreneurs at the beginning of the nineteenth century, can be disastrous in the conduct of multinational corporations towards the end of the twentieth.[11] What in nature would be the evolution of a new species, in human affairs is merely the transformation of an institution. My point is simply that as diligent scientists can overlook the evidence calling for a revision of accepted theory, so too men of affairs can overlook the evidence for significantly changed institutions.

There is a further difference between natural process and human affairs. When natural laws are not observed, one concludes, not that nature has gone astray, but that scientists have been mistaken. When the legitimating precepts of a human institution are not observed, matters are more complex, for one has to reckon not only with the adequacy of the precept but also with the honesty of men. If intelligent self-interest has a defensible meaning, it can also be a cloak for bias—for the individual bias of the individual that grabs what he can get away with; for the far more insidious bias of the group insensitive to the rights of outsiders and unaware that its own function has diminished or disappeared; for the general bias of mankind, at best ready to listen to the dictates of common sense, but impatient and even contemptuous of criticism that rests on a theoretical source. And the sundry aspects of this threefold bias, as I have argued elsewhere,[12] can arise not only in the sphere of economics but

b bureaucratic administration
4 defects

also in that of government, not only in politics but in any of the areas into which political benevolence may extend, not only in things secular but also in things sacred.

The large establishment and its bureaucratic administration, then, suffer from four defects. Its products and its services are specified by universals, but the good is always more concrete than a set of universals. Its mode of operation is rigid with little tolerance for discretionary adaptation. Its capacity for the more alert observation and the more critical reflection that generate revised ideas and remodeled operations seems no greater than that attributed to the scientific community by Thomas Kuhn.[13] Its size, finally, its complexity, and its solidarity with other large establishments and bureaucracies provide a broad field for the ingenuity of egoists, the biases of groups, the disastrous oversights of 'practical' common sense.

I write no more than prolegomena. But if today social alienation exists, the bureaucratic establishment is clearly a candidate for scrutiny. Injustice breeds hatred. A monopoly of power and initiative breeds resentment. The 'black box' of vast and intricate complexity precludes the understanding that might set a limit to criticism.

3. THE SECOND ENLIGHTENMENT[14]

The Enlightenment—it becomes just the first Enlightenment if a second is recognized—was carried socially and culturally. Socially by the movement that would sweep away the remnants of feudalism and a lingering absolutism by proclaiming liberty, fraternity, equality. Culturally by the triumph of Newton, who did for mechanics what Euclid had done for geometry and whose success led philosophers to desert rationalism and swell the ranks of empiricists.

That movement has lasted into our own day and still enjoys a dominant position. But, as it were, from within it there has developed an antithesis, no less massive though, as yet, it has not crystalized. To it I refer when I speak of a second enlightenment.

Culturally its first underpinnings came with the relativization of Euclidean geometry: from being regarded as the unique deduction of necessary truth from self-evident principles it became just one of many possible geometric systems deduced from freely chosen postulates. Newton's mechanics suffered a similar fate when Einstein's special relativity was accepted; the necessary laws of nature gave way before Heisenberg's uncertainty principle; and the iron laws of economics could be ignored by Lord Keynes in the great depression of the thirties. Moreover, the new significance granted statistics replaced Darwin's chance variation by the probability of the emergence of new forms, while his survival of the fittest became the higher probabilities of survival. A deductivist world of mechanist determinism was making way for the probability schedules of a world in process from lower to higher species and ecosystems.

By rejecting pure reason yet granting a primacy to practical reason Kant had sought a middle ground between empiricism and rationalism. The absolute idealists endeavored to bring about a new rationalist avatar, but the fertility of their suggestiveness was to survive with little acceptance of their abstruse systems. Instead there came Schopenhauer's priority of will and representation, Kierkegaard's surrender to faith, Newman's first toast to conscience, Dilthey's *Lebensphilosophie* and Nietzsche's will to power, Blondel's philosophy of action and Ricoeur's philosophy of will, with similar tendencies found in pragmatists, personalists, phenomenologists, existentialists.

This philosophic assertion of human freedom and autonomy was matched by a counterpart in human studies. Philosophies of history that dispensed with historians were countered by the German Historical School. Its ideal had been formulated by August Boeckh as the interpretative reconstruction of the constructions of mankind. Its deep intuition was that meaning and values have a constitutive and controlling role in human living. Its procedure was empirical without being empiricist. For its basis was the total remains of a culture, whether linguistic, literary, epigraphical, archeological, numismatic; and its background was the whole of previous studies, grammatical, phonetic, chronological, comparative, critical, constructive. Its goal was an understanding that rose out of the data and fitted them in their entirety and particularity as well as was possible at any given time. Its incompletely successful theoretician was Wilhelm Dilthey who grounded the distinction between the *Natur-* and the *Geistes-wissenschaften*.

While the approach to human studies through hermeneutics and history has never become dominant to the west of Germany, pockets

are emerging in which reductionist positivism is set aside. Abraham
Maslow in psychology belongs to a 'third force' that shuns both the
experimental psychologist's concentration on the subhuman and the
clinical psychologist's on the abnormal.[15] Freud's mechanist assumptions have been exorcised by various types of hermeneutic.[16]
Talcott Parsons has stressed that it was not theologians but sociologists that put out of court the old-style speculations of anthropolo-
gists on religion,[17] and assigns, as does Robert Bellah, a notable role
to religion in the continuity of a system of social action.[18] Finally, to
mention a point to which we shall return, the correlation between
brain waves and various states of consciousness, discovered by Hans
Berger in the twenties, has brought to light physiological differences
between ordinary consciousness, internally focused states, drowsi-
ness, and deep sleep.[19]

Such in summary fashion is the second enlightenment. It is a
profound transformation in mathematics and natural science. It is
paralleled by a transformation in philosophy. It is complemented by
the vast development in human studies stemming from the initiatives
of the German Historical School. It has found allies in sociological
and psychological tendencies away from the reductionist postulate
of positivist philosophy.

Of itself this second enlightenment is culturally significant. But
it may have as well a social mission. Just as the first enlightenment
had its carrier in the transition from feudal to bourgeois society, so
the second may find a role and task in offering hope and providing
leadership to the masses alienated by large establishments under bureaucratic management.

An exploration of this possibility would call for another *Ency-
clopédie*. Let me just mention the pointed relevance of a single contemporary work, *The American Condition*, by Richard Goodwin,[20]
and turn at once to certain features of religious consciousness in this
sociocultural situation.

4. EMERGING RELIGIOUS CONSCIOUSNESS

In his *The Coming Convergence of World Religions*[21] Robley
Edward Whitson draws attention to a thrust towards world community in contemporary consciousness. Let me quote:

Without parallel in the past, contemporary civilization is coming to be centered upon consciousness of man as community: the significance of man in personal relationship—not the isolated individual nor the subordinating society. . . . Perhaps this is the most impressive element in the development of the first half of the century: materialist individualism, exalting the pragmatic good in the isolated value of possession, pleasure, security—the individual as opposed to others, morally unrelated; and subordinating totalitarianism, identifying all reality in the will of one as leader, as consensus, as collective dictatorship—the individual absorbed in anti-relational conformism.

In the latter half of the century we find that our choice does not rest between these two. It seems, rather, that opposition to both is stimulating an awareness of a positive correspondence between man as individual and as social: community. And an immediate consequent of even the most rudimentary recognition of human community is the further recognition of human unity, not simply in terms of external pressures and circumstances pragmatically forcing man to come together, but as emerging consciousness of what man really is, and hence the consciousness that these ''external'' factors are not determinative causes, but dynamic reflections of the human condition.

Yet human unity . . . is still clearly at its beginnings, still mostly dream. But perhaps now we can see it as dream in the psychological sense—a sign from within the hidden inward side of our process of consciousness revealing our fuller life history—rather than a dream in the sense of theoretical ideal. The thrust toward unity in contemporary civilization is unique precisely because it has emerged in our consciousness from our real, experiential history, not from an abstract social theory. We can see this best in terms of problems. The sense of reality we have about human unity does not rest upon what has been achieved, but upon the appalling problems experienced (and only partly resolved) in the first half of the century and upon the problems now arising as we seek unity.[22]

I have quoted Dr. Whitson at such length because he brings out so well the mating of external and internal factors in emerging consciousness: consciousness like the dream emerging from the unconscious as an intimation of a reality to be achieved; alienation both from the isolated individualism of misconceived freedom and from the imposed conformity of totalitarianism; the attraction of an idea only in the bud, of community.

An even longer passage would have to be quoted to do justice to the remarkable consensus achieved in the meetings of the Research Group on "Philosophy and the Study of Religion" at the last World Congress of Philosophy held at Varna, Bulgaria, in September 1973. There a wide range of participants, representing not only the major religions of the world but also different forms of Marxism and humanism and including the presence of the Moscow Institute for Atheism and Religion, gave unanimous approval to a seven-point formulation drawn up by our colleague in the present symposium, Dr. Raimundo Panikkar.[23]

Concurrent testimony could be inferred, I believe, from the widespread interest in the books of the late Pierre Teilhard de Chardin. Their appeal was not merely ecumenical but universalist. Their influence continues through all those that found in Teilhard the word or example that brought to focus some deeper aspiration of their own.

Less well known is another Jesuit, an Irishman, who had been studying and teaching at Sophia University in Tokyo for over twenty years. His most recent book, *Silent Music: The Science of Meditation*,[24] continues his exploration of western and eastern mysticism begun in *The Mysticism of the Cloud of Unknowing*,[25] and continued in *The Still Point*[26] and *Christian Zen*.[27] His trajectory has been from the interpretation of a medieval English mystic through a comparison of Zen enlightenment with Christian contemplation to the advocacy of Zen techniques for the promotion of Christian mysticism. He has frequented Zen monasteries and prayed under Zen masters and in recent years has made summer forays in America. His latest work begins from the rapid diffusion of the meditation movement, scientific study of brain waves and correlated states of consciousness, and biofeedback techniques. From psychic states of 'expanded consciousness' through their benefits and dangers he advances to an area that, as experience, is common to East and West, morally uplifting, cosmic in orientation but, when interpreted, takes on the distinctiveness of diverse traditions. It is at this point that we meet what, on the one hand, is religious in its distinctiveness and, so to speak, its essence but, on the other hand, has not yet become the infrastructure incorporated within an interpretative suprastructure.

Let me attempt to elucidate the significance of this virtual isolation of religious experience by placing it in a quite different context. Some five years ago Dr. Panikkar wrote: *diacritical theology*

> The Buddhist would like to believe in the whole message of
> Christ, and he sincerely thinks he could accept it and even un-
> derstand it better if it could be purified from what he considers
> to be its theistic superstructure. The Hindu will wonder why he
> has to join a physical and cultural community simply because of
> his belief in the divinity of Christ and in his resurrection. The
> 'death of God' theologian, or whatever name we may choose for
> him, will say that it is precisely because Christ is the Savior that
> he can dispense with any conception of a transcendent God or a
> physical miracle.[28]

Without suggesting that the 'death of God' theologian need be a
mystic, one may observe that there is not too great a difference between Dr. Johnston's awareness of a religious experience that is incorporated in different interpretations and, on the other hand, what
remains when the opposing interpretations are removed.

Now it is precisely this common factor that Dr. Panikkar would
take as the basic or starting point in his proposal of a "Metatheology
or Diacritical Theology as Fundamental Theology."[29] He holds that
there exists ". . . that human primordial relatedness which occurs
when dealing with ultimate problems." He stresses that he is not assuming ". . . that there must be a kind of objectifiable common
ground or certain universally formulable common statements." He
continues: "I am only pleading for a really open dialogue—one in
which the meeting ground may have itself first to be created—where
in the very intermingling of religious currents, ideas and beliefs, a
more powerful stream of light, service, and better understanding
will emerge."[30]

A similar basis seems to lie behind Dr. Whitson's contention
that theologians should promote his coming convergence of world
religions. He writes:

> The peculiarity of this convergence process is that we must not
> think we are leaving or abandoning traditions for someone else's
> or for a new construction, but we are bringing traditions into
> contact with the expectation that when they are no longer iso-
> lated we will be able to discover how each in its own authentic-

ity has even greater significance in interaction with the others. . . . We are also assuming that the historic traditions are being called into unity and hence that this is integral to their authenticity. The theological task is to discern this calling in the historic development of the tradition to this point and creatively to project at least something of what a fulfilment of this calling could mean for the tradition in question and the others converging with it.[31]

A context for these statements may be surmised from the fact that Dr. Whitson published *Mysticism and Ecumenism* in 1966 and *Shaker Theological Sources* in 1969.

Let us now move from universalist to ecumenist concern. In August 1969 the Central Committee of the World Council of Churches granted membership to the Kimbanguist church of the Congo.[32] As representative of indigenously developing African Christianity, it calls for our attention and has been described by George B. Thomas in *Idoc International*.[33] The product of a Christian mission school, Simon Kimbangu finally yielded to a long and repeated call to preach Christ to his African brothers in April 1921. His mission was to be one of greater fidelity to Christ, his preaching was confirmed by gifts of healing, and he attracted numbers so great that the authorities intervened. On a number of charges he was condemned to death on September 12, 1921, but this sentence was commuted to life imprisonment, and so in prison he languished until he died on October 12, 1951.[34] The segregation of the leader failed to destroy the movement. Kimbanguists were persecuted. Masters of oral tradition, they went underground until such time as the black man could worship God in his way.[35] In 1956 it chanced to become known among the blacks that the Congo had signed the United Nations Declaration of the Rights of Man. This seems to have acted as a signal. Organized Kimbanguist protest kept escalating until the colonial authorities capitulated to Kimbanguist demands. From December 24, 1959, public prohibitions and public persecutions ceased. In January 1960 Kimbanguist schools were officially recognized. In June the Congo became independent and its government granted official recognition to the Kimbanguist church.[36]

Its belief is in God the Father, in Jesus Christ the Son, in the Holy Spirit, the witness of fulfillment of the power of God, the rev-

elation in the Old and New Testaments. Simon Kimbangu is a witness as a prophet in whom the Spirit of God was manifested and has
opened the revelation of Christ through African religious experience
in fresh ways.[37]

Alienated by persecution and by exclusion from the Christian
mission churches, the Kimbanguist church has developed its own
native symbols.[38] It is elaborately organized but in indigenous fashion and under indigenous leadership.[39] The impression one gathers is
of deep populist roots, a sincere Christian outlook on life, intense religious devotion, strong organization, and the readiness of an independent body to cooperate with other Christian groups.

5. SCHEMATIC FRAMEWORK

There occur experiences commonly named religious.

Their emergence into consciousness may be anything from
slight and unnoticed to absorbing, fascinating, dominating.

Of themselves they pertain to an infrastructure, i.e., religious
experience does not occur with a label attached; of itself it is not formulated. To characterize it as infrastructure, however, regards only
its relation to its formulation. By no means is it implied that it is in-
ferior to any other experience or operation.

Any formulation is in the context of some tradition and milieu;
diverse formulations reflect different traditions; and as yet the world
religions do not share some common theology or style of religious
thinking.

The long-term approach to such a common style would seem to
be along the lines of Dr. Panikkar's diacritical theology and/or Dr.
Whitson's convergence of religions. The former regards more especially the initiation of the effort; the latter the need for development beyond present positions.

Hence, at the present time specific discussion of emerging religious consciousness has to proceed on the basis of some convention. If it is not to be merely generic, it has to adopt the formulation
of some particular tradition at least as a temporary or momentary
convention. Commonly this could be the formulation of the group
that is carrying on the discussion or the one most relevant to the material being discussed.

When the choice falls on Christianity, the following points may be noted:

A classical formulation of Christian religious experience may be found in St. Paul's statement that God's love has flooded our inmost heart through the Holy Spirit he has given us (*Rom. 5:5*).

As infrastructure it is the dynamic state of being in love in an unrestricted fashion, a conscious content without an apprehended object.

Its suprastructure, however, is already extant in the account of Christian origins: God sending his only Son for our salvation through death and resurrection and the sending of the Spirit.

The distinctiveness of Christianity lies in this suprastructure. To it the adherents of non-Christian religions may wish to ascribe the characterization of religious experience as being in love.

There is to Christianity an aspiration to universalism, e.g., *I Tim. 2:4*. Perhaps the simplest explanation of this universalism would be that (1) the salvation of the Christian is in and through charity, and (2) this gift as infrastructure can be the Christian account of religious experience in any and all men.

From this basis one may proceed to a general account of emerging religious consciousness, whether universalist, or ecumenist, or 'bottled effervescence,' or alienated by secular or ecclesiastical bureaucracy, or seeking the integration of religious awakening with a fuller development of the second enlightenment, or distorted by human obtuseness, frailty, wickedness.

Paper presented at the Second International Symposium on Belief, Baden/Vienna, January 1975; also presented for the McMartin Memorial Symposium, Carleton University, Ottawa, October 12–13, 1978. Previously published in *Studies in Religion,* Vol. IX (1980), pp. 3–15; Italian translation, "Tra particolarismo e universalismo . . .," in Rocco Caporale, ed., *Vecchi e Nuovi Dei* . . .(Turin: Valentino, 1976); French translation, "Prolégomènes à l'étude de la conscience religieuse . . .," in Bernard Lonergan, *Les voies d'une théologie méthodique* . . . (Montréal: Bellarmin, 1982).

Notes

1. Jolande Jacobi, *Complex/Archetype/Symbol in the Psychology of C. G. Jung,* tr. by Ralph Manheim (London: Routledge and Kegan Paul, 1959), pp. 6–19.

2. *Ibid.*, pp. 19–30.

3. E. Neumann, *The Origins and History of Consciousness*, 1970.

4. G. Adler, *The Living Symbol*, 1961.

5. *George Herbert Mead on Social Psychology: Selected Papers*, ed. by Anselm Strauss (Chicago: The University of Chicago Press, 1964; first published, 1956, as *The Social Psychology of George Herbert Mead*).

6. B. Lonergan, *Insight*, 1957.

7. Raymond Hostie, *Religion and the Psychology of Jung*, tr. by G. R. Lamb (New York: Sheed & Ward, 1957), p. 72.

8. Karen Horney, *The Neurotic Personality of Our Time* (New York: W. W. Norton, 1937), p. 69.

9. Wilhelm Stekel, *Compulsion and Doubt*, tr. by Emil A. Gutheil (New York: Liveright Publishing Corporation, 1949), Vol. I, p. 229.

10. Aristotle, *Nicomachean Ethics*, V, 10, 1137b 27.

11. Richard Barnet and Ronald Müller, "Multinational Corporations," *New Yorker*, December 2 and 9, 1974.

12. B.Lonergan, *Insight*, pp. 218–242.

13. T. S. Kuhn, *The Structure of Scientific Revolutions*, 1970.

14. For the notion of a second enlightenment I am indebted to a paper presented by Frederick Lawrence at a workshop sponsored by the Philosophy and Theology Departments of Boston College, June 17–21, 1974. (Ed.: This paper was published as " 'The Modern Philosophic Differentiation of Consciousness' or What Is the Enlightenment?" in Fred Lawrence (ed.) *Lonergan Workshop*, Vol. II [Chico, Cal.: Scholars Press, 1981], pp. 231–279.)

15. On 'third force' see Abraham H. Maslow, *Toward a Psychology of Being*, 1962, p. vi (p. ix in 2nd ed., 1968).

16. Ernest Becker, *The Denial of Death* (New York: The Free Press, 1973). Herbert Fingarette, *The Self in Transformation: Psychoanalysis, Philosophy, & the Life of the Spirit* (New York: Harper Torchbook, 1965; first published, 1963). Paul Ricoeur, *Freud and Philosophy: An Essay on Interpretation*, tr. by Denis Savage (New Haven: Yale University Press, 1970); and, *The Conflict of Interpretations: Essays in Hermeneutics*, ed. by Don Ihde, with various translators (Evanston: Northwestern University Press, 1974).

17. Talcott Parsons, "The Theoretical Development of the Sociology of Religion," in his *Essays in Sociological Theory*, 1966, pp. 197–210.

18. Talcott Parsons, "Introduction" (to Part IV: Culture and the Social System) in *Theories of Society: Foundation of Modern Sociological Theory*, ed. by Talcott Parsons et al. (New York: The Free Press, 1965; first published, 1961), pp. 963–993; see p. 983. R. Bellah, *Beyond Belief*, 1970, p. 12.

19. William Johnston, *Silent Music: The Science of Meditation* (New York: Harper & Row, 1974), p. 32.

20. Richard N. Goodwin, *The American Condition* (Garden City, New York: Doubleday, 1974).

21. Robley Edward Whitson, *The Coming Convergence of World Religions* (New York, etc.: Newman, 1971).

22. *Ibid.*, pp. 17–18.

23. Raimundo Panikkar, "Have 'Religions' the Monopoly on *Religion?*" *Journal of Ecumenical Studies,* Vol. XI (1974), pp. 515–517.

24. W. Johnston, *Silent Music,* 1974.

25. William Johnston, *The Mysticism of The Cloud of Unknowing: A Modern Interpretation,* with a Foreword by Thomas Merton (New York: Desclée, 1967).

26. W. Johnston, *The Still Point: Reflections on Zen and Christian Mysticism* (New York: Fordham University Press, 1970).

27. W. Johnston, *Christian Zen* (New York: Harper & Row, 1971).

28. Raimundo Panikkar, "Metatheology or Diacritical Theology as Fundamental Theology," *Concilium,* Vol. XLVI (1969), pp. 43–55; see p. 49.

29. *Ibid.*, pp. 43–55.

30. *Ibid.*, p. 52.

31. R. E. Whitson, *The Coming Convergence of World Religions,* 1971, pp. 168–169.

32. William H. Crane, "The Kimbanguist Church and the Search for Authentic Catholicity," *The Christian Century,* Vol. LXXXVII (1970), pp. 691–695.

33. George B. Thomas, "Kimbanguism: African Christianity," *Idoc International: North American Edition,* No. 21 (13 March, 1971), pp. 2–29.

34. *Ibid.*, pp. 3–9, 12.

35. *Ibid.*, pp. 9–12.

36. *Ibid.*, pp. 12–14.

37. *Ibid.*, pp. 15–16.

38. *Ibid.*, pp. 23–25.

39. *Ibid.*, pp. 16–17.

6

Christology Today:
Methodological Reflections

Jesus of Nazareth, known as a man, confessed as Son of God, Christ, Lord, Savior, has been the focus and the basis of Christian faith from its origins down to the present time. But as Claude Geffré has put it, we are living in a new age of theology.[1] If our faith has been ever the same, still it has also regularly put forth different expressions to meet the exigences of different times. A new age of theology brings with it new expressions no less in Christology than in other areas of belief. It is with what is new in Christology that my methodological reflections will be concerned.

In an age of novelty method has a twofold function. It can select and define what was inadequate in former procedures and, at the same time, indicate the better procedures that have become available. But it may also have to discern the exaggerations or deficiencies to which the new age itself is exposed. Indeed, inasmuch as theological development is dialectical, contemporary risks and dangers are apt to provide, if not the highest motive, at least the most efficacious incentive towards a renewal of theological method.

It is with such an incentive in mind that occasionally throughout this paper I shall refer to Piet Schoonenberg who in 1969 published a book that originally appeared in Dutch, that immediately was translated into German, that two years later came out in English and, after a further lapse of two years, was issued in French.[2]

It was in between the English and the French translations on February 21, 1972, that the Sacred Congregation for the Doctrine of the Faith decided to oppose certain recent errors and issued an explicit reaffirmation of the doctrines of the council of Chalcedon and of the third council of Constantinople.[3] Nor would it be altogether rash to surmise whose errors the Congregation had in mind, for Fr. Schoonenberg had favored replacing the doctrinal pattern of these councils with ". . . that of God's complete presence in the human person Jesus Christ with his own human will and actions."[4]

More in sympathy with Fr. Schoonenberg than with the Roman Congregation Klaus Reinhardt in the *Internazionale katholische Zeitschrift* for May/June 1973 published an extensively documented article. In it he contrasted the old Christology, which believed Jesus Christ to be the Son of God made man, with an incipient new Christology, which thought of Jesus more simply as the true, the exemplary, the new man.[5] Moreover, in the same month in *Orientierung* Fr. Schoonenberg adumbrated the contents of a book on which he was working by enumerating thirty-six propositions. One is led to expect a tome that will try to do away with the Trinitarian and Christological doctrine that has been taught by the church for over fifteen hundred years.[6]

My purpose, however, is not controversial and negative but positive and didactic. I shall be concerned with seven related topics. Three regard prolegomena in psychology, history, philosophy. Two more deal with Christological method in its religious and its theological aspects. A sixth deals with the meaning of Chalcedon, and the seventh will try to meet the main issue, namely: Can one be truly a man without being a human person? It is an issue that is all the more grave now that we have set Scholasticism aside without as yet putting in its place any commonly accepted doctrine.

1. THE FIRST PROLEGOMENON: PSYCHOLOGY

Scholastic psychology was a metaphysical psychology. It was a doctrine of the essence of the soul, of its potencies, of their informing habits and acts, and of the objects of the acts. So little did consciousness enter into this psychology that Aristotle treated in the same work the psychology of men, of animals, and of plants.

Traditionally it has been this psychology that has underpinned theological accounts of the person of Christ, of his human perfections, and of the grace given all men but superabundantly to him.

The basically metaphysical approach in this traditional psychology and theology stems from the Aristotelian view that other sciences were subalternate to metaphysics, that the basic terms and principles of metaphysics held *mutatis mutandis* for all beings, and consequently that these terms and laws formed the nucleus around which particular sciences constructed their further determinations.

There is no need on the present occasion to discuss the validity of Aristotelian architectonics. Suffice to say that, if the contemporary challenge to traditional Christology is to be met, then one must go beyond a metaphysical view of the person, a metaphysical account of human perfection, a metaphysical account of the life of grace. One must do so, for the essence of the challenge is an assumption (1) that a person is the psychological subject of interpersonal relations, (2) that human development is entry into a symbolic world, a world mediated by meaning, (3) that one cannot be truly a human being without being a human person.

By such "going beyond" I mean not a rejection of metaphysics but its inclusion within the dynamic unity of a foundational methodology. Within that unity all cognitional procedures would be recognized, each would retain its proper autonomy, and all would be related within the critical architectonic of transcendental method. And the term, transcendental, would refer not only to objects (one, true, real, good) and not only to the *a priori* of the subject but to both together, to the *a priori* of the subject's questions and to the range of objects disclosed in answers.[7]

Now when psychology is conceived not as subalternate to metaphysics but as a science in its own right, then it proceeds from the data of consciousness. Its basic terms name conscious operations. Its basic relations name conscious processes. Its account of truly human development is of conscious subjects moving cumulatively through their operations to the self-transcendence of truth and love.

On this view of human development advance ordinarily is from below upwards. It is from experiencing through inquiry to understanding; from intelligent formulations through reflection to judgment; from apprehended reality through deliberation to evaluation, decision, action.

Still the ordinary process is not the exclusive process. Man's insertion in community and history includes an invitation for him to accept the transformation of falling in love: the transformation of domestic love between husband and wife; the transformation of human love for one's neighbor; the transformation of divine love that comes when God's love floods our inmost heart through the Holy Spirit he has given us (*Rom. 5:5*).

Such transforming love has its occasions, its conditions, its causes. But once it comes and as long as it lasts, it takes over. One no longer is one's own. Moreover, in the measure that this transformation is effective, development becomes not merely from below upwards but more fundamentally from above downwards. There has begun a life in which the heart has reasons which reason does not know. There has been opened up a new world in which the old adage, *nihil amatum nisi prius cognitum*, yields to a new truth, *nihil vere cognitum nisi prius amatum*.

It was such transforming love that enabled Paul to say: ''. . . the life I now live is not my life, but the life which Christ lives in me'' (*Gal. 2:20*). It is on the analogy of such transforming love that perhaps we can gain some imperfect understanding of the mystery that the life lived by Jesus of Nazareth really was the fully human life of the second person of the Blessed Trinity.

2. THE SECOND PROLEGOMENON: PHILOSOPHY

Contemporary Catholic theology deprecates any intrusion from philosophy. The result inevitably is, not no philosophy, but unconscious philosophy, and only too easily bad philosophy.

So Fr. Schoonenberg explains that he contends for a Christology of presence.[8] Very plausibly this makes for a pastoral Christology, for everyone knows what is meant by presence, but only philosophers talk about being. Still before we go along with Fr. Schoonenberg's rejection of Chalcedon and of the third council of Constantinople, it may be well for us to pause for an instant in an effort to grasp just what one means by presence. Quickly one finds more than one meaning.

For all of us have lived from infancy in a world of immediacy, a world of sights and sounds, of tastes and smells, of touching and feeling, of joys and sorrows. It was from within that world (as described by Jean Piaget) that we first developed operationally by assimilating new objects to objects already dealt with, by adjusting old operations to new occasions, by combining differentiated operations into groups, and by grouping groups in an ascending hierarchy.

But also within that operational development we came to listen, endeavored to repeat, managed to understand, began to speak, to converse, to learn from others. Thereby we gradually moved out of our original world of immediacy into a world mediated by meaning. It was quite a new world that included the past and the future as well as the present, the possible and probable as well as the actual, rights and duties as well as facts. It was an incredibly rich and varied world, and it was extended by literature and history, by philosophy and science, by religion and theology.

Not only do the two worlds differ vastly in their content. They differ no less in their cognitional procedures and in the criteria governing valid procedure. The world of immediacy is a world of data, of what is given to sense and given to consciousness. It is a world as yet without names or concepts, without truth or falsity, without right or wrong. Its criteria lie quite simply in the presence or absence of successful functioning.

In contrast the world mediated by meaning goes beyond experiencing through inquiry to ever fuller understanding, beyond mere understanding through reflection to truth and reality, beyond mere knowing through deliberation to evaluated and freely chosen courses of action. Now mere experiencing has to be enhanced by deliberate attention. Chance insights have to submit to the discipline of the schoolroom and to the prescriptions of method. Sound judgment has to release us from the seduction of myth and magic, alchemy and astrology, legend and folktale; and it has to move us to the comprehensive reasonableness named wisdom. Most of all we have to enter the existential sphere, where consciousness becomes conscience, where the cognitional yields to the moral and the moral to the religious, where we discern between right and wrong and head for holiness or sin.

No one is simply ignorant of these two worlds, of their different procedures, of the differences between their respective criteria. But commonly this advertence is not thematic; it is only lived. As the Scholastics put it, men possess it not *signate* but only *exercite*. And because the possession is only latent and implicit, confusions easily arise. Besides the presence of parents to their infant child, there also is the presence of the parents to one another. No one would fail to notice the difference between these two instances of presence. But when a theologian gets along with a minimal philosophy, he can tell us without further ado that he argues for a Christology of presence. When the absence of philosophy is taken as proof of sincere pastoral concern, many will be entranced by his proposal.

But the fact is that the presence of Christ to us is not presence in the world of immediacy: ''Happy are they who never saw me and yet have found faith'' (*John 20:29*). The fact is that divine revelation comes to us through the mediation of meaning. It comes through meaning transmitted by tradition, meaning translated from ancient to modern tongues, meaning here clarified and there distorted by human understanding, meaning reaffirmed and crystalized in dogmas, meaning ever coming to life in God's grace and God's love.

So little can Fr. Schoonenberg get away from the mediation of meaning that the first ten of his thirty-six propositions published in *Orientierung* lay down laws for theological thought and expression. We are told that we can proceed from this world up to God but not in the opposite direction. We can learn about the Trinity from revelation, but we are not to begin from the Trinity and proceed to think about Christ. In brief, theological thought is to observe the traffic laws of a one-way street and, it is claimed, by such obedience Trinitarian doctrine will become concrete, related to human life, and relevant to preaching.[9]

But this claim, I feel, would be more attractive if it were not involved in vast oversimplifications. However much the one-way traffic law may suit a Christology of presence, it runs counter to the structure and procedures of the world mediated by meaning. Human development more commonly is from below upwards but more importantly, as we have urged, it is from above downwards. Logic would have us argue from the *causa essendi* no less than from the *causa cognoscendi,* from the sphericity of the moon to its phases as well as from the phases to the moon's sphericity. In a contemporary transcendental method one clarifies the subject from objects and one clarifies the objects from the operations by which they are known. In each of the empirical sciences one proceeds not only from the data of observation and experiment to the formulation of laws, but also from the ranges of theoretical possibility explored by mathematicians to physical systems that include empirical laws as particular cases. In theology, finally, one proceeds not only from the data of revelation to more comprehensive statements but also from an imperfect, analogous yet most fruitful understanding of mystery to the syntheses that complement a *via inventionis* with a *via doctrinae*.[10]

3. THE THIRD PROLEGOMENON: HISTORY

There is the history that is written and the history that is written about. Today the history that is written is the work of an ongoing community of professional specialists, developing their proper skills and techniques, setting their own standards, and making their standards effective through a long and exacting apprenticeship of graduate studies. History in this contemporary sense largely was the creation of the nineteenth century, and its acceptance in the Catholic church has occurred only slowly and gradually in the present century. It found its way first into church history, then into patristic and medieval studies, and finally in recent decades into biblical studies.

Where earlier history was a matter of believing testimony, contemporary history is a matter of understanding evidence. Any relic or trace of the past may be evidence, but what it might be evidence for emerges only from the accumulated expertise of the history-writing community, and what it actually does establish results only from a consensus based on investigations that have been carried out by competent researchers and submitted to the scrutiny of competent reviewers.

This contrast between precritical belief in testimony and critical understanding of evidence is of the greatest theological significance. When the New Testament is viewed as testimony to be believed because it is credible, then the greatest emphasis will be placed on the words of Jesus Christ himself, for they are supremely credible, while a fundamentalist adherence will spread indiscriminately over every aspect of every word and sentence because all are divinely inspired. Then the theologian has only to open his Bible to find convincing proof for whatever preconceived ideas he may happen to entertain. But when the New Testament is viewed as evidence, then one need hardly believe what the Synoptic Gospels affirm if one is concerned to differentiate stylistic features, discern successive strata, and compose a history of the synoptic tradition. Then what Jesus really said and did belongs to a stratum still earlier than any to be verified in the successive contributions to the synoptic tradition, and the Jesus of history becomes either Bultmann's itinerant rabbi who eventually was crucified or, more recently, the hopefully fuller figure that is the objective of the new quest of the historical Jesus.

In the light of this shift from history as belief to history as science, one is to find in the New Testament in the first instance evidence on the language and the beliefs that were current in the territory and at the time of the writing and diffusion of the various books that make up the New Testament. At a second instance evidence is provided for earlier times and places insofar as earlier strata may be found in later writing and their provenance may be established. In a third instance what antedates established strata and origins is a matter not so much for historical science as for historical inference.

From a theological viewpoint this means that scripture as inspired is mainly evidence on the faith of the early church. In the first instance it reveals what was believed at the time a given book was written, diffused, accepted. At a second instance it reveals what was believed at the time and place of earlier strata found in later writings. At a third instance it provides premises for inferences on still earlier knowledge or belief.

So at the present time, according to Fr. Raymond Brown, New Testament scholars that may be named moderate conservatives distinguish between an implicit and an explicit Christology in the Jesus of history. An implicit Christology does not attribute to Jesus himself any of the titles the New Testament ascribes to him but does find Christological doctrine implicit in his preaching the kingdom of God and in the authority and power he displayed. An explicit Christology would attribute to Jesus himself some of his New Testament titles and these the less significant ones. Between these two views Fr. Brown expects moderate conservatives to be divided for the rest of this century.[11]

To specific implications of scholarly history for Christological thought we shall presently return. But it has a presupposition to which we may advert at once. Medieval and later theology conceived the psychology of Christ as man not merely in ontological terms but also on the basis of the perfections that on *a priori* grounds were considered befitting a divine person. Today we have to attend more to the words of scripture (*Heb. 4:15*) as cited by the council of Chalcedon (*DS* 301): "similar to us in all things save sin." If we are to think of Jesus as truly a man, we have to think of him as a historical being, as growing in wisdom, age, and grace in a determinate social and cultural milieu, as developing from below as other human beings and from above on the analogy of religious development.

4. CHRISTOLOGY: A RELIGIOUS QUESTION

The extension of modern historical methods into the biblical field constrains theologians to drop some of their former procedures and to develop new ones. Such is a basic feature of the problem of method in contemporary theology. Concretely it means that theologians may not just read a passage of scripture and at once discover in it the verification of traditional ideas. More gravely it means that the interpretation of scripture is not a static pool of information but a moving stream of cumulative and progressive investigation. The problem of method, then, is to find the approach that can select what is valid in current views without becoming involved in positions open to radical change. Some delineation of that approach, as it concerns Christology, I must now attempt.

A first step is a simple reflection that embraces in their complementarity *both* man as attentive, as intelligent, as reasonable, as responsible *and* the human world as given and as structured by intelligence, by reasonable judgment, by decision and action. In this first step there is merely recalled what I may refer to as a post-Kantian transcendental method.

The second step notes that while all fully human behavior involves attention, intelligence, reasonableness, and responsibility, still different inquiries have different emphases and so different goals and different presuppositions. So it is that the textual critic, the exegete, and the historian proceed from the same data to quite different conclusions. So too it is that historians may start from the same data to reach three quite different types of historical affirmation or negation. There is the goal of history conceived by von Ranke as ascertaining the facts, telling how it really happened, *wie es eigentlich gewesen*. There is the goal of history conceived by

Lord Acton as passing moral judgment on the deeds of societies and
their leaders. There is the goal of religious history, of *Heilsgeschichte,* that would discern in facts and moral actions what pertained to the salvation of mankind.

I have distinguished five different genera of inquiry. All five
can be applied to the New Testament. The textual critic can special-
ize in the manuscript tradition. The exegete can master all related literatures and bring them to bear on an understanding of this or that
section of the text. The factual historian can assemble the factual
statements in the New Testament, submit them to his critical scrutiny, and seek to fit them in the context of other known contemporary events. The ethically oriented historian can compare the moral
attitudes of New Testament personages with those of other human
communities or he can subsume them under some moral code to
praise them or blame them. But while all of these approaches have
their significance and value, none of them deals with what mani-
festly is the principal concern of the New Testament. For first and
last, the New Testament is a book with a message; the message is
presented in a great variety of manners, in narratives and parables, in
precepts and counsels, in exhortations and warnings. The message is
depicted as emanating from the man, Jesus, who suffered, died, was
quickened from the dead, and now sits at the right hand of the Father
in heaven. The message announces the imminent coming of the
kingdom of God, and, as it challenged Jew and Greek two millennia
ago, so too today it challenges us with a last word about last things.
As Saul on the way to Damascus heard a voice saying: "Saul, Saul,
why do you persecute me?"[12] so each of us is to hear from the same
voice either of two verdicts. That verdict may be: ". . . anything
you did for one of my brothers here, however humble, you did for
me." But again it may be: ". . . anything you did not do for one of
these, however humble, you did not do for me."[13]

Our third step continues the second. We began from the exigence of a post-Kantian transcendental method that attends not just
to the object, not just to the subject, but to each in itself and in its dependence on the other. We proceeded from that generality to the currently common view that the New Testament pertains to the genus,
Heilsgeschichte, that it centers on a *kerygma* addressed to *Existenz.*
We have now to note that the message is at once simple, radical, and

intensely personal, that it stands in correlation with the response it elicits, that in that response there emerges the message as message-for-us.

The message then is simple, as simple as the "Follow me" addressed to Simon and Andrew, to James and John, to Levi the publican.[14] It is as radical as the counsel to leave father and mother and all one possesses, to renounce wealth and honors, to put up with every indignity, day after day to take up one's cross.[15] Simple and radical, the message is intensely personal. It is "Follow *me*," "for my sake and for the Gospel," "for the sake of my name," "for the sake of the kingdom of God,"[16] that is, for the kingdom for which Jesus himself lived and died.

To such a message the essential answer is action. The critical issue is not just the data, not just their interpretation, not just the question of fact, but deliberation, decision, deed. So the relevant answer is action as recounted in the Acts of the Apostles, in their joy in being found worthy to ". . . suffer indignity for the sake of the Name."[17] It is action as in the journeys and preaching, the stripes and prisons, as well as in the letters of St. Paul.

Answer by action begets further answering action. It comes in the words of those touched by Peter's first sermon, "Friends, what are we to *do?*[18] as earlier it had come, according to John, in Peter's own words, "Lord, to whom shall we go? Your words are words of eternal life."[19] It comes, as Heinrich Schlier has effectively set forth, with acclamations acknowledging Jesus as Lord, with confessions that God has quickened him from the dead, with gradually developing and expanding formulas of belief.[20] Finally, as Franz Mussner has added, it was to provide a context for such acclamations, such confessions, such formulas, to clarify their meaning and preclude misinterpretations, that memories of Jesus' earthly ministry were recalled and gospels were written.[21]

Such, then, is our third step, and plainly it leads to a fourth. The third step placed the New Testament in the genre of salvation history, and it placed our response to it on the existential level of confrontation, deliberation, evaluation, decision, deed. But the New Testament not only is a religious document calling for religious living; it also is a personal invitation and the appropriate response to it is a personal commitment. So ineluctably there arises the question, Who is this Jesus? It is the question asked by the storm-tossed disciples when the winds and seas obeyed him.[22] It is the question he himself raised at Caesarea Philippi.[23] It is the question recurrent in the Gospel of John, when Jesus spoke to the Samaritan woman at Jacob's well,[24] when the Jews questioned the man cured at the Sheep-Pool in Jerusalem,[25] when Jesus contrasted those that belong to the world below with those belonging to the world above,[26] when Jesus revealed himself to the man born blind,[27] when the people asked who this Son of Man is that is to be lifted up.[28]

5. CHRISTOLOGY: THE THEOLOGICAL QUESTION

As a religious and personal question, the question of Christology antedates New Testament times. But in our time it also is a theological question, and it has to deal with certain prior issues. There is the contrast between the Jesus of history and the Christ of faith. There is the suggested option between a functional and an ontological Christology. There is the problem of uniting the concern of the inquiring subject with the objective wealth of scriptural scholarship. On each of these topics something must be said.

The contrast between the Jesus of history and the Christ of faith may be approached from the distinction already drawn of three kinds of historical writing, namely, writing that deals mainly (1) with questions of fact, or (2) with moral issues, or (3) with matters pertaining to salvation. Now different writing supposes difference in competence. A historian trained to deal with questions of fact also is competent to deal with factual issues that serve to introduce matters pertaining to the second and third style of historical writing. But this does not necessarily imply that he will possess the moral sensibility or the religious concern that will fit him for an open and adequate treatment of matters proper to these further fields. In brief, he can treat certain aspects of the Jesus of history, but he may be unequal to discerning the Christ of faith or to determining the factual presuppositions of the Christ of faith.

Similarly, a religious person will readily discern the Christ of faith but, unless he has been trained in the techniques of scientific history, he will be prone to a fundamentalist interpretation of the New Testament. For him any question of the Jesus of history, as understood by scientific history, will be a matter not of science but of unbelief and infidelity. Nonetheless, there are not only possible but also actually existing religious persons, committed to the Christ of faith, yet also fully cognizant of the nature and procedures of scientific history. They are aware that the New Testament was written by men of faith and addressed to men of faith; they are aware that the authors of the books in the New Testament expressed themselves far more in the vocabulary of their own later day than in the less evolved vocabulary possible in the time of the Jesus of history. And so they not only present the Christ of faith but also join in the new quest for the historical Jesus.[29]

For the secularist, then, the Jesus of history easily becomes a shadowy figure, since so much in the New Testament only excites his incredulity. For the fundamentalist, on the other hand, the Christ of faith is so sufficient that efforts to reconstruct the thought and language of the Jesus of history are regarded as mistaken and superfluous. But this radical opposition tends to vanish when (1) religious people correct their precritical views of history and (2) learned people come to recognize in the New Testament contemporary and so firsthand evidence on the beliefs of the early church.

It is in this coincidence that there is to be found the clue to Christological method. This we have characterized as selecting what is valid in current views without becoming involved in positions open to radical change. Now what is open to radical change, is the incipient and still tentative reconstruction of the thought and language of the Jesus of history. What can be valid in current views is based on the contemporary and so firsthand evidence we possess on the beliefs of the early church. By discerning Christian tradition in that evidence, by coming to grasp its immanent structure and intelligibility, by leaving open the questions still to be settled by the reconstruction of the Jesus of history, the theologian, I submit, will find a first and basic component in a methodically developing Christology.

A second determination of Christological method comes from asking whether New Testament Christology is ontological or functional. Our answer will be that it is neither merely functional nor yet strictly ontological.

A merely functional Christology acknowledges no more than a series of religious events. There is factual evidence that people in New Testament and later times believed Jesus to have risen from the dead. Such acts of believing are historically established. They constitute the set of events referred to as Christology.[30]

Now this is all true enough but it ignores the notion of salvation history. It is not a factual history of acts of believing. It is history of what happened on the evidence believers discern in the light of faith. But there was no question for the New Testament writers that the Jesus who was condemned and crucified, who died and was buried, also rose from the dead. One may agree with them or one may disagree; but if one disagrees, one will not attempt Christian salvation history; one will limit oneself to factual history.[31]

At the same time New Testament Christology is not strictly ontological. It purports to deal with persons that really existed and with events that really occurred. But it does not go into the hermeneutics of its message and, least of all, does it go into that recondite department of hermeneutics that involves one in cognitional theory, epistemology, and metaphysics.

A third determination of Christological method is reached from a consideration of its heuristic structure. But let me begin by an example. Down the ages there have been accepted quite different views on the nature of fire. For Aristotelians it was one of the four elements. For chemists prior to Lavoisier it was attributed to phlogiston. Subsequently to Lavoisier it has been explained as a process of oxydization. The answers differed greatly from one another, but nonetheless they were answers to the same question. What then was that question?

It involved two elements. There were on the side of the object the data on fire, the sensible flames, their sensible effects. But there also was on the side of the subject inquiring intelligence (1) wanting to know what would be known when the data were understood, (2) entertaining answers as long as they seemed to cover all the data, and (3) rejecting answers that eventually were found wanting and entertaining different answers that subsequently seemed to cover all the data.

A heuristic structure, then, is a conjunction both of data on the side of the object and of an operative criterion on the side of the subject. Accordingly, a Christological heuristic structure will be a similar conjunction giving rise to the succession of Christologies set forth in New Testament writings and further developed in the formulations of individuals and of communities down the ages. On the side of the data one discerns three points: (1) that Jesus is named time and again from different viewpoints and in different contexts the Son of God;[32] (2) that we through faith are sons of God and by baptism are one in Christ (*Gal. 3:26–28*), that God sent his only Son that we might acquire the status of sons as is proved to us by the sending of the Spirit of Christ crying in our hearts "Abba! Father!" (*Gal. 4:3–7; Rom. 8:14–17*); and (3) that the Spirit we have received from God knows all and has been given us that we may know all that God of his own grace gives us (*I Cor. 2:10–16; John 14:16, 17, 26*).

In correspondence with such data there arises in the Christian subject his or her heuristic structure. In many contexts and from many viewpoints Jesus was named the Son of God, and that gives rise to the multiple question: How are we in our own minds to understand Jesus as Son of God? Are we to suppose it is a mythic or merely honorific title such as was given to kings? Or does it simply denote the mission of the Messiah? Or does it point to an inner reality such as is our own divine sonship through Christ and in the Spirit, so that as God in us is the Spirit, so God in Jesus is the Word? Or does the sonship of Jesus mean, as the church for centuries has understood it, that Jesus was truly a man leading a truly human life but his identity was the identity of the eternal Son of God consubstantial with the Father?

The heuristic structure then presents a multiple question. Still there is not only question but also criterion. Our own experience of our own sonship provides a first criterion, for if the Spirit in us is God, surely God was in Jesus too. Further the Spirit of God in us enables us to discern what the spirit of the world cannot discern. It is in the progressive clarification of Christian experience and in the continuous exercise of spiritual discernment in the Christian community that Christological doctrine developed.

For Christologies have been many. They have conformed to the diverse strata represented in New Testament writing. They endeavored to meet the needs of Gentiles that had reached a philosophic monotheism. They reacted against Gnostics and Marcionites by defending the Old Testament's creator God and by allegorizing anthropomorphic accounts of his doings. They suffered from involvement in the world-of-immediacy of Stoic naivete and in the seductive halfway house of Middle Platonism. For over fifteen centuries they found a static equilibrium in the definitions of Nicea, Ephesus, Chalcedon, and the third council of Constantinople. But in our time of hermeneutics and history, of psychology and critical philosophy, there is an exigence for further development. There are windows to be opened and fresh air to be let in. It will not, I am convinced, dissolve the solid achievement of the past. It will, I hope, put that achievement on a securer base and enrich it with a fuller content.

6. THE MEANING OF CHALCEDON

The meaning of Chalcedon is not obscure. It teaches, in its opening paragraph, one and the same Son our Lord Jesus Christ: the same perfect in divinity and the same perfect in humanity: truly God and the same truly man . . .; consubstantial with the Father according to his divinity, and the same consubstantial with us according to his humanity . . .; before all ages begotten of the Father according to his divinity, and in the last days, for our sake and for our salvation, the same according to his humanity born of the Virgin Mary mother of God (*DS* 301).

It remains that the clarity of Chalcedon has an essential condition, for it can be clear only if it has a meaning, and it can have a meaning only if dogmas have a meaning. But today there is no lack of people that consider dogmas meaningless. In principle they reject all dogmas from Nicea and the rest of the Greek councils through the medieval councils to Trent and the Vatican. Others would distinguish: the dogmas represent a thought form that in its day was meaningful; but now that day is over. Such perhaps is the opinion of Bernhard Welte who has associated with Nicea the beginning of a type of metaphysics that conforms to the aberration denounced by Heidegger as a forgetfulness of being.[33] Others finally do not seem to advert to the very notion of dogma, to the notion that propositions can be true or false and as true or false refer or do not refer to reality.

Fr. Schoonenberg seems to belong to this last group. He discusses not the dogma of Chalcedon but what in the English translation is called the pattern of Chalcedon and in the German *das Modell*.[34]

Now I have no doubt of the significance of patterns or models or schemata in exegetical and historical study. They serve admirably to direct attention to resemblances and to bring together texts that share a common feature despite differences of expression and of context. So in patristic study Aloys Grillmeier made excellent use of the patterns, God-Man and *Logos-Sarx*. So in New Testament studies one can classify Christologies by the perspective they represent: there are texts that begin from Jesus' earthly ministry and look forward to his passion, death, and resurrection or to his future coming; there are texts that begin with the now risen Lord seated at the right hand of the Father; there are texts that begin from heavenly origins, recount his earthly mission, and terminate with his reign from heaven.

However, the significance of patterns is no more than preliminary. Further evidence is needed before one can conclude that different patterns mean more than different occasions or different contexts. When more is established, one still has to ask whether there is being corrected a defect in language, or in conception, or in understanding; and if the defect is in understanding, then whether it was the nature of man that was misunderstood, or some revealed teaching that was overlooked, or adherence to Christ that was at fault.

So from the nature of the case a discussion of patterns has to face deeper issues. The deeper issue at Chalcedon is that its decree is dogmatic and that its pattern results from earlier dogmatic decrees. It results from the affirmation of Nicea that the Son is consubstantial with the Father, that he is not made but begotten (*DS* 125). It results from the rejection by Nicea of those that claimed there was a time when the Son did not exist or that he did not exist before he was begotten (*DS* 126). It results from Ephesus[35] and from the *Formula unionis* on which Alexandrines and Antiochenes agreed in the spring of 433 that Jesus Christ the only Son of God was consubstantial with the Father according to his divinity and consubstantial with us according to his humanity (*DS* 272).

7. PERSON TODAY

I do not believe that Fr. Schoonenberg does justice to the dogmas of the church. I do not believe that he does justice to the very conditions of possibility of man's living in a world mediated by meaning. But I have no doubt that he raises an issue—very real in systematic theology and very urgent in pastoral theology—when he asks whether one can lead a truly human life without being a human person.

The dogmas in fact teach one person in two natures. All along they imply that the one person is divine, and in the third council of Constantinople—not to mention the second—this is explicitly affirmed (*DS* 554–555). If in earlier ages it was enough to adore the mystery, if from the medieval period some metaphysical account of person and nature were all that was sought, it remains that in our age of psychology and critical philosophy, of hermeneutics and history, something both different and more exacting is required. We have to be able to say what it means for a divine person to live a fully human life.

To this end I shall attempt to offer some explanation of the statement: the person of Christ is an identity that eternally is subject of divine consciousness and in time became subject of a human consciousness. I shall speak (1) of identity, (2) of human consciousness, (3) of human subjectivity, (4) of divine subjectivity, and (5) of the compatibility of one identity with the two subjectivities.

By *identity* I understand the third of the three meanings of *one*. There is *one* in the sense of instance: a first instance is one; a second makes two; still another and there are three; and so on to infinity.

There next is *one* in the sense of intelligible unity. There are many phases of the moon, for its appearance changes night by night. But there is only one moon, for the many appearances have a single explanation: the moon is spherical.

Thirdly, there is *one* in the sense of one and the same. It is the one that presupposes the intelligible unity already mentioned but adds to it an application of the principles of identity and contradiction. So it is one in the sense of the old definition: *indivisum in se et divisum a quolibet alio*. Such is the "one and the same" of the Chalcedonian decree.

Next, consciousness. Man's sensitive, intellectual, rational, and moral operations have two distinct but related characteristics. They are both intentional and conscious. Insofar as they are intentional, they make objects present to us. Insofar as they are conscious, they make us present to ourselves. However, if I have used the same word, present, twice, I also have used it in two different senses. Intentionality effects the presence of an object to the subject, of a spectacle to a spectator. Consciousness is a far subtler matter: it makes the spectator present to himself, not by putting him into the spectacle, not by making him an object, but while he is spectator and as subject.

For adult consciousness subject and object are already distinct. But the distinction is not primordial. For Aristotle coincidence preceded distinction: sense in act is the sensible in act; and intelligence in act is the intelligible in act. Today detailed cognitional theory complements this Aristotelian opinion by conceiving human knowledge as a process of objectification. More radically, educators and moralists have ever urged people to become their true selves, and their contention finds more than an echo in Jungian thought. It can depict a genesis of the ego under the guidance of the archetypes;[36] it views complexes on the analogy of the ego and so has an explanation of multiple personality;[37] it describes an individuation process from a life centered on the ego to a life centered on the self.[38] Here analytic psychology is complemented by social psychology, by personalist reflection, and by post-Hegelian and post-Marxist thought, which concur in teaching that one becomes a person in one's dealings with other persons.[39] Nor can theologians resist such various testimonies, since Jesus himself is credited with the saying: ". . . a grain of wheat remains a solitary grain unless it falls into the ground and dies; but if it dies it bears a rich harvest" (*John 12:24*).

In brief, we cannot conceive subject and object as fixed and immutable things. The world mediated by meaning is not just reality but reality as known, where the knowing is ever in process. The subject that mediates his world by meaning similarly is in a process of self-realization through self-transcendence. So in man we have to distinguish and verify all three meanings of *one:* a man is one as an instance of the human species; he is one as an intelligible unity in an ongoing process; finally, he is one as one and the same, as identity, as himself and nobody else. Further, as we distinguish three meanings of *one* in man, so too we need a distinction between subject and subjectivity. For man's self-realization is by self-transcendence. Without difference there is no self-transcendence. Without identity it is not one's own but some other self that is realized. So we shall reserve the term, subject, to denote the identity. We shall employ the term, subjectivity, to denote the intelligible unity that already is teleologically what it eventually is to become.[40]

We have treated three of our five topics: identity, human consciousness, and human subjectivity. Before going further, we may note that part of our objective has already been attained. For in a truly human life there is identity. I am no longer an infant, a child, a boy, a young man, but however great the differences in my truly human living, I am still the same I that I was from the beginning. Nor is this identity diminished by the fact that the differences are not confined to differences in abilities and skills and habits, that they involve the becoming and the stability of my ego, my personality, what I can call myself. For such differences regard not the identity of the subject but his subjectivity.[41] He remains himself though he truly transcends himself.

But we must now turn to the main component in the hypostatic union. Can one speak intelligibly of three distinct and conscious subjects of divine consciousness? I believe that one can, but to do so one must take the psychological analogy of the Trinitarian processions seriously, one must be able to follow the reasoning from processions to relations and from relations to persons, and one has to think analogously of consciousness.

The psychological analogy, then, has its starting point in that higher synthesis of intellectual, rational, and moral consciousness that is the dynamic state of being in love. Such love manifests itself in its judgments of value. And the judgments are carried out in decisions that are acts of loving. Such is the analogy found in the creature.

Now in God the origin is the Father, in the New Testament named *ho Theos*,[42] who is identified with *agapē* (*I John 4:8,16*). Such love expresses itself in its Word, its Logos, its *verbum spirans amorem*,[43] which is a judgment of value. The judgment of value is sincere, and so it grounds the Proceeding Love that is identified with the Holy Spirit.

There are then two processions that may be conceived in God; they are not unconscious processes but intellectually, rationally, morally conscious, as are judgments of value based on the evidence perceived by a lover, and the acts of loving grounded on judgments of value. The two processions ground four real relations of which three are really distinct from one another; and these three are not just relations as relations, and so modes of being,[44] but also subsistent,[45] and so not just paternity and filiation but also Father and Son. Finally, Father and Son and Spirit are eternal; their consciousness is not in time but timeless; their subjectivity is not becoming but ever itself; and each in his own distinct manner is subject of the infinite act that God is, the Father as originating love, the Son as judgment of value expressing that love, and the Spirit as originated loving.

Perhaps now we can begin to discern, however imperfectly, the possibility of a single divine identity being at once subject of divine consciousness and also subject of a human consciousness.

For though this implies that a man lived a truly human life without being a human person, still the paradox of this implication is removed by the distinction between identity and subjectivity. Though his identity was divine, still Jesus had a truly human subjectivity that grew in wisdom and age and grace before God and men (*Luke 2:52*) and that was similar to our own in all things save sin (*DS* 301). Nor is the timeless and unchanging subjectivity proper to the divine identity in conflict with the developing subjectivity of a human life. For as Chalcedon would put it, though the identity is without distinction or separation, still the subjectivities are without modification or confusion (*DS* 302).

Moreover, the human subjectivity of Christ conforms to the divine. For the eternal Word is Son, and it is that very Son that introduced into human language prayer to God not simply as Father but as a child's Father, as Abba; and as the Son as man prayed to Abba, so we in the Spirit of the Son also cry, Abba! Father! Again, as the eternal Word is the eternally true expression of the value that God as *agapē* is, so the Word as man by obedience unto death again expressed that value by revealing how much God loved the world (*John 3:16*). Finally, in his resurrection and exaltation he beckons us to the splendor of the children of God for which up to now "the whole created universe groans in all its parts as if in the pangs of childbirth" (*Rom. 8:22*). In that beckoning we discern not only the ground of our hope but also the cosmic dimension in the new creation of all things in Christ Jesus our Lord.

8. CONCLUSION

To give an account of the meaning of person today, I have had to attempt what never can be more than some analogous and so imperfect understanding of the mysteries of the Trinity and the Incarnation (*DS* 3016). From the nature of the case, however, such high matters awaken perplexity as much as satisfaction. For this reason it will be well to conclude with a brief and clear-cut statement of the root difference between Fr. Schoonenberg's position and my own.

I would grant that Fr. Schoonenberg began from impeccable premises: Jesus was a man; Jesus was a person. From these premises Fr. Schoonenberg concluded that Jesus was a human person. So certain was he of this conclusion that he felt it could overrule any apparently conflicting doctrine, be it scriptural, traditional, or conciliar. Specifically he insisted: "What is said of the pre-existent divine person can never nullify this one and human person."[46] On this basis he proceeded to his mystifying exegesis of scripture, tradition, and the councils.

While I grant Fr. Schoonenberg's two premises, I maintain that his conclusion presupposes not two but three premises. For his assertion that Jesus was a human person means not simply that Jesus was a person and a man but effectively that Jesus was a person and a man and only a man. If it does not mean "only a man," then there is no conflict with faith in the preexistent divine person who became a man. And if it does mean "only a man," then its source is not Christian preaching but Ebionite heresy. Such is the dilemma in which I find Fr. Schoonenberg's position; and I do not find that he has confronted it fairly and squarely.

A lecture at the Colloque de Christologie, Université Laval, Québec, March 22, 1975. Previously published in Raymond Laflamme and Marcel Gervais (eds.), *Le Christ Hier, Aujourd'hui et Demain* (Québec: Les Presses de l'Université Laval, 1976), pp. 45–65; French translation, "La christologie aujourd'hui . . .," in Bernard Lonergan, *Les voies d'une théologie méthodique . . .* , 1982.—Here and elsewhere in the volume, "DS" refers to Denzinger-Schönmetzer; see note 41 to this chapter.

Notes

1. C. Geffré, *Un nouvel âge de la théologie,* 1972.

2. Piet Schoonenberg, *Hij is een God van Mensen* ('s-Hertogenbosch: Malmberg, 1969); *Ein Gott der Menschen* (Zürich, etc.: Benziger, 1969); *The Christ: A Study of the God-Man Relationship in the Whole of*

Creation and in Jesus Christ, tr. by Della Couling (New York: Herder and Herder, 1971); *Il est le Dieu des hommes* (Paris: Cerf., 1973).

3. *Acta Apostolicae Sedis,* Vol. LXIV (1972), pp. 237–241.

4. *The Christ,* p. 136; *Ein Gott,* p. 146. I had best note that the concern of this paper is not with Fr. Schoonenberg as world-famous catechist but simply and solely with Fr. Schoonenberg as theologian. In catechetics, and more generally in communications (see my *Method in Theology,* Ch. 14), the rule is pluralism, for one has to express the Christian message in the language and style appropriate to a given class of people in a given culture. Still such pluralism does not imply that there are many, diverse Christian messages; and it is the task of the theologian to ascertain just what is the one message that the many communicators present to the many different audiences.

5. Klaus Reinhardt, "Die Einzigartigkeit der Person Jesu Christi: Neue Entwurfe," *Internazionale katholische Zeitschrift,* Vol. II (1973), pp. 206–224; "In What Way Is Jesus Christ Unique?" *Communio: International Catholic Review,* Vol. I (1974), pp. 343–364.

6. Piet Schoonenberg, "Trinität—Der vollendete Bund: Thesen zur Lehre vom dreipersönlichen Gott," *Orientierung,* Vol. XXXVII (1973), pp. 115–117.

7. Basic presentation in B. Lonergan, *Insight,* 1957, and *Method,* 1972; the transition from Aquinas in *Verbum,* 1967, and *Grace and Freedom,* 1971.

8. *The Christ,* p. 93; *Ein Gott,* p. 98. See my "The Dehellenization of Dogma," *Theological Studies,* Vol. XXVIII (1967), pp. 336–351, reprinted in Bernard J. F. Lonergan, *A Second Collection,* ed. by Wm. F. J. Ryan and Bernard J. Tyrrell (London: Darton, Longman & Todd, 1974; Philadelphia: Westminster, 1975), pp. 11–32.

9. "Diese Begrenzung aber macht die Trinitätslehre konkret, auf die Menschen bezogen und für die Verkündigung dienstbar," *op. cit., Orientierung,* 1973, p. 115, thesis 9.

10. Aquinas composed his *Summa Theologiae* in the *via doctrinae;* see the *Prologus.* It corresponds to the functional specialty, *Systematics,* of my *Method in Theology.* The *via inventionis* would cover the first four or perhaps five previous specialties.

11. Raymond E. Brown, "Who Do Men Say That I Am? Modern Scholarship on Gospel Christology,'" *Horizons,* Vol. I (1974), pp. 35–50; see pp. 47–49.

12. *Acts 9:4.*

13. *Matt. 25:40, 45.*

14. *Mark 1:17, 20; 2:14; Matt. 4:19, 22; 9:9; Luke 5:11, 27.*

15. *Mark 10: 17–31; Matt. 19: 16–30; 10: 34–39; 8: 20, 22; Luke 18: 18–30; 14: 25–33.*

16. *Mark 10: 29; Matt. 19: 29; Luke 18: 29.*

17. *Acts 5: 41.*

18. *Acts 2: 37.*

19. *John 6: 68.*

20. Heinrich Schlier, "Die Anfänge des christologischen Credo," in *Zur Frühgeschichte der Christologie: Ihre biblischen Anfänge und die Lehrformel von Nikaia,* ed. by Bernhard Welte (Quaestiones Disputatae, 51, Freiburg, etc.: Herder, 1970), pp. 13–58.

21. Franz Mussner, "Christologische Homologese und evangelische Vita Jesu," *ibid.,* pp. 59–73.

22. *Mark 4: 41.*

23. *Mark 8: 27.*

24. *John 4: 10.*

25. *John 5: 12.*

26. *John 8: 23.*

27. *John 9: 35–38.*

28. *John 12: 34.*

29. *Rückfrage nach Jesus: Zur Methodik und Bedeutung der Frage nach dem historischen Jesus,* ed. by Karl Kertelge (Quaestiones Disputatae, 63, Freiburg, etc.: Herder, 1974). For general background see Reginald H. Fuller, *The Foundations of New Testament Christology* (London: Lutterworth, and New York: Scribner's, 1965).

30. See Josef Ernst, "Personale oder funktionale Christologie," *Münchener theologische Zeitschrift,* Vol. XXIII (1972), pp. 217–240.

31. Note, however, Alan Richardson, *History Sacred and Profane* (London: SCM, 1964), Ch. 6, where the argument for the resurrection of Christ is basically an extrapolation from factual history.

32. See the series of articles on "Jesus Christus—Gottessohn" in *Theologische Quartalschrift,* Vol. CLIV (1974), pp. 203–278. On the successive meanings of "Son of God" in the New Testament, see Fuller, *op. cit.* (above, note 29).

33. Bernhard Welte, "Die Lehrformel von Nikaia und die abendländische Metaphysik," *Zur Frühgeschichte der Christologie* (above, note 20), pp. 100–117. Far more substantial is the preceding paper by Friedo Ricken, "Das Homousios von Nikaia als Krisis des altchristlichen Platonismus," *ibid.,* pp. 74–99. I should say that there is, not explicit systematic thought, but an implicit dialectic in ante-Nicene and Nicene theology. Without being technically Stoics the apologists were involved in Stoic naivete, much as Fr. Schoonenberg is involved in the world of immediacy. To

correct this naivete Origen turned to Middle Platonism and reached a thoroughgoing Trinitarian subordinationism. Nicea took its stand on preaching the word of God, and its *homoousios* meant, as Athanasius put it: "What is true of the Father, also is true of the Son, except that the Son is not Father" (*Oratio III contra Arianos*, 4: *Patrologia Graeca*, Vol. XXVI, 329A). The formula became liturgical in the Roman Preface for Trinity Sunday: "Quod enim de tua gloria, revelante te, credimus, hoc de Filio tuo, hoc de Spiritu sancto sine differentia discretionis sentimus." See my *De Deo Trino*, Vol. I (Rome: Gregorian University Press, 1964), pp. 40–112. (Editor: this section is now in English, *The Way to Nicea: The Dialectical Development of Trinitarian Theology*, tr. by Conn O'Donovan [London: Darton, Longman & Todd, 1976; Philadelphia: Westminster, 1977]; see pp. 36–137.)

34. In *The Christ*, pp. 51–66 are concerned with "The Chalcedonian Pattern and the Objections Against It." On that basis Fr. Schoonenberg proceeds to develop a hermeneutic that ensures a human person in Christ by bracketing God's eternal Son.

35. The decisive session of Ephesus is found in Eduard Schwartz, *Acta Conciliorum Oecumenicorum*, Tome I, Vol. I, Pars 2 (Berlin: W. de Gruyter, 1927), pp. 12–35. The condemnation of Nestorius resulted from the conformity of Cyril's letter with the decree of Nicea and the opposition of Nestorius' letter to the same decree. The letters are in Schwartz, *op. cit.*, Pars 1, pp. 25–28 and 29–32; also in *Patrologia Graeca*, Vol. LXXVII, 44–49 and 49–57. From the letters it is clear that it is not classical Christology but Nestorian Christology that starts from two distinct natures and endeavors to join them in one individual. The contrary view was expressed by Klaus Reinhardt, *op. cit.* (note 5, above), on p. 210 in *Internazionale katholische Zeitschrift* and pp. 348–350 in *Communio*.

36. E. Neumann, *The Origins and History of Consciousness*, 1970.

37. J. Jacobi, *Complex/Archetype/Symbol*, 1959, pp. 6–19.

38. G. Adler, *The Living Symbol*, 1961.

39. David Rasmussen, "Between Autonomy and Sociality," *Cultural Hermeneutics*, Vol. I (1973), pp. 3–45; see pp. 3–25.

40. As the moon is the intelligible unity in the four-dimensional manifold of positions and phases, so human subjectivity is the intelligible unity in the multi-dimensional manifold of the conscious events of a lifetime.

41. Those with a metaphysical bent may ask whether in one and the same identity there are or are not many subjectivities. The simplest answer is to revert to an earlier controversy. In one and the same man are there three substantial forms, one biological, a second sensitive, and the third intellectual? Or is there just one, which is intellectual, but capable of fulfilling the functions of the other two as well as its own? Now just as the councils (Denzinger-Schönmetzer, *Enchiridion Symbolorum, Definitionum*

et Declarationum de rebus fidei et morum, 33rd ed., Barcelona: Herder, 1965, nos. 902, 1440) affirm that the intellective soul is the one form of the body in man, so we acknowledge in one man only one subjectivity which, however, manifests itself in time and by degrees in accord with the norms of human development. In Christ, however, who is both divine and human, there is both a divine and a human subjectivity, though but a single identity, and a single human subjectivity.

42. Karl Rahner, "Theos in the New Testament," *Theological Investigations,* Vol. I, tr. by Cornelius Ernst (London: Darton, Longman & Todd, 1961), pp. 79–148.

43. St. Thomas Aquinas, *Sum. Theol.,* I, q. 43, a. 5 ad 2m; *In I Sent.,* d. 27, q. 2, a. 1 sol.

44. On the historical and systematic aspects of this see my *De Deo Trino,* Vol. I, p. 198, and Vol. II (also published by the Gregorian University Press, 1964), pp. 193–196.

45. The three really distinct real relations in God are identical with the divine essence (Denzinger-Schönmetzer, *Enchiridion,* no. 804) and so subsistent. Hence the real relation as relation is a mode of being; but the relation as subsistent is a person. Cf. St. Thomas Aquinas, *Sum. Theol.,* I, q. 33, a. 2 ad 1m. Fr. Schoonenberg would have it that there are three modes of the divine being that in the economy of salvation are related to one another and to us as three persons, *op. cit., Orientierung,* 1973, p. 116, thesis 28.

46. *The Christ,* p. 82; *Ein Gott,* p. 87.

7

Healing and Creating in History

The topic assigned me reads: Healing and Creating in History.

What precisely it means or even what it might mean, does not seem to be obvious at first glance. An initial clarification appears to be in order.

We have to do with healing and creating *in history*. But no particular kind of history is specified, and so we are not confined to religious or cultural or social or political or economic or technological history. Again no people or country is mentioned, neither Babylonians nor Egyptians, Greeks nor Romans, Asians nor Africans, Europeans nor Americans. It would seem, then, that we have to do with healing and creating in human affairs. For human affairs are the stuff of history, and they merit the attention of the historian when they are taken in a relatively large context and prove their significance by their relatively durable effects.

Now if "history" may be taken broadly to mean human affairs, it is not too difficult to obtain at least a preliminary notion of what is meant by the other two terms in our title, "healing" and "creating." For there comes to hand a paper by Sir Karl Popper entitled "The History of Our Time: An Optimist's View."[1] In it he opposes two different accounts of what is wrong with the world. On the one hand, there is the view he attributes to many quite sincere churchmen and, along with them, to the rationalist philosopher, Bertrand Russell. It is to the effect that our intellectual development has outrun our moral development. He writes:

> We have become very clever, according to Russell, indeed too clever. We can make lots of wonderful gadgets, including tele-

100

vision, high-speed rockets, and an atom bomb, or a thermonu-
clear bomb, if you prefer. But we have not been able to achieve
that moral and political growth and maturity which alone could
safely direct and control the uses to which we put our tremen-
dous intellectual powers. This is why we now find ourselves in
mortal danger. Our evil national pride has prevented us from
achieving the world-state in time.

To put this view in a nutshell: we are clever, perhaps too
clever, but we also are wicked; and this mixture of cleverness
and wickedness lies at the root of our troubles. [2]

In contrast, Sir Karl Popper would argue that we are good, perhaps
a little too good, but we are also a little stupid; and it is this mixture
of goodness and stupidity that lies at the root of our troubles. After
avowing that he included himself among those he considered a little
stupid, Sir Karl put his point in the following terms:

> The main troubles of our time—and I do not deny that we live in
> troubled times—are not due to our moral wickedness, but, on
> the contrary, to our often misguided moral enthusiasm: to our
> anxiety to better the world we live in. Our wars are fundamen-
> tally religious wars; they are wars between competing theories
> of how to establish a better world. And our moral enthusiasm is
> often misguided, because we fail to realize that our moral prin-
> ciples, which are sure to be over-simple, are often difficult to
> apply to the complex human and political situations to which we
> feel bound to apply them. [3]

In upholding this contention Sir Karl was quite ready to descend to
particular instances. He granted the wickedness of Hitler and Stalin.
He acknowledged that they appealed to all sorts of hopes and fears,
to prejudices and envy, and even to hatred. But he insisted that their
main appeal was an appeal to a kind of morality. They had a message; and they demanded sacrifices. He regretted that an appeal to
morality could be misused. But he saw it as a fact that the great dic-
tators were always trying to convince their people that they knew a
way to a higher morality.

Now one may agree with Lord Russell. One may agree with Sir
Karl. Indeed, there is no difficulty in agreeing with both, for the
Christian tradition lists among the effects of original sin both a dark-

ening of intellect and a weakening of will. But whatever one's opinion, it remains that there is a profound difference between diagnosing a malady and proposing a cure. Whether one stresses with Lord Russell the conjunction of clever but wicked or with Sir Karl the conjunction of good but stupid, one gets no further than diagnosis. On the other hand, when one speaks of healing and creating, one refers to positive courses of action. To this positive aspect of the issue, we now must turn.

The creating in question is not creating out of nothing. Such creating is the divine prerogative. Man's creating is of a different order. Actually, it does not bring something out of nothing, but it may seem to do so. William James, the American psychologist and philosopher, has described three stages in the career of a theory. First, ". . . it is attacked as absurd; then it is admitted to be true, but obvious and insignificant; finally it is seen to be so important that its adversaries claim that they themselves discovered it."⁴ Such a theory is creative.

Let me illustrate this need for human creating from the contemporary economic situation. Last year there was published a thick volume by Richard Barnet and Ronald Müller with the title, *Global Reach,* and the subtitle, *The Power of the Multinational Corporations.* Its thirteen chapters fell into three parts. The first set forth the aims of the multinational corporations: they propose to run the world, for they can do the job and our little national governments are not equipped to do so. The second set of chapters delineated what the multinational corporations were doing to the underdeveloped countries: they have been making them more hopelessly worse off than otherwise they would be. The third set finally asked what these corporations, which in the main are American, have been doing to the United States; the answer is that they are treating the States in the same way they are treating the underdeveloped countries and, in the long run, the effects will be the same as in the rest of the world.

Now if the multinational corporations are generating worldwide disaster, why are they permitted to do so? The trouble is that there is nothing really new about multinational corporations. They aim at maximizing profit, and that has been the aim of economic enterprise since the mercantile, the industrial, the financial revolutions ever more fully and thoroughly took charge of our affairs. The alternative to making a profit is bankruptcy. The alternative to maximizing profit is inefficiency.[5] All that the multinational corporation does is maximize profit not in some town or city, not in some region or country, but on the global scale. It buys labor and materials in the countries where they are cheapest. Its credit is unimpeachable and so it can secure all the money it wants from whatever banks or money markets are in a position to create it. Its marketing facilities are a global network and to compete one would have first to build up a global network of one's own. The multinational corporation is a going concern. It is ever growing and expanding. It is built on the very principles that slowly but surely have been moulding our technology and our economics, our society and our culture, our ideals and our practise for centuries. It remains that the long-accepted principles are inadequate. They suffer from radical oversights. Their rigorous application on a global scale, according to Barnet and Müller, heads us for disaster. But as the authors also confess: "The new system needed for our collective survival does not exist."[6] When survival requires a system that does not exist, then the need for creating is manifest.

While it can take a series of disasters to convince people of the need for creating, still the long, hard, uphill climb is the creative process itself. In retrospect this process may appear as a grand strategy that unfolds in an orderly and cumulative series of steps. But any retrospect has the advantage of knowing the answers. The creative task is to find the answers. It is a matter of insight, not of one insight but of many, not of isolated insights but of insights that coalesce, that complement and correct one another, that influence policies and programs, that reveal their shortcomings in their concrete results, that give rise to further correcting insights, corrected policies, corrected programs, that gradually accumulate into the all-round, balanced, smoothly functioning system that from the start was needed but at the start was not yet known.

This creative process is nothing mysterious. It has been described by Jane Jacobs in her *The Economy of Cities*,[7] as repeatedly finding new uses for existing resources. It has been set forth in the grand style by Arnold Toynbee under the rubric of "Challenge and Response" in his *A Study of History*, where the flow of fresh insights takes its rise from a creative minority, and the success of their implementation wins the devoted allegiance of the rank and file.[8]

I have spoken of insights, and I had best add what I do not

mean. An insight is not just a slogan, and an ongoing accumulation
of insights is not just an advertising campaign. A creative process is
a learning process. It is learning what hitherto was not known. It is
just the opposite of the mental coma induced by the fables and jin-
gles that unceasingly interrupt television programs in our native land
and even in the great republic to the south of us.

Again, insights are one thing, and concepts are quite another.
Concepts are ambiguous. They may be heuristic, but then they
merely point to unspecified possibilities, as highly desirable as justice, liberty, equality, peace—but still just empty gestures that fail to
reveal how the possibilities might be realized and what the realization concretely would entail. Again, concepts may be specific, but
then they are definite, rounded off, finished, abstract. Like text-
books on moral theology they can name all the evils to be avoided
but get no further than unhelpful platitudes on the good to be
achieved. For the good is never an abstraction. Always it is concrete.[9] The whole point to the process of cumulative insight is that
each insight regards the concrete while the cumulative process heads
towards an ever fuller and more adequate view. Add abstraction to
abstraction and one never reaches more than a heap of abstractions.
But add insight to insight and one moves to mastery of all the eventualities and complications of a concrete situation.

The creative process culminates in system, but the system is
only system on the move. It never reaches static system that comes
into existence and remains forever after. So it is that, when the flow
of fresh insights dries up, when challenges continue and responses
fail to emerge, then the creative minority becomes the merely dominant minority and the eagerness of the rank and file, that exulted in
success, turns into the sullenness of an internal proletariat frustrated
and disgusted by the discovery that a country in which, more and
more, everything had worked has become a country in which, more
and more, nothing works. Such is the disenchantment that, to use
Toynbee's terms, brings to an end the genesis of a civilization and
introduces first its breakdowns and eventually its disintegration.

But, one may ask, why does the flow of fresh insights dry up?
Why, if challenges continue, do responses fail? Why does a minority
that was creative cease to be creative and become merely dominant?

There are many intermediate answers that correspond to the
many and varied circumstances under which civilizations break

down. But there is one ultimate answer that rests on the intrinsic limitations of insight itself. For insights can be implemented only if people have open minds. Problems can be manifest. Insights that solve them may be available. But the insights will not be grasped and implemented by biased minds. There is the bias of the neurotic fertile in evasions of the insight his analyst sees he needs. There is the bias of the individual egoist whose interest is confined to the insights that would enable him to exploit each new situation to his own personal advantage. There is the bias of group egoism blind to the fact that the group no longer fulfills its once useful function and that it is merely clinging to power by all the maneuvers that in one way or another block development and impede progress. There is finally the general bias of all 'good' men of common sense, cherishing the illusion that their single talent, common sense, is omnicompetent, insisting on procedures that no longer work, convinced that the only way to do things is to muddle through, and spurning as idle theorizing and empty verbiage any rational account of what has to be done.[10]

Not only is there this fourfold exclusion of fresh insights by the neurotic, by the bias of individual and, worse, of group egoism, and by the illusory omnicompetence of common sense. There also is the distorting effect of all such bias on the whole process of growth. Growth, progress, is a matter of situations yielding insights, insights yielding policies and projects, policies and projects transforming the initial situation, and the transformed situation giving rise to further insights that correct and complement the deficiencies of previous insights. So the wheel of progress moves forward through the successive transformations of an initial situation in which are gathered coherently and cumulatively all the insights that occurred along the way. But this wheel of progress becomes a wheel of decline when the process is distorted by bias. Increasingly the situation becomes, not the cumulative product of coherent and complementary insights, but the dump in which are heaped up the amorphous and incompatible products of all the biases of self-centered and shortsighted individuals and groups. Finally, the more the objective situation becomes a mere dump, the less is there any possibility of human intelligence gathering from the situation anything more than a lengthy catalogue of the aberrations and the follies of the past. As a diagnosis of terminal cancer denies any prospect of health restored, so a social dump is the end of fruitful insight and of the cumulative development it can generate.

I have spoken of creating in history and of its nemesis. But my topic also calls for a few words on healing. In fact, the genesis and breakdown of civilization occupy only the first six of the ten volumes Toynbee devoted to his *A Study of History*. In the last four there emerges a new factor, for out of the frustration and disgust of the internal proletariat there come the world religions and a new style of human development.

For human development is of two quite different kinds. There is development from below upwards, from experience to growing understanding, from growing understanding to balanced judgment, from balanced judgment to fruitful courses of action, and from fruitful courses of action to the new situations that call forth further understanding, profounder judgment, richer courses of action.

But there also is development from above downwards. There is the transformation of falling in love: the domestic love of the family; the human love of one's tribe, one's city, one's country, mankind; the divine love that orientates man in his cosmos and expresses itself in his worship. Where hatred only sees evil, love reveals values. At once it commands commitment and joyfully carries it out, no matter what the sacrifice involved. Where hatred reinforces bias, love dissolves it, whether it be the bias of unconscious motivation, the bias of individual or group egoism, or the bias of omnicompetent, shortsighted common sense. Where hatred plods around in ever narrower vicious circles, love breaks the bonds of psychological and social determinisms with the conviction of faith and the power of hope.

What I have attributed to love and denied to hatred, must also be denied to any ambiguous and so deceptive mixture of love and hatred. If in no other way at least from experience we have learnt that professions of zeal for the eternal salvation of souls do not make the persecution of heretics a means for the reconciliation of heretics. On the contrary, persecution leads to ongoing enmity and in the limit to wars of religion. In like manner wars of religion have not vindicated religion; they have given color to a secularism that in the English-speaking world regards revealed religion as a merely private affair and in continental Europe thinks it an evil.

Again, while secularism has succeeded in making religion a marginal factor in human affairs, it has not succeeded in inventing a vaccine or providing some other antidote for hatred. For secularism is a philosophy and, no less than religion, it may lay claim to absolutes of its own. In their name hatred can shift from the religious group to the social class. So the professions of tolerance of the eighteenth-century Enlightenment did not save from the guillotine the feudal nobility of France, and the Marxist march of history in Russia has attended to the liquidation not merely of the bourgeoisie but also of the Romanovs, the landowners, and the kulaks.[11]

As healing can have no truck with hatred, so too it can have no truck with materialism. For the healer is essentially a reformer: first and foremost he counts on what is best in man. But the materialist is condemned by his own principles to be no more than a manipulator. He will apply to human beings the stick-and-carrot treatment that the Harvard behaviorist, B. F. Skinner, advocates under the name of reinforcement. He will maintain with Marx that cultural attitudes are the by-product of material conditions and so he will bestow upon those subjected to communist power the salutary conditions of a closed frontier, clear and firm indoctrination, controlled media of information, a vigilant secret police, and the terrifying threat of the labor camps. Again, while Christians accord to God's grace the principal role in touching men's hearts and enlightening their minds, it would seem that the true believer in the gospel according to Marx must be immersed in proletarian living conditions, on the ground that only such material conditions can confer upon him the right thinking and righteous feeling proper to proletarian class consciousness.[12]

Healing then is not to be confused with the dominating and manipulating to which the reforming materialist is confined by his own principles. It has to be kept apart from religious hatred of heretical sects and from philosophic hatred of social classes.[13] But besides these requirements, intrinsic to the nature of healing, there is the extrinsic requirement of a concomitant creative process. For just as the creative process, when unaccompanied by healing, is distorted and corrupted by bias, so too the healing process, when unaccompanied by creating, is a soul without a body. Christianity developed and spread within the ancient empire of Rome. It possessed the spiritual power to heal what was unsound in that imperial domain. But it was unaccompanied by its natural complement of creating, for a single development has two vectors, one from below upwards, creating, the other from above downwards, healing. So when the Roman empire decayed and disintegrated, the church indeed lived on. But it lived on, not in a civilized world, but in a dark and barbarous age in which, as a contemporary reported, men devoured one another as fishes in the sea.

If we are to escape a similar fate, we must demand that two requirements are met. The first regards economic theorists; the second regards moral theorists. From economic theorists we have to demand, along with as many other types of analysis as they please, a new and specific type that reveals how moral precepts have both a basis in economic process and so an effective application to it. From moral theorists we have to demand, along with their other various forms of wisdom and prudence, specifically economic precepts that arise out of economic process itself and promote its proper functioning.

To put the same points in negative terms, when physicists can think on the basis of indeterminacy, economists can think on the basis of freedom and acknowledge the relevance of morality. Again, when the system that is needed for our collective survival does not exist, then it is futile to excoriate what does exist while blissfully ignoring the task of constructing a technically viable economic system that can be put in its place.[14]

Is my proposal utopian? It asks merely for creativity, for an interdisciplinary theory that at first will be denounced as absurd, then will be admitted to be true but obvious and insignificant, and perhaps finally be regarded as so important that its adversaries will claim that they themselves discovered it.

A lecture in the series, Anniversary Lectures, The Thomas More Institute, Montreal, May 13, 1975. Previously published in *Bernard Lonergan: 3 Lectures* (Montreal: Thomas More Institute Papers/75, 1975), pp. 55–68.

Notes

1. Karl Popper, *Conjectures and Refutations: The Growth of Scientific Knowledge* (New York: Harper Torchbooks, 1968; first published, 1962).

2. *Ibid.,* p. 365.

3. *Ibid.*, p. 366.

4. William James, *Pragmatism* (London: Longmans, 1912), p. 198. Quoted by Louis Mink, *Mind, History, and Dialectic: The Philosophy of R. G. Collingwood* (Bloomington/London: Indiana University Press, 1969), p. 255.

5. Where, of course, inefficiency means by definition the failure to maximize profit.

6. Richard J. Barnet and Ronald E. Müller, *Global Reach: The Power of the Multinational Corporations* (New York: Simon and Schuster, 1974), p. 385.

7. Jane Jacobs, *The Economy of Cities* (New York: Random House, Vintage Books, 1970; first published, 1969).

8. For an incomplete list of the critiques of Toynbee's *A Study of History*, see that work, Vol. XII: *Reconsiderations* (London/New York: Oxford University Press, 1961), pp. 680–690. With *Reconsiderations* available, the critics are far less impressive.

9. As the Scholastics put it: *Bonum ex integra causa, malum ex quocumque defectu.*

10. I have written at greater length on bias in *Insight*, pp. 191–206, 218–242, 627–633, 688–693. In the Hegelian-Marxist tradition bias is treated obliquely under the name of alienation.

11. For background see the penetrating analysis by Christopher Dawson, "Karl Marx and the Dialectic of History," *The Dynamics of World History*, ed. by John J. Mulloy (London: Sheed and Ward, 1957), pp. 354–365. The chapter appeared originally in Dawson's *Religion and the Modern State*, 1935.

12. For Marx, morality is relative to social class. As Dawson trenchantly put it: "Hence it would seem that the only real immorality is to betray the interests of one's own class, and that a man like Karl Marx himself, or F. Engels, who serves the interests of another class even if it be the class of the future, is no social hero, but an apostate and a traitor. He has become a bad bourgeois but he can never become a good proletarian unless he is economically and sociologically absorbed into the proletariat" (*op. cit., The Dynamics of World History*, pp. 362–363).

13. Of course, though racism and nationalism are prephilosophic, they can be imagined as absolutes and generate abundant hatred.

14. Moral precepts that are not technically specific turn out to be quite ineffectual, as Christian Duquoc has pointed out in his *Ambiguité des théologies de la sécularisation: essai critique* (Gembloux: Duculot, 1972). See his remark on *The Secular City* by Harvey Cox on p. 67; also pp. 103 ff. and 113 ff. on the Pastoral Constitution of the second Vatican council, *Gaudium et Spes*.

Part Two

Lectures on Religious Studies and Theology

Preface

The topic for these lectures was suggested to me by the great interest awakened by Charles Davis' paper on "The Reconvergence of Theology and Religious Studies." It was read to the Canadian Society for the Study of Religion, Toronto, 1974. When it was published in the bilingual journal, *Studies in Religion/Sciences Religieuses,*[1] not only was it preceded by a two-page editorial but also it was followed by the comments and rejoinders of no less than five professors.

To pursue that discussion, however, was not my intention. To have done so would have been highly commendable in a seminar, for there a multiplicity of viewpoints fits in readily enough with a variety of active participants. But a lecture series demands greater unity and, more importantly, it provides the opportunity for working out a single but complex viewpoint.

Such an opportunity, I felt, should not be missed. I had already published a book, *Method in Theology,* which I had conceived on interdisciplinary lines. Might not some similar conception be relevant to the relations between religious studies and theology? Might not this pair be regarded neither as simply identical, nor again as alternative and mutually exclusive options, but as at once distinct and complementary?

At least there seems to be a certain plausibility to such an approach. Religious studies and theology are not identical but distinct. The theologies tend to be as many and diverse as the religious convictions they express and represent. In contrast, religious studies envisage all religions and, so far from endeavoring to arbitrate between opposed religious convictions, commonly prefer to describe and understand their rituals and symbols, their origins and distribution, their history and influence.

But many may readily grant the distinction yet hesitate before acknowledging complementarity. Indeed, I myself would agree with their hesitation if it arises from complementarity, not as an ideal for the future, but as an account of the common practise of the past. But precisely because my personal interest is method, I am inclined to discern in the practise of the past the beginnings of a new practise for the future.

Insofar as religious studies have been shifting from detached description to understanding and even empathy, insofar as Friedrich Heiler has ventured to view the history of religions as a preparation for the cooperation of religions,[2] insofar as such cooperation has begun to be realized in ecumenical dialogue, in the clustering of diverse theological schools, in Christian ascetics frequenting Zen monasteries, in that measure there have emerged the signs of the times that invite a methodologist to explore the foundations for an interdisciplinary approach to religious studies and theology.

Need I say that questions of method are practical. So my purpose in these lectures is not to demonstrate what is necessary. It is not to forecast what is probable. It is solely to invite you to share in the exploration of a proposal. For practical issues regard possible courses of action. They set forth objects of free choice. They have their pros and cons. Only with time do they advance in clarity and precision. Only with a lag do they begin to gain acceptance. Only when they are put in practise and the fruits of practise are found to be good, does acceptance spread and performance become common.

I have acknowledged my debt to Professor Charles Davis and explained my methodological purpose. It remains that I express my gratitude to those that set things in motion. My thanks then to the Committee for the Donald Mathers Memorial Lectureship for the warm invitation they extended to me; to the Committee Chairman, Professor John D. Cook, for the many services he rendered me both before and, above all, during my stay in Kingston; to the audience that on three successive nights braved first a blustery snowstorm and then the ensuing rain and slush to encourage me with their generous attention.

8

First Lecture: Religious Experience

Traditionally man was defined with abstract generality as the *zoon logikon,* the *animal rationale,* the rational animal. More concretely today he is regarded as the symbolic animal, whose knowledge is mediated by symbols, whose actions are informed by symbols, whose existence in its most characteristic features is constituted by a self-understanding and by commitments specified by symbols. On the abstract view man was understood as nature. On the relatively recent view man is understood as historic: for the symbols that inform his being vary with the cultures into which he is born, and the cultures themselves change with the passage of time. They emerge, they develop, they flourish, they influence one another, they can go astray, vanish with their former carriers, only to reappear with fresh vitality and vigor grafted upon new hosts.

The symbolic animal in his endless manifestations is the object of human studies. In the multiplicity of human studies one department is religious studies. It is a singular department, for its symbols are human indeed, since they express the spirit of man, yet at the same time commonly they purport to refer to what is beyond man, what is beyond anything in this world that man can observe and thereby come to study and to know.

It is the singularity of religious symbols that gives rise to the distinction between religious studies and theology. For religious studies leave to theology questions concerned with what is believed to be more than man, what is not of this world. They confine their attention, as does the whole of modern science, to what is within this world, to the things man experiences, and even to human experiencing itself. Nor is there any doubt, in my opinion, about the general soundness of this restriction. For modern sciences are defined by their methods and their fields and, clearly enough, the same method cannot be employed both in investigating what lies within human experience and in investigating what lies beyond it.

1. THE AMBIGUITY OF EXPERIENCE

It remains that the distinction I have drawn raises further questions. Some of them are philosophic or theological. But the one that calls for immediate attention has to do with the ambiguity of the word, experience. For that word commonly is used as a synonym for knowledge and, indeed, for thorough and especially for practical knowledge. So we speak of men of experience and thereby we mean men that have long been engaged in some trade or profession, some art or craft, and have come to possess a full and balanced knowledge of the ins and outs of their calling.

But there is another meaning at times given to the word, experience, and it is this meaning that concerns us here. It occurs in certain analyses of the various components that together make up human knowing. It is employed to denote an infrastructure within knowing, and its significance resides in a contrast between this infrastructure and a suprastructure.

To take a first illustration, any scientist will distinguish sharply between his hypothesis and the data to which he appeals. To the data the hypothesis adds a suprastructure of context, problem, discovery, formulation. But the data, as appealed to, are not yet the infrastructure. For, as appealed to, the data are named. That naming supposes a scientific suprastructure both of technical language and of the scientific knowledge needed to employ the technical language accurately. In turn, the technical language and the scientific knowledge presuppose an earlier ordinary language and the commonsense style of knowing that were employed in learning the science in the first place. Only when one goes behind ordinary language and commonsense knowing does one come to the infrastructure in its pure form. It is pure experience, the experience underpinning and distinct from every suprastructure. As outer experience it is sensation as distinct from perception. As inner experience it is consciousness as distinct not only from self-knowledge but also from any introspective process that goes from the data of consciousness and moves towards the acquisition of self-knowledge.[3]

No doubt, a distinction between consciousness and self-knowledge may seem paradoxical. But I think a brief excursion into cognitional theory will take one from the paradox to the simple fact. We all are conscious of our sensing and our feeling, our inquiring and our understanding, our deliberating and deciding. None of these activities occurs when one is in a coma or in dreamless sleep. In that basic sense they are conscious. Still they are not yet properly known. They are just an infrastructure, a component within knowing that in large part remains merely potential. It is only when we heighten consciousness by adverting not only to objects but also to activities, when we begin to sort out the activities, to assign them their distinctive names, to distinguish and to relate, only then that we begin to move from the mere infrastructure that is consciousness to the compound of infra- and supra-structure that is man's knowledge of his own cognitional process.

What I have illustrated from cognitional theory, also may be illustrated from psychiatry. There is Carl Rogers' client-centered therapy. It aims to provide the patient with an ambiance in which he feels at ease, permits his feelings to emerge, comes to distinguish them from other inner events, to compare different feelings with one another, to add recognition to their recurrence, to bestow names upon them, to manage gradually to encapsulate within a suprastructure of language and knowledge, of confidence and assurance, an infrastructure of feelings that by themselves had been an occasion for turmoil, disorientation, dismay, disorganization.

Again, but from a different viewpoint, a student of Carl Jung's has remarked that, for Jung, consciousness means reflective consciousness. Jung, he claims, refuses to name the contents of inner activities conscious unless the subject relates them explicitly and consciously to his own ego.[4]

In contrast to Jung, Karen Horney writes: ". . . there is no strict alternative between conscious and unconscious, but . . . there are . . . several levels of consciousness. Not only is the repressed impulse still effective—one of the basic discoveries of Freud—but also in a deeper level of consciousness the individual knows about its presence." After making this point, Karen Horney proceeded to pin it down with a technical term: she would use the word, register, when she meant that we know what is going on within us without our being aware of it.[5]

In similar vein Wilhelm Stekel wrote: "Our thinking is a polyphony. There are always several thoughts working simultaneously, one of which is the bearer of the leading voice. The other thoughts represent the medium and low voices. . . . In this framework the whole material with which we deal in analysis is capable of becoming conscious. It is to be found predominately in the lower voices. . . . To quote Klages, the thing in question (the matter repressed) is not so much a thing that is not thought as one that is not recognized."[6]

We meet with a similar testimony when we turn from the clinical psychologists concerned with people who are unwell to the so-called 'third force' concerned with people who are conspicuously healthy.[7] The late Abraham Maslow, onetime president of the American Psychological Association, set about investigating peak experiences. At first he supposed that such experiences occurred only rarely and then in exceptional individuals. But, as his investigation advanced, he discovered that peak experiences really were common, that most people had them, but that few were aware of the fact. In other words, like other experiences, peak experiences pertain to the infrastructure.[8] It is one thing to have a peak experience. It is something else again to advert to it, to compare it with other experiences, to note its singularity, to draw up a scale of higher and lower, to assign this type of experience to the topmost rank, and to label it a peak experience. All such adverting, comparing, evaluating, labeling pertain to a suprastructure. Without them one can very well have peak experiences but without them one will not be explicitly aware of what was going on.

So in another area we have a parallel to Wilhelm Stekel's polyphony and Karen Horney's many levels of consciousness. But in matters psychological what really clinches the issue is one's own personal experience. Of course, you must not expect me to tell you what your own personal experience has been. All I can do is suggest lines of inquiry. For instance, are you aware of having made free choices? What was going forward when the question of choosing arose? Was it merely that some people were urging you to this and others urging you to that? Was it ever that within you there was a polyphony of higher and medium and lower voices, that they were not in harmony but discordant, that for your own inner peace you had to make up your mind and decide once and for all in favor of this or that alternative? Or again, to take a different example that some may find more familiar, have you ever been to a lecture, followed it attentively for a while, and then discovered that your mind was wandering off on some other topic? Have you been reading a book and found yourself thinking of some quite different matter? Or to become a bit theological, have you been to church and found yourself distracted in your prayer?

2. THE CULTIVATION OF RELIGIOUS EXPERIENCE

Because man is a symbolic animal, his development is only partly a matter of his genes. All its higher reaches depend upon his historical milieu with its techniques of socialization, acculturation, education. Where the kitten or puppy is born with built-in instincts and skills, the human infant is born with a helplessness that leaves room for an indefinite plasticity. Its capacities can be shaped along any of the lines that have been devised or may be devised by systems of symbols. Since such systems admit all but endless diversification and refinement, excellence in any walk of life is ever a matter of effort, training, education, encouragement, support.

What is true of the rest of human living, also is true of religious living. The sower, we read, went out to sow his seed, and some fell by the wayside, some among thorns, some on stony ground, but some on good soil where it brought forth fruit now thirty-, now sixty-, now a hundred-fold. The seed, we are told, is the word, for the word is the tool of the symbolic animal. The ground is human consciousness in the polyphony of its many levels. But consciousness does not heed when absorbed in outer cares, or distracted by pleasures, or hardened in waywardness. And even when it is fruitful, its fruitfulness will vary with the cultivation it has received.

In time there emerge professional cultivators: ascetics and mystics, seers and prophets, priests and ministers. There is sought the transformation of consciousness that makes possible a human life that is a life of prayer. There is found the inspiration that speaks to the heart of a tribe or clan, a nation or people. There is worked out a stable organization that diffuses the transformation of consciousness of the ascetic or mystic and that radiates the inspiration of the prophet or seer. There is fostered the piety of a people that fears God. Religion becomes an institution, a distinct and palpable reality. It is a region of human culture, an integral part of the social order, an explicitly acknowledged part in a tribal or national tradition.

Religious studies take us back behind the institutionalization of religion to a prior age. Mircea Eliade has discerned archaic techniques of ecstasy in the shamanism of the central Asian plateau. He has described man's being-in-the-world when religion had not yet become a thing apart but rather penetrated the whole of living. Then places and ways formed an intelligible unity, not through road maps and street signs, but through their relations to a sacred place that was their center. Then the intervals of time were marked off, not by calendars and clocks, but by daily rituals and periodic festivals. Then the symbolic ordering that is the major constituent of human living was communicated, not through systems of public education, but through the traditional myths that told of the beginning of the world, of human destiny, of laudable deeds and abominable ways.

I have been contrasting major stages in the cultivation of religious experience: the sacralization of the universe and of the whole of human living in preliterate times; the emergence of religion as a distinct institution with its schools of ascetics, its prophetic traditions, its priesthoods; the contemporary phase in which much institutional religion appears to be in decline, the universe has been desacralized, and human living secularized.

But it would be a mistake, I think, to concentrate on such differences to the neglect of what is more fundamental. For in the main such differences represent no more than the ongoing process in which man's symbols become ever more differentiated and specialized. What is fundamental is human authenticity, and it is twofold. There is the minor authenticity of the human subject with respect to the tradition that nourishes him. There is the major authenticity that justifies or condemns the tradition itself. The former leads to a human judgment on subjects. The latter invites the judgment of history upon traditions. Let us dwell briefly on both these forms.[9]

As Kierkegaard asked whether he was really a Christian, so divers men can ask themselves whether or not they are genuine Catholics or Protestants, Moslems or Buddhists, Platonists or Aristotelians, Kantians or Hegelians, artists or scientists. They may answer that they are, and their answers may be correct. But it also can happen that they answer affirmatively and nonetheless are mistaken. In that case there will be a series of points in which what they are coincides with what the ideals of the tradition demand. But there also will be another series marked by a greater or less divergence. These points of divergence tend to be overlooked. Whether from a selective inattention, or a failure to understand, or an undetected rationalization, the divergence exists. What I am is one thing, what a genuine Christian is is another, and I am unaware of the difference. My unawareness is unexpressed. Indeed, I have no language to express what I really am, so I use the language of the tradition I unauthentically appropriate, and thereby I devaluate, distort, water down, corrupt that language.

Such devaluation, distortion, corruption may occur only in scattered individuals, and then there occurs unauthenticity in its minor form. But it may also occur on a more massive scale, and then the words are repeated but the meaning is gone. The chair is still the chair of Moses, but it is occupied by scribes and Pharisees. The theology is still Scholastic, but the Scholasticism is decadent. The religious order still reads out the rules and studies the constitutions, but one may doubt whether the home fires are still burning. The sacred name of science is still invoked, but one can ask with Edmund Husserl whether any significant scientific ideal remains, whether it has not been replaced by the conventions of a clique. Then the unauthenticity of individuals generates the unauthenticity of traditions. Then if one takes the tradition as it currently exists for one's standard, one can do no more than authentically realize unauthenticity. Such is unauthenticity in its tragic form, for then the best of intentions combine with a hidden decay.

So it is that commonly men have to pay a double price for their personal attainment of authenticity. Not only have they to undo their own lapses from righteousness but more grievously they have to discover what is wrong in the tradition they have inherited and they have to struggle against the massive undertow it sets up. Such resentment against the human condition offers some explanation, perhaps, of the attraction exercised by Rousseau's picture of the noble savage or, again, of the ever recurrent hopes that an earthly paradise would be ushered in by the revolutionary obliteration of the human past. But really the problem is not tradition but unauthenticity in the formation and transmission of tradition. The cure is not the undoing of tradition but the undoing of its unauthenticity.

The cure is not the undoing of tradition, for that is beyond our power. It is only through socialization, acculturation, education, that we come to know that there is such a thing as tradition, that it has its defects, its dangers, its seductions, that there are evils to be remedied. To learn as much is already to be a product of the tradition, to share its biases, to be marked in a manner that we can change only in the light of what we have learnt and in the directions that such learning opens up. However much we may react, criticize, endeavor to bring about change, the change itself will always be just another stage of the tradition, at most a new era, but one whose motives and whose goals—for all their novelty—will bear the imprint of their past. The issue is not tradition, for as long as men survive, there will be tradition, rich or impoverished, good and evil. The issue is the struggle of authenticity against unauthenticity, and that struggle is part and parcel of the human condition, of our being animals yet equipped to live not just by instinct but principally by the symbols by which we express our self-understanding and our commitments.

3. THE IMMANENT CONTEXT OF RELIGIOUS EXPERIENCE

In a public lecture at the University of Toronto in January 1968, Professor Wilfred Cantwell Smith began by remarking that much fruitful energy had been devoted to exploring man's many religious traditions and to reconstructing the history of the overt data on man's religious living. Both in detail and in wide compass the observable forms have been observed and the observations have been recorded. But Professor Smith went on to claim that a further, a more important, and a more difficult question must be raised. To live religiously is not merely to live in the presence of certain symbols but, he urged, it is to be involved with them or through them in a quite special way—a way that may lead far beyond the symbols, that may demand the totality of a person's response, that may affect his relation not only to the symbols but to everything else, to himself, to his neighbor, to the stars.

Now just what is to be understood by man's relationship to the stars is a question for theology rather than religious studies. But we have been led rather naturally from a consideration of religious experience to the various ways in various cultures that men seek to promote religious experience and, no less naturally, we have been led from such group activity and its historical prolongations to the question of human authenticity. Now while authenticity is not a topic alien to any aspect of human living, still it does attain special prominence in religious texts and monuments. Feelings of guilt, a sense of one's uncleanness, denunciations of unfaithfulness, all express failures to be authentic. Rituals of repentance, confessions of sinfulness, prayers for deliverance, testify to the desire for a reestablished authenticity. The posture and, above all, the features of the statue of the Buddha at prayer radiate a serenity that reveals what might be meant by authenticity attained. In brief, it has seemed to me that the notion of authenticity possesses a twofold relevance: it is relevant to the interpretation of recurrent elements in the observable phenomena collected and catalogued by students of religion; but it also is relevant to the inner commitment to which Professor Smith has invited our attention.

What, then, is commitment? Negatively, one might perhaps say that it is absent in the man or woman that just drifts through life, content to do what everyone else is doing, to say what everyone else is saying, to think what everyone else is thinking, where the "everyone else" in question is just drifting too. Out of that company of drifters one steps when one faces the problem of personal existence, that is, when one finds out for oneself that one has to decide for oneself what one is to do with oneself, with one's life, with one's five talents or two or lonely one. *matt 5:25*

Commonly such a discovery, such a decision, such a program of self-actualization becomes effective and irrevocable when one falls in love. Then one's being becomes being-in-love. Such being-in-love is not without its antecedents, its causes, its conditions, its occasions. But once it has blossomed forth and as long as it lasts, it takes over. It becomes the immanent and effective first principle. From it flow one's desires and fears, one's joys and sorrows, one's discernment of values, one's day-to-day decisions and deeds.

Being-in-love is most conspicuous in the home: in the love of husband and wife, of parents and children. Love gave rise to the marriage. Love gave rise to the offspring. Love keeps the family an ongoing, joyful affair. Nor is love unconnected with authenticity. A love that is not genuine is not the 'true love' that provides the recurrent theme in our older novels and poems and songs. Again, if today the institution of marriage is assailed, still authenticity can be invoked both to bolster and to repel the attack: to bolster it on the ground that the traditional institution has become unauthentic; to repel it on the ground that the innovators are lacking in the simpler authenticity of an earlier time.

Besides love in the home there is love of country. Here too our thinking has taken on the complexity of modern life. One is apt to brush aside as jingoism any old-style allegiance to one's country right or wrong. But in the measure that one does so, not only is one questioning the authenticity of once unquestioned loyalties, but also there is commonly to be found not an abolition but only a displacement of loyalty. It is no longer one's country that is given a blank cheque but a better social order within the country or better relations with other countries abroad. In brief, the exigence of authenticity leads to a reformulation but not an abolition of our allegiances where abuses have crept in or newer insights been gained.

Besides the love of home and the love of country there is a third love. To it there testifies a great religious tradition that proclaims: "Hear, O Israel: the Lord our God is the only Lord; love the Lord your God with all your heart, with all your soul, with all your mind, and with all your strength" (*Mark 12: 29–30*). Of such love St. Paul spoke as God's love flooding our inmost heart through the Holy Spirit he has given us (*Rom. 5: 5*). To the power of that love the same apostle bore witness with the words: ". . . there is nothing in death or life, in the realm of spirits or superhuman powers, in the world as it is or the world as it shall be, in the forces of the universe, in heights or depths—nothing in all creation that can separate us from the love of God in Christ Jesus our Lord" (*Rom. 8: 38–39*).

We have been asking about religious conviction and we spoke first of mere drifting, then of its efficacious opposite, a being-in-love that becomes the first and dominant principle in one's living, finally of the different modes of being-in-love, the love of intimacy that animates the family, the love of one's neighbor that animates a people, and the love of God which seems to be characteristic of authentic religious conviction in a great religious tradition of the Middle East and the West.

Whether such love pertains to religious conviction in other religious traditions, is a large and intricate question.[10] For the present we must pass it by, not only because of its diversity and complexity, but more fundamentally because to me it seems a mistaken method to seek generalization before one has tried to understand the particular. Accordingly, I propose to stick to the topic of this section, namely, the immanent context of religious experience, and so go on to ask in what manner God's love flooding our hearts is a human experience and just how it fits into human consciousness.

First, then, it is an experience, not in the broad sense that refers to the coming together and compounding of many conscious elements, but rather in the technical sense that refers to a single element and so constitutes not a structure but an infrastructure.

Secondly, consciousness is like a polyphony, or like a concerto that blends many themes in endless ways. So too religious experience within consciousness may be a leading voice or a middle one or a low one; it may be dominant and ever recurrent; it may be intermittently audible; it may be weak and low and barely noticeable. Again, religious experience may fit in perfect harmony with the rest of consciousness; it may be a recurrent dissonance that in time increases or fades away; it may vanish altogether, or, at the opposite extreme, it may clash violently with the rest of experience to threaten disruption and breakdown. As the metaphor from music offers an enormous variety of suggestions, so too the lives of men and women present every degree and shade in the intensity of religious experience, in the frequency of its recurrence, in the harmony or dissonance of its conjunction with the rest of consciousness.

Thirdly, as religious experience is found to vary when one compares one individual with another, so too it may be found to develop in the lifetime of this or that individual. Hence there was long repeated the traditional distinction of three stages in the inner life. Beginners were said to be in the purgative way, for theirs was the initial task of reducing and, as far as possible, eliminating the conflict between their religious commitment and the other themes recurrent in their consciousness. Next came the illuminative way in which the significance and implications of religious commitment were ever more fully apprehended and understood. Finally, there was listed a unitive way in which potential conflicts were under control, the full significance of religious commitment was understood and accepted, and in mortal beings there could be verified the harvest of the Spirit catalogued by St. Paul: "love, joy, peace, patience, kindness, goodness, fidelity, gentleness, and self-control" (*Gal. 5: 22*).

Lastly, there are the somewhat intricate relationships between religious development and cognitive development in man. In its spontaneous unfolding cognitive development may be characterized as from below upwards: it proceeds from the data of experience through the unifications and relational networks spun by understanding towards a process of verification that ends with a verdict of acceptance or rejection. Moreover, there is a certain necessity to this order of development: without the unifications and relational networks spun by understanding there is nothing for a process of verification to test; and without the data of experience there is nothing for understanding to unify or relate. It remains, however, that these operations occur within a context and that this context is all the more complex and extensive the richer the culture and the more nuanced the social arrangements one has inherited. Nor is this context just some inert datum that attains influence only in the measure that it is noted, understood, verified, evaluated. Rather it exerts a major influence on the interest that motivates our attention, on the language that selects what we can name and study, on the preunderstanding that underpins our further advance, on the opinions that have to be revised before anything novel or new can be entertained or accepted.

So it is that besides development from below upwards there also is development, if not from above downwards, at least from within an encompassing, enveloping worldview or horizon or blik. Clearly enough this fact is particularly embarrassing in religious studies. For in the measure that the student is committed religiously, he can be expected to be predisposed in favor of religion. In the measure he is uncommitted, he can be feared to lack the resources needed for adequate interpretation.

The dilemma is real enough. What has to be observed is that it turns upon two quite distinct issues. Insofar as doubt is cast on the authenticity of the person that has become religiously convinced and committed, I must ask you to await the outcome of tomorrow's consideration of the validity of religious knowledge. But insofar as you ask how religious commitment arises, perhaps you will find some beginnings towards an answer in the three topics we have considered this evening.

They were, first, the ambiguity of experience: it can be taken to mean the whole of knowledge; but it can also mean an element within a larger compound, an infrastructure that easily is unnoticed until it is rounded off in combination with a manifold of further elements.

Secondly, there was the cultivation of religious experience. We are self-completing animals: at birth we are alive and perhaps kicking; but we become normal human beings only by mastering vast systems of symbols and adapting our muscles, our nerves, our cerebral cortex, to respond to them accurately and precisely. The cultivation of religious experience is its entry into harmony with the rest of one's symbolic system, and as symbolic systems vary with the culture and the civilization, so too does the cultivation of religious experience.

Finally, we took our clue to the nature of religious commitment from the Hebraic and Christian tradition. We found it to be a type of love, distinct from the love of intimacy, distinct from loyalty to one's fellows, for it grounds both domestic and civil devotion by reconciling us, by committing us, to the obscure purposes of our universe, to what Christians name the love of God in Christ Jesus.

This chapter, with the two following chapters, were originally The Donald Mathers Memorial Lectures, given at Queen's University, Kingston, Ontario, March 2, 3, and 4, 1976, under the general title, Religious Studies and Theology. This first lecture was previously published (without the Preface) in Thomas A. Dunne and Jean-Marc Laporte (eds.), *Trinification of the World: A Festschrift in Honour of Frederick E. Crowe* (Toronto: Regis College Press, 1978), pp. 71–83; French translation, ''L' expérience religieuse,'' in Bernard Lonergan, *Les voies d'une théologie méthodique . . .* , 1982.

Notes

1. Vol. IV, no. 3 (1974–1975), pp. 203–236; Davis' paper, 205–221, with responses by Gregory Baum, Kenneth Hamilton, William O. Fennell, Paul Younger, and William Hordern, pp. 222–236.

2. Friedrich Heiler, ''The History of Religions as a Preparation for the Co-operation of Religions,'' in *The History of Religions: Essays in Methodology,* ed. by Mircea Eliade and Joseph M. Kitagawa (Chicago: The University of Chicago Press, 1959 and 1962), pp. 132–160.

3. For a fuller account, B. Lonergan, *Collection*, 1967, pp. 221–239.

4. R. Hostie, *Religion and the Psychology of Jung*, 1957, p. 72.

5. K. Horney, *The Neurotic Personality of Our Time*, 1937, p. 69.

6. W. Stekel, *Compulsion and Doubt*, 1962, p. 229.

7. On 'third force' see A. Maslow, *Toward a Psychology of Being*, 1962, p. vi (p. ix in 2nd ed., 1968).

8. Abraham H. Maslow, *Religions, Values, and Peak-Experiences* (New York: Viking Press, 1970), pp. 22, 86, 88–90.

9. The next two paragraphs repeat what I wrote in *Collection*, 1967, pp. 246–247.

10. I ventured to say something on this topic in *A Second Collection*, 1975, pp. 149–151.

9

Second Lecture: Religious Knowledge

Three questions may be put regarding religious knowledge. First, there is a question of fact. Second, there is a question of philosophic possibility. Third, there is a practical question.

The question of fact is whether religious people know anything that nonreligious people do not know. With the question of fact we are not concerned tonight and we shall not be concerned tomorrow. It is an enormously complicated and intricate issue that must be left to departments of religious studies and/or theology.

The question of philosophic possibility is our concern tonight. It asks what could be meant by affirming the validity or objectivity of religious knowledge. Our answer will be in terms of the inner conviction that men and women of any time or place may attain. To an account of such inner conviction there will be added a survey of the many ways in which such conviction is formulated as human cultures advance in self-understanding and self-knowledge.

The third practical question adverts to the conditions and requirements of setting up an academic discipline. It confronts the issue whether or not religious conviction at the present time and in the present state of scientific knowledge has to be regarded as at best a private affair. Alternatively it envisages the conditions under which the study of religion and/or theology might become an academic subject of specialization and investigation. This third practical question will concern us in our third and final lecture tomorrow.

I have been blocking off our present topic by contrasting it with a question of fact and a question of academic appropriateness. The question of academic appropriateness we leave to tomorrow. The question of the factual validity of this or that religion we leave to religious authorities and academic experts with more than three lectures at their disposal for the communication of their views.

It remains that something be said about the connection between yesterday's topic and today's. Yesterday we began by noting a distinction between single elements that are merely an infrastructure within human experience and the larger context within which they may flourish, or intermittently recur, or tend to vanish. We went on to consider the cultivation of religious experience. There was considered the sacralization of man's world in preliterate societies when religious thought and affect penetrated the organization of man's apprehension of his world, the structure of his social arrangements, the content of his cultural and moral aspirations. There was contrasted the emergence of religious specialists, of ascetics and mystics, of seers and prophets, of priests and ministers; of their role as the religious leaven in human experience, of the formation of religious groups and the genesis of their rituals, their beliefs, their precepts. There was raised the question of authenticity in its twofold form: the authenticity of the individual in his appropriation of his religious tradition; and the authenticity of that tradition itself which becomes questionable when the failures of individuals become the rule rather than the exception, when vital reinterpretation is corrupted by rationalization, when heartfelt allegiance more and more gives way to alienation. Finally, we raised the question of religious commitment, illustrated its nature from the precept of loving God above all found in both the Book of Deuteronomy and the Gospel according to Mark, but postponed the agonizing question that arises in such a time as our own, namely, how can one tell whether one's appropriation of religion is genuine or unauthentic and, more radically, how can one tell one is not appropriating a religious tradition that has become unauthentic.

To that question, yesterday postponed, we now turn. Our remarks will fall under two main headings. First, we shall attempt to describe the experience of authenticity in terms of self-transcendence. Secondly, we shall attempt to relate the inner conviction of authenticity, generated by self-transcendence, with the various notions of validity or objectivity entertained in successive stages of man's cultural development.

1. SELF-TRANSCENDENCE

In various ways clinical psychologists have revealed in man's preconscious activity a preformation, as it were, and an orientation towards the self-transcendence that becomes increasingly more explicit as we envisage successive levels of consciousness.

Perhaps most revealing in this respect is a distinction drawn by the existential analyst, Ludwig Binswanger, between dreams of the night and dreams of the morning.[1] He conceives dreams of the night as largely influenced by somatic determinants such as the state of one's digestion. But in dreams of the morning the subject is anticipating his waking state; however fragmentary the dream and however symbolic its content, he is anticipating his world and taking his own stance within it.

It remains that it is on awaking that we begin to be pushed or pulled beyond ourselves. Our felt needs and our multiform sensations, our memories of satisfactions and our anticipations of their repetition, engage us irrevocably in an ongoing interplay with our immediate environment.

A further level of self-transcendence emerges from the exercise of intelligence, the learning of language, the construction of a world mediated by meaning. Thereby man moves out of the habitat of an animal and into the universe that adds the distant to what is near, the past and future to what is present, the possible and the probable to what is actual. By unifying and relating, by constructing, by discovering seriations, by extrapolating and generalizing, there are gradually pieced together the remarks of parents and the lore of one's peers, the tales of travelers and the stories of great deeds, the revelations of literature, the achievements of science, the meditations of holy men and women, the reflections of philosophers and even perhaps theologians.

But the constructions of intelligence without the control of reasonableness yield not philosophy but myth, not science but magic, not astronomy but astrology, not chemistry but alchemy, not history but legend. Besides the questions of intelligence, such as why and what and how and what for and how often, there are further questions of reflection that arch the eyebrows and ask whether this or that really is so. Then the issue is, not more bright ideas, not further insights, but marshaling and weighing the evidence and presenting the sufficient reason that makes doubting unreasonable just as its absence would make assenting merely rash. Only in virtue of this further level of consciousness can we set aside myth and magic and astrology and alchemy and legend and begin to live by philosophy and science and astronomy and chemistry and history. It is a decisive stage in the process of self-transcendence when we not merely think of the universe but begin to know what the universe really is. In other words, man always lives in his world for his being is a being-in-the-world. But it is far from always true that the world in which he is, is a world that really exists.

Beyond the data of experience, beyond questions for intelligence and the answers to them, beyond questions for reflection concerned with evidence, truth, certitude, reality, there are the questions for deliberation. By them we ask what is to be done and whether it is up to us to do it. By them is effected the transition from consciousness to conscience, from moral feelings to the exercise of responsibility, from the push of fear and the pull of desire to the decisions of human freedom. So it is that on the level of deliberating there emerges a still further dimension to self-transcendence. On previous levels there stood in the foreground the self-transcendence of coming to know. But deliberation confronts us with the challenge of self-direction, self-actualization, self-mastery, even self-sacrifice.

Already I have spoken of consciousness as a polyphony with different themes at different intensities sung simultaneously. Now I would draw attention to the different qualities, to what Gerard Manley Hopkins might call the different self-taste, on the successive levels: the spontaneous vitality of our sensitivity, the shrewd intelligence of our inquiring, the detached rationality of our demand for evidence, the peace of a good conscience and the disquiet released by memory of words wrongly said or deeds wrongly done. Yet together they form a single stream, and we live its unity long before we have the leisure, the training, the patience to discern in our own lives the several strands.

The basic unity of consciousness reaches down into the unconscious. It is true that conflicts do arise, as the psychiatrists have insisted. But this truth must not be allowed to distract us from a far profounder and far more marvelous harmony. In man, the symbolic animal, there is an all but endless plasticity that permits the whole of our bodily reality to be fine-tuned to the beck and call of symbolic constellations. The agility of the acrobat, the endurance of the athlete, the fingers of the concert pianist, the tongue of those that speak and the ears of those that listen and the eyes of those that read, the formation of images that call forth insights, the recall of evidence that qualifies judgments, the empathy that sets our own feelings in resonance with the feelings of others—all bear convincing testimony that self-transcendence is the eagerly sought goal not only of our sensitivity, not only of our intelligent and rational knowing, not only of our freedom and responsibility, but first of all of our flesh and blood that through nerves and brain have come spontaneously to live out symbolic meanings and to carry out symbolic demands.

As self-transcendence is the meaning of each of the many levels of human reality, so too it is the meaning of the whole. But that meaning of the whole, when realized concretely, is falling in love. So the experience of being-in-love is an experience of fulfillment, of complete integration, of a self-actualization that is an unbounded source of good will and good deeds. Such is the love of man and wife, of parents and children. Such is the loyalty of fellow citizens to their commonwealth. Such is the faith that has its fount in the love with which God floods our hearts through the Holy Spirit he has given us.

Love, loyalty, and faith can all be questioned. When they are authentic, readily, I feel, they are esteemed beyond price. But so easily they are unauthentic, whether from the failures of the individual or, tragically, from the individual's authentic appropriation of an unauthentic tradition.

Still, even if only in principle they can be authentic, then at least in principle they point to an answer to our question. For the man or woman intent on achieving self-transcendence is ever aware of shortcomings, while those that are evading the issue of self-realization are kept busy concealing the fact from themselves. But our question has been the grounds of the inner conviction that informs religious living and the answer we have come up with is that self-transcendence is so radically and so completely the inner dynamism of human reality that one cannot but be aware when one is moving

towards it and, on the other hand, one cannot but feel constrained to
conceal the fact when one is evading the abiding imperative of what
it is to be human.

[handwritten margin notes: example / What does 2 enrich / whom?]

2. INNER CONVICTION AND OBJECTIVE TRUTH

At first blush inner conviction and objective truth stand at opposite poles. Inner conviction is subjective. Objective truth is the
truth about what is already-out-there-now for everyone to see and
grasp and handle. It is public truth, and the publicity is spatial. Precisely because it is spatial, because in principle it can be tested by
anyone, it is beyond doubt or question.

Still questions do arise. One can distinguish between the world
of immediacy and the world mediated by meaning. The world of immediacy includes all the data of sense and all the data of consciousness. It consists of two parts: the totality of the data of sense is the
sphere of objectivity that is spatial, public, in principle open to anyone's inspection; the totality of the data of consciousness is an aggregate of distinct and segregated subjectivities none of which can
inspect what is going on in any of the others.

To be contrasted with this world of immediacy there is the
world mediated by meaning. It consists of all that is to be known by
asking questions and arriving at correct answers. It is a world unknown to infants but gradually introduced to children as they learn to
speak, to boys and girls as they study in school, to students and
scholars in centers of learning.

Man the symbolic animal lives in both of these worlds. As animal he lives in the world of immediacy and, like Macbeth, is liberated from his fantasies when he adverts to the sure and firm-set
earth on which he treads. As symbolic, he both suffers from the fantasies and brings about his liberation, for that consists not merely in
the pressure on the soles of his treading feet but also in his certainty
that the earth is firm-set and will not give way under his tread.

Still man the symbolic animal has long been a puzzle to man the
philosopher. Insofar as philosophers search for simplicity and coherence, they opt for one of the two worlds and attempt to get along
without the other. Empiricists opt for the world of immediacy, and

proceed to empty out from the world mediated by meaning everything that is not immediately given. Rationalists take their stand on
demonstrative argument and, if they go along with the ancient Eleat-
ics, will argue that there cannot be more than one being and that that
one being cannot undergo any change.

But both of these are extreme positions. Empiricists usually
find it convenient to take an occasional excursion into the world mediated by meaning, at the very least to expound and prove their own
position. Rationalists can advert to the fact that questions are raised
with respect to the data of experience and that answers are confirmed
by pointing to data that show what they say. So they are led to supplement the apodictic power of demonstration with the intuitions of
sense and/or consciousness. But both empiricist excursions into
meaning and rationalist appeals to intuition are compromises. They
renege on their initial premise of simplicity and coherence. They
point the way to a new starting point that acknowledges the complexity of man the symbolic animal.

The so-called ''new'' starting point is, of course, very old. It
goes back to Plato and Aristotle. It reached crises in the medieval
controversy between Augustinians and Aristotelians and in the later
victory of modern science over Aristotelian constructions. It heads
into a quite different starting point in the twentieth century in which
the notion of method aspires to a foundational role.

In search, then, of the meaning of the phrase, objective truth, I
propose to speak, first, of the limitations of the Aristotelian notion of
science, secondly, of the shift in the sciences that conceives necessity, truth, certitude more as remote ideals than proximate achievements, thirdly, of the ascendency of method and the partial eclipse
of logic in contemporary investigations.

3. FROM ARISTOTLE'S *Posterior Analytics* TO NEWTON'S *Principia*

In his study of *The Origins of Modern Science: 1300–1800,*
Herbert Butterfield has argued, convincingly, I feel, that from the
beginning of the fourteenth century onwards many elements of modern science were discovered by experimenters, but the experimenters themselves were unable to break loose from Aristotelian

preconceptions and set up an appropriate conceptual framework of their own.

Now the achievement of Newton's *Principia* was precisely that it established such a framework and did so in a manner that stood its ground for the next two centuries. It remains, however, that the very title of Newton's masterpiece, *Philosophiae Naturalis Principia Mathematica,* bears an Aristotelian imprint. For the title suggests that Newton's mechanics is not an autonomous science standing in its own right but a set of mathematical principles for the department of philosophy called natural philosophy. In this respect the title is misleading. What Newton achieved was the vindication of mechanics as an autonomous science. But what he could not bring about was the total refashioning of the Aristotelian ideal that became possible between two and three centuries later.

I must begin by noting that the *Posterior Analytics* never were normative for Aristotle's own philosophic thinking or scientific work. They represent one of his great discoveries. They express it under the grave limitations of the science of his day. It was their unhappy fate to provide glib talkers with ready answers and serious thinkers with baffling problems until the reality of scientific achievement brought to light a more solidly grounded notion of scientific knowledge.

With the first stage of that transformation we are now concerned. If its triumph was Newton, still its goal was not Aristotelian theoretical knowledge but the practical utility praised by Francis Bacon in his *Novum Organum.* Its conceptual framework took its inspiration not from Aristotle's metaphysics but from Galileo's program of mathematicizing nature. Its field of inquiry was defined not by Aristotle's intellect, capable of fashioning and becoming all, but by the cautious rule of the Royal Society that excluded questions that neither observation nor experiment could solve.

In that movement there were two chief complaints against the Aristotelians. It was urged that they were concerned not with real things but with words. It was felt that the Aristotelian priority of metaphysics constituted an insuperable barrier to the development of experimental science. The validity of both complaints can, I think, be argued from a consideration of the *Posterior Analytics.*

In the second chapter of the first book of that work one is aware that Aristotle's basic concern is with causal necessity. We think we understand, he notes, when we know the cause, know that it is the cause, and know that the effect cannot be other than it is.[2] But straightway this concern with things and their causes is transposed into syllogistic theory. We are told how knowledge of causal necessity is expressed in appropriate subjects and predicates, premises and conclusions, and thereby manifests its nature as science. We are told how one science can find its principles in the conclusions of another more general science. But when at the end of the second book it is asked how the initial premises are obtained on which the whole deductive structure has to rest, we are told about a rout followed by a rally. The line breaks. *Sauve qui peut!* But as the fleeing line scatters in every direction, somewhere someone will turn and make a stand. Another will join him, and then another. The rally begins. The pursuing enemy now is scattered. Victory may be snatched from the jaws of defeat.[3] I think this military analogy is sound enough. For it represents the chance accumulation of clues that can combine into a discovery. But it is not at all clear that a necessary truth will be discovered and not a mere hypothesis, a mere possibility that has to be verified if it is to merit the name not of truth but of probability. If the only premises the *Posterior Analytics* can provide are just hypotheses, verifiable possibilities, then we have many words about causal necessity but no knowledge of the reality.

Further, the syllogistic approach distinguished philosophy and science simply as the more and the less general. It followed that together they formed a seamless robe with the basic terms and basic relations of philosophy ramifying through the less general fields and robbing them of their autonomy. But experimental science has to be autonomous. For experiment yields correlations. Correlations consist in relations between terms. The terms and relations determined experimentally were the mass-velocities and mass-accelerations of Newton's mechanics; they were to be the electric and magnetic field vectors of Maxwell's equations; and the *corpus Aristotelicum* knew nothing about them.

4. FROM LOGIC TO METHOD

The Aristotelian hegemony had been broken, but Aristotelian notions not directly challenged by the new science lived on in quiet possession of the field of common assumptions. Among them was the view that science consisted in true and certain knowledge of causal necessity. Indeed, Newton's deduction of the orbits of the moon and of the planets was regarded as a stunning confirmation of that view. Laplace's proof that a planetary system periodically returned to an initial situation went hand in hand with his assurance that, in principle, any situation in the universe could be deduced from any other earlier or later situation. Right into the twentieth century it was common to speak of the necessary laws of nature and even of the iron laws of economics. Even in our own day there have been loud complaints that Thomas Kuhn's work on *The Structure of Scientific Revolutions* was an advocacy of irrationalism.[4]

But the logic of the matter is simple. Verification is not proof. For verification is an affirmation of what follows from scientific hypothesis, theory, system. But to affirm the consequent of an hypothesis, settles nothing about the truth of the antecedent from which the consequent follows. A logical conclusion is to be had only when the attempt to verify turns up contrary instances; for then one denies the consequent and from that denial there follows the denial of the antecedent. Accordingly, the principles and laws of an empirical science, no matter how frequently they are verified, may be esteemed ever more probable but may not be considered to be definitively established.

Moreover, the progress of modern science points in the same direction. Newton was acclaimed because he was considered to have done for mechanics what Euclid had done for geometry. But in the nineteenth century it became clear that Euclidean geometry could no longer be considered the one and only possible geometry. In the twentieth the repeated verification of Einstein's special relativity made it probable that a non-Euclidean geometry was the appropriate conceptualization in physics.

Similarly, Laplace's determinism was found to have shaky foundations. For Heisenberg's relations of indeterminacy (or uncertainty) reveal a knowledge that is not less but greater than the knowledge offered by classical laws. Formerly, indeed, probability was thought to be no more than a cloak for our ignorance. But now the tables are turned. For classical laws hold only under the blanket proviso, other things being equal. So it is that classical predictions can be notably mistaken because they fail to foresee the interference of some alien factor. But, further, the verification of classical laws is never exact: no more is demanded than that actual measurements fall within the limits set by a theory of probable errors of observation. In brief, classical theory consists of two parts: there is the classical law, and it sets an ideal norm from which actual measurements do not diverge systematically; there is the theory of measurement and it sets the limits within which errors of observation may be considered probable. But, as Patrick Heelan has pointed out, the same two aspects are contained within the single formalism proposed by quantum mechanics. For the single formalism admits two interpretations: one interpretation yields an ideal norm from which actual measurements do not diverge systematically; the other interpretation of the same formalism informs us of the distribution of the divergence from the norm.[5]

But quantum mechanics is not some limiting case or isolated instance. Thermodynamics had already drawn upon statistical theory. Darwinian thought easily moved from chance variations to probabilities of emergence and from the survival of the fittest to probabilities of survival. A statistical view of the emergence, distribution, and survival of the forms of plant and animal life naturally suggests a similar approach in the investigation of the emergence and distribution of the chemical elements and compounds. Finally, what seems true of nature seems also to hold for man's knowledge of nature: as natural forms evolve in accord with schedules of probabilities, so too man's grasp of natural forms and of their evolution develops in accord with the probabilities of new discoveries.

There has occurred, then, a transition from logic to method. It has occurred in the field of natural science. It does not, by any means, involve an elimination of logic: for it still is logic that cares for the clarity of terms, the coherence of propositions, the rigor of inferences. But it does involve a shift in the significance of logic. For Aristotle in his *Posterior Analytics* made his demonstrative syllogism the central piece in his construction both of the nature of science and of the relations between sciences. That construction has turned out to be a procrustean bed on which science cannot lie. So far from providing the key to the whole nature of science, logic has to be content with the task of promoting clarity, coherence, and rigor in the formulation and application of hypotheses and theories. Further, while it is essential that this task be properly performed, still the significance of that performance is measured not by logic itself but by method. For an empirical science is not confined to logical operations with respect to terms, propositions, inferences. It includes observation, description, the formulation of problems, discovery, processes of experimentation, verification, revision. Within the larger whole logic ensures the clarity of terms, the coherence of propositions, the rigor of inferences. And the more successfully it performs that task, the more readily will there come to light not the definitive immutability but the defects of current views and the need to seek more probable opinions.

5. GENERALIZED EMPIRICAL METHOD

We were dissatisfied with mere inner conviction and so we asked whether it bore any relation to objective truth. We have been pondering successive stages in the liquidation of the brave view presented in Aristotle's *Posterior Analytics*. We have come up with a science that yields, not objective truth, but the best available opinion of the day.

But, if science does not give us objective truth, where are we to go? At this point each man has to become his own philosopher, and so I have no more to offer than my own solution to the issue. I have called it a generalized empirical method.[6]

Generalized empirical method is a method. It is a normative pattern of related and recurrent operations that yield ongoing and cumulative results. It regards operations, and so it is not just a list of materials to be combined in a cake or a medicine. It regards recurrent operations, and so the same method can be employed over and over again. It yields ongoing and cumulative results, and so it differs from the New Method Laundry which keeps on repeating the same result whenever it is used. Such cumulative results set a standard, and because the standard is met, the pattern of related operations is normative: it is the right way to do the job.[7]

Generalized empirical method envisages all data. The natural sciences confine themselves to the data of sense. Hermeneutic and historical studies turn mainly to data that are expressions of meaning. Clinical psychology finds in meanings the symptoms of conflicts between conscious and preconscious or unconscious activities.

Generalized empirical method operates on a combination of both the data of sense and the data of consciousness: it does not treat of objects without taking into account the corresponding operations of the subject; it does not treat of the subject's operations without taking into account the corresponding objects.[8]

As generalized empirical method generalizes the notion of data to include the data of consciousness, so too it generalizes the notion of method. It wants to go behind the diversity that separates the experimental method of the natural sciences and the quite diverse procedures of hermeneutics and of history. It would discover their common core and thereby prepare the way for their harmonious combination in human studies. From various viewpoints man has been named the logical animal, the symbolic animal, the self-completing animal. But in each of these definitions man is regarded as an animal, and so he is an object for the natural sciences. At the same time, he is regarded as logical or symbolic or self-completing; he lives his life in a world mediated by meaning; and so he is a proper object for hermeneutic and historical studies. What then is the common core of related and recurrent operations that may be discerned both in natural science and in human studies?

In the natural sciences the key event is discovery. Whether we recall Archimedes' *Eureka* or the legend of Newton associating a falling apple with a falling moon, whether we turn from epoch-making discoveries to the larger field of less surprising but no less essential contributions, we ever find ourselves at the point where natural science has made a quantum leap. Something new has emerged. Again, in hermeneutics the key event is understanding: for the theorist of hermeneutics was Schleiermacher, and he got beyond the various rules of thumb of classical scholars and biblical exegetes by expounding a discipline based on the avoidance of misunderstanding and thereby the avoidance of misinterpretation. In history, again, the key operation is understanding, and so it was that Johann Gustav Droysen extended the procedures of hermeneutics to the whole of history by observing that not only individuals but also families, peoples, states, religions express themselves. Nor is understanding alien to common sense. It is the everyday experience of seeing what you mean, getting the point, catching on, seeing how things hang together. Indeed, when we esteem people for their intelligence, it is because of the ease and frequency with which they understand; and when we suspect that they may be a bit retarded, it is because they understand only rarely and then slowly.

However, understanding is only one of the many components that have to be combined to constitute an instance of human knowledge. It presupposes data, whether given to sense or given in consciousness: for our understanding always is an insight, a grasp of intelligible unity or intelligible relationship; and a grasp of unity presupposes the presentation of what needs unification, as a grasp of intelligible relationship presupposes the presentation of what can be related. Again, such insight or grasp presupposes inquiry: that search, hunt, chase for the way to piece together the merely given into an intelligible unity or innerly related whole. Nor is it enough to discover the solution. One also must express it adequately. Otherwise one will have had the mere experience of the occurrence of a bright idea, but one will not have the power to recall it, use it, apply it. There is a further point to such expression whether in word or deed. Insights are a dime a dozen. For the most part they occur, not with respect to data in all their complexity, but with respect to merely schematic images. Dozens of such images are needed to approximate to what actually is given, and so it is that the expression of insight has to be followed by a very cool and detached process of reflection that marshals the relevant evidence and submits it to appropriate tests before laying claim to any discovery or intention.

Such in briefest outline is the normative pattern of recurrent and related operations that yield ongoing and cumulative results in natural science, in hermeneutics, in history, in common sense. It will be noted that the operations involved occur consciously: in dreamless sleep one does not experience or inquire or understand or formulate or reflect or check or pass judgment. Not only are the operations conscious. There also is a dynamism that moves one along from one operation to the next. There is the spontaneity of sense. There is the intelligence with which we inquire in order to understand and, once we have understood, there is the intelligence with which we formulate what we have grasped. There is the reasonableness with which we reflect on our formulations, check them out, pronounce in the light of the evidence we have brought to light. Such spontaneity, intelligence, reasonableness are themselves conscious. So it is that both the operations and the relations that unite them in a normative pattern are given in consciousness.

But their givenness, of itself, is only infrastructure. It is not yet human knowledge but only one component within an item of knowledge of which the remainder as yet is only potential. To make that remainder actual one has *first* to attend to one's attending, note how spontaneously it fixes upon what gives delight, promises pleasure, threatens danger, recall the long years at school when teachers labored to sublimate our animal spirits and harness them to different, allegedly higher pursuits, so that now without too much pain one can sit through a whole lecture and even listen to most of it. *Secondly,* one has to advert to one's own intelligence, its awareness when one is failing to understand, its dissatisfaction with explanations that do not quite explain, its puzzled search for the further question that would clear the matter up, its joy when a solution comes to light, its care to find the exact expression to convey precisely what understanding has grasped. In brief, attending to one's own intelligence brings to light a primitive and basic meaning of the word, normative, for the intelligence in each of us prompts us to seek understanding, to be dissatisfied with a mere glimmer, to keep probing for an ever fuller grasp, to pin down in accurate expression just what we so far have attained. In similar fashion, *thirdly,* attending to one's own reasonableness reveals an equally primitive and basic but complementary type of normativeness. Ideas are fine, but no matter how bright, they are not enough. The practical man wants to know whether they will work. The theoretical man will wonder whether they are true: he will test their inner coherence, compare them with what he otherwise considers established, work out their implications, devise experiments to see whether the implications are verifiable, and if no flaw can be found, he will grant, not that they are true, but only that they seem probable. Our reasonableness demands sufficient evidence, marshals and weighs all it can find, is bound to assent when evidence is sufficient, and may not assent when it is insufficient. *Finally,* there is the normativeness of our deliberations. Between necessity and impossibility lies the realm of freedom and responsibility. Because we are free, we also are responsible, and in our responsibility we may discern another primitive and basic instance of normativeness. It is, so to speak, the reasonableness of action. Just as we cannot be reasonable and pass judgment beyond or against the evidence, so too we cannot be responsible without adverting to what is right and what is wrong, without enjoying the peace of a good conscience when we choose what is right, without suffering the disquiet of an unhappy conscience when we choose what is wrong.

It is time to conclude. We have been asking whether there is any connection between inner conviction and objective truth. By inner conviction we have meant not passion, not stubbornness, not wilful blindness, but the very opposite; we have meant the fruit of self-transcendence, of being attentive, intelligent, reasonable, responsible; in brief, of being ruled by the inner norms that constitute the exigences for authenticity in the human person. But for objectivity we have distinguished two interpretations. There is the objectivity of the world of immediacy, of the already-out-there-now, of the earth that is firm-set only in the sense that at each moment it has happened to resist my treading feet and bear my weight. But there also is the objectivity of the world mediated by meaning; and that objectivity is the fruit of authentic subjectivity, of being attentive, intelligent, reasonable, responsible.

In my opinion, then, inner conviction is the conviction that the norms of attentiveness, intelligence, reasonableness, responsibility have been satisfied. And satisfying those norms is the highroad to the objectivity to be attained in the world mediated by meaning and motivated by values.

This, the second in the Queen's University lectures of 1976, was previously published in Fred Lawrence (ed.), *Lonergan Workshop,* Vol. I (Missoula, Montana—now Chico, Cal.: Scholars Press, 1978), pp. 309–327; French translation: "La connaissance religieuse," in Bernard Lonergan, *Les voies d'une théologie méthodique . . . ,* 1982.

Notes

1. Ludwig Binswanger, *Le rêve et l'existence,* Introduction and notes by Michel Foucault (Tournai : Desclée, 1954).

2. Aristotle, *Posterior Analytics,* I, 2, 7lb 9–12.

3. *Ibid.,* II, 19, 100a 10–14.

4. Imre Lakatos and Alan Musgrave (eds.), *Criticism and the Growth of Knowledge* (Proceedings of the International Colloquium in the Philosophy of Science, London, 1965, Vol. IV; Cambridge: At the University Press, 1970).

5. Patrick Heelan, *Quantum Mechanics and Objectivity: A Study of the Physical Philosophy of Werner Heisenberg* (The Hague: Martinus Nijhoff, 1965), pp. 53–54, 38.

6. B. Lonergan, *Insight,* 1957, pp. 243–244, and cf. p. 72.

7. See the first chapter in B. Lonergan, *Method in Theology,* 1972.

8. Distinguish three meanings of the term, transcendental: the most general and all-pervasive concepts, namely, *ens, unum, verum, bonum,* of the Scholastics; the Kantian conditions of the possibility of knowing an object *a priori;* Husserl's intentionality analysis in which *noēsis* and *noēma,* act and object, are correlative.

10

Third Lecture:
The Ongoing Genesis of Methods

There is no need for me to tell you that today the word, theology, denotes not some well-defined form of thought but rather an aggregate
of quite different and often quite nebulous forms. In contrast, religious studies seem to present a more determinate and uniform front,
though even there, one may feel, there exist stirrings and strivings
that may be all the more significant because they are mainly potential.

If this estimate of the present situation is correct, then mani-
festly there can be no simple answer to the question before us. One
might compare or contrast some particular type of theology with
some particular direction in religious studies. But when both terms
are left in their full generality, then the issue has to shift from statics
to dynamics.

Such a shift is not just a vague dodge. For a quite static view of
the nature of the sciences and of their relations to one another can be
had from Aristotelian analysis in terms of material and formal objects. In contrast, a quite dynamic view of the same matter is had
when sciences are conceived in terms of method and field, and methods are not fixed once for all but keep developing, differentiating,
regrouping as the exigences of advance may demand.

It is into the ongoing genesis of methods that we must plunge,
for it is precisely this process that explains both the disarray of contemporary theologies and the less apparent though perhaps not less
significant stirrings in religious studies.

Accordingly we begin from the origin of this dynamic of methods in the scientific revolution of the sixteenth and seventeenth centuries. Next, we shall take issue with the danger or suspicion of relativism by indicating the foundations on which the succession of methods may be based. Thirdly, we shall argue that increasing specialization entails increasing limitation and that increasing limitation serves to define the possibility and encourage the actuality of additional, distinct, even disparate methods. Fourthly, it will appear that the more human studies turn away from abstract universals and attend to concrete human beings, the more evident it becomes that the scientific age of innocence has come to an end; human authenticity can no longer be taken for granted. Fifthly, we ask whether there is any method that can deal with the unauthentic as well as the authentic, with the irrational as well as the rational; and some such approach we designate by the Greek name, praxis. Finally, in the light of praxis, we attempt to relate religion, theology, and religious studies, where these three are considered not as static abstractions but as the dynamic entities they partly are and partly can be.

1. LEARNING: MODERN STYLE

In the introduction to his account of *The Origins of Modern Science* Herbert Butterfield noted that the scientific revolution of the sixteenth and seventeenth centuries overturned the authority in science not only of the middle ages but also of the ancient world. He concluded that that revolution ''outshines everything since the rise of Christianity and reduces the Renaissance and Reformation to the rank of mere episodes, mere internal displacements, within the system of medieval Christendom.''[1]

Now I have already had occasion to point out certain elements in that revolution. It aimed at utility, and so it was concerned with everyday materials, their manipulation, their mastery, through a process of trial and error. It demanded autonomy: its basic terms and relations were to be mathematical in their origins and experimental in their justification. It was concerned not with words but with reality and so it excluded questions that could not be resolved by an appeal to observation or experiment. On all three counts it ran counter to the ideal set forth in Aristotle's *Posterior Analytics*. Despite an initial concern with understanding things, that work devoted its efforts to the construction of a theory of science out of the terms, relations, inferences constitutive of the demonstrative syllogism. Instead of developing science by combining mathematical notions with their experimental verification, the *Posterior Analytics* conceived philosophy and science as a single, logically interlocking unity, in which philosophy was to provide the sciences with their basic terms and principles. Instead of directing men's minds to practical results, Aristotle held that science was concerned with necessary truth, that what can be changed is not the necessary but the contingent, and so the fruit of science can be no more than the contemplation of the eternal truths it brought to light.[2]

Such was modern science at its origins. But it continued to develop and thereby to reveal further differences. Notable among these was its departure from an earlier individualistic view of science. Aristotle's sets of syllogisms were highly compact affairs, and so he had no difficulty in thinking of science as an acquired habit tucked away in the minds of individuals. Cartesian thought took its stand on an initial universal doubt and proceeded as a search for ideas so clear and distinct as to beget certitude. The program of the eighteenth-century Enlightenment was to appeal to reason, proclaim science, and purge people's minds of the prejudices inflicted upon them by tradition.

But if such individualism still lives in the assumptions of many in the twentieth century, the carrier of a science today is a social group. No individual knows the whole of modern mathematics, or the whole of physics, or the whole of chemistry, or the whole of biology. Such knowledge is possessed not by an individual but by the members of a group. They have passed successfully through the initiation ritual of a Ph.D. They are familiar with a technical language which they alone speak and understand. They know the correct procedures to be followed in their investigations and the ideals that should govern their thinking. They are master of the novel conceptual systems introduced by the pioneers and the renovators of their field. They belong to the appropriate associations, attend the congresses, read the journals, consult the libraries, contribute to the publications, and design the tools and equipment they may need. A modern science is a specialization.[3] The scientists are specialists. Their function is to keep their tradition alive and flourishing. Hans-Georg Gadamer startled many when in his great book, *Wahrheit und*

Methode, first published in 1960, he contended that to interpret a literature one had to inherit or find one's way into a literary tradition. But what holds for the humanities, also holds for the sciences. If Butterfield is right in thinking modern science the most striking event since the beginning of Christianity, the eighteenth century was right in rejecting an earlier tradition only because it launched a new tradition.

Initially, of course, the new tradition was not yet a tradition. Nor was it easy for it later on to advert to its traditional character. For there lurked in men's minds the Aristotelian assumption that science was clear and certain knowledge of causal necessity. What could be more clear and certain than the verified deduction of the orbits of the moon and of Mars? What could be more necessary than conclusions that were demonstrated? Only when Euclid and Newton and Maxwell bowed to Riemann and Einstein and Heisenberg, did it become obvious that earlier mistakes could not be knowledge of necessity and that, like earlier views, the new systems were not deductions from necessary truths but verified conclusions from hypothetical theories.

Aristotle, then, was quite right in holding that a science that consisted in the grasp of necessary truth had to be purely theoretical and could not be practical. But from the start modern science intended to be practical. Today there are many steps along the way from basic research to pure science, from pure science to applied, from applied to technology, from technology to engineering. But the multiplicity does not obscure the underlying unity. For us good theory is practical, and good practise is grounded in sound theory. Where the Aristotelian placed his reliance on first principles he considered necessary, the modern scientist places his reliance ultimately not on his basic laws and principles but on his method. It was the method that brought forth the laws and principles in the first place, and it will be the method that revises them if and when the time for revision comes.

2. FOUNDATIONS

So we are brought up against a problem of foundations. If method can revise the principles and laws on which a successful science has been constructed, so too, it would seem, methods themselves are open to correction and revision. If methods too can be revised, then is not the whole of science just a vast structure resting upon sand?

Here, I believe, there is room for a valid distinction. There are the particular methods adapted to the needs and opportunities of particular fields. As such needs and opportunities come to light, methods themselves undergo further adaptation. They become more specialized. They develop new techniques and refine old ones. They incorporate fresh stratagems, models, mappings, seriations. But all such changes and modifications come under a higher law. As the revisions of existing theories, so too the developments of existing methods are just fresh instances of attending to the data, grasping their intelligibility, formulating the content of the new insights, and checking as thoroughly as possible their validity. In brief, underpinning special methods there is what I have named generalized empirical method. Its operations are the operations we can verify each in his own consciousness. And the normative pattern that relates these operations to one another is the conscious dynamism of sensitive spontaneity, of intelligence raising questions and demanding satisfactory answers, of reasonableness insisting on sufficient evidence before it can assent yet compelled to assent when sufficient evidence is forthcoming, of conscience presiding over all and revealing to the subject his authenticity or his unauthenticity as he observes or violates the immanent norms of his own sensitivity, his own intelligence, his own reasonableness, his own freedom and responsibility.

Now it will be felt that this appeal to generalized empirical method really is an appeal to individual subjectivity and that individual subjectivity, so far from offering a secure foundation, gives rise to serious doubts and grave uneasiness.

But once more a distinction must be drawn. There is the subject correlative to the world of immediacy, and the subject correlative to the world mediated by meaning and motivated by value. The world of immediacy is very much like Hume's world in which there is discerned neither permanence nor causality nor necessity. The subject correlative to the world of immediacy is the subject locked up in his immediate experience of the data of sense and of the data of consciousness. His knowledge is just infrastructure, and his actions flow directly from appetites. His capacity to communicate is uninformed by intelligence, unguided by reason, uncontrolled by responsibility.

Now if individual subjectivity is understood to mean the subject as correlative to the world of immediacy, then I heartily agree that individual subjectivity, so far from offering a secure foundation, gives rise to serious doubts and well-founded uneasiness.

However, I must point out that generalized empirical method appeals not to the individual subjectivity that is correlative to the world of immediacy but to the individual subjectivity that is correlative to the world mediated by meaning and motivated by value.

I must add that the subject in this sense, so far from being locked up in immediate experience of the data of sense and the data of consciousness, moves in a universe with which he is acquainted—according to the measure of his personal development—by common sense, by science, by human studies, by philosophy, perhaps even by theology.

Further I would urge that while the experience of the subject correlative to the world of immediacy is a purely private affair, privacy in the world mediated by meaning has to be contrived and defended and even then it is limited. In that world one is taught by others and, for the most part, what they know they have learnt from others, in an ongoing process that stretches back over millennia. In that world one not merely experiences but understands and manifests one's understanding in one's words and deeds, thereby to invite the approval or correction of one's betters, the admiration or the ridicule of one's peers. Common sense is not an individual idiosyncrasy. Scientific discoveries that are not published, scrutinized, accepted, remain unknown and without issue. Exegetes and historians may secure the privacy of their findings by consigning them to the flames, but only if their findings are published, only if they are read, only if they attain the recognition of the community of specialists in their field, only then do they begin to exert some influence on subsequent exegetical or historical investigation or teaching.

However, while I believe that attention, intelligence, reasonableness, responsibility take individuals out of the isolation and privacy of the experiential infrastructure, I must not be thought to suggest that this liberation towards truth, reality, objectivity, excellence is automatic or foolproof. It is not. Man is called to authenticity. But man attains authenticity only by unfailing fidelity to the

but the historical process

exigences of his intelligence, his reasonableness, his conscience. What is far more grave, is that the shortcomings of individuals can become the accepted practise of the group; the accepted practise of the group can become the tradition accepted in good faith by succeeding generations; the evil can spread to debase and corrupt what is most vulnerable while it prostitutes to unworthy ends what otherwise is sound and sane. Then the authentic, if any have survived, are alienated from their society and their culture. The courageous look about for remedies but find none that even appear equal to the task. The average man, who knows he was not born to be a hero, decides he has no choice but to go along with things as they are. And the more numerous the people who concur with that decision, the less is the hope of recovery from unauthenticity, the greater is the risk of the disintegration and the decay of a civilization.

Since disintegration and decay are not private events, even generalized empirical method is experimental. But the experiment is conducted not by any individual, not by any generation, but by the historical process itself.

3. FROM METHOD TO METHODS

A modern science is characterized more by its method than by its field, for the field tends to expand to include every area in which the method can be applied successfully.

At the same time, the more a method is developed, the more it becomes specialized. In certain areas its success is conspicuous, in others success is modest and even rare. In such cases probably a different development of method is needed, and so where there had been one more general method, now there are two more specialized methods. In this fashion the scientific revolution of the sixteenth and seventeenth centuries was a general methodical breakthrough that since has divided and subdivided into all the specialized branches of natural science.

It remains, however, that not all empirical methods emerge as differentiations within the basic procedures of the natural sciences. The clear-cut instance of this leap to another genre is provided by historical studies as they developed in Germany in the nineteenth century. The background that gave this movement its sweep and profundity is to be traced to the French Enlightenment and the post-Kantian idealists. But if it took over the Enlightenment's dedication to human progress, it abhorred its abstract thinking. If it agreed with Hegel's insistence on concreteness and his concern with world history, it repudiated his *a priori* methods.

It was this movement that launched the study of the history of religions, and it will not be out of place to indicate its basic ideas as they were unfolded by Friedrich Wolf, Friedrich Schleiermacher, August Boeckh, Johann Gustav Droysen, and Wilhelm Dilthey.[4]

Friedrich Wolf, when still a student, demanded the creation of a new faculty, philology. He conceived it as a philosophico-historical study of human nature as that nature was exhibited in antiquity. To this end in his own teaching later on at Halle he brought together in his courses a whole series of distinct disciplines: literature, antiquities, geography, art, numismatics; and he informed them with the critical spirit that produced his *Prolegomena to Homer*.

Friedrich Schleiermacher found the hermeneutics of his day to be little more than two sets of rules of thumb: those followed by biblical exegetes and those employed by classical scholars. He reconceived it as a general art of avoiding misunderstanding and misapprehension. By that negative formulation he nonetheless gave to understanding, *Verstehen,* its basic role in the theoretical development of historical studies.

August Boeckh was a pupil of both Wolf and Schleiermacher. He developed their ideas in composing an *Encyclopedia and Methodology of the Philological Sciences*. In it philology was conceived in the grand manner, a manner at once precise, penetrating, and comprehensive. In a definition to which presently we shall recur, philology was to be the interpretative reconstruction of the constructions of the human spirit.

Johann Gustav Droysen generalized the notion of expression. Not only individuals express themselves in their speech and writings. There is a sense in which families, peoples, states, religions may be said to express themselves. Accordingly, history may be conceived as the interpretation of such group expression, and Boeckh's ideas on philology may be applied to the writing of history.

Wilhelm Dilthey brought the matter to its fine point. He contended that *Das Leben selbst legt sich aus*. Human living is itself its own interpretation. In other words, the expression, which the exegete or the historian interprets, is itself the product of understanding, namely, the understanding people have of themselves, their situation, their role, the human condition.

At once it follows that there is a profound difference between natural science and historical study. Both the scientist and the historian would understand: the scientist would understand nature; the historian would understand man. But when the scientist understands nature, he is not grasping nature's understanding of itself; for though nature is intelligible, it is not intelligent. But when the historian understands man, his understanding is a recapturing of man's understanding of himself. This recapturing is interpretation. It differs from the understanding that it recaptures, for it makes thematic, puts in words, an understanding that was not thematized but lived. Yet in another fashion it corresponds to what it recaptures; for it envisages an earlier situation and recounts how an individual or group understood that situation and revealed themselves by their understanding of it.

In Dilthey we have an echo of Vico's claim that it is human affairs that men best understand, for human affairs are the product of human understanding. Again, in Dilthey we have an anticipation of R. G. Collingwood's view that historical knowledge is a reenactment of the past. Finally, we have only to shift our gaze from the interpreter to the persons under scrutiny, to arrive at a phenomenological ontology. The endless variety exhibited in human living has its root in the endless variety of the ways in which people understand themselves, their situation, and the human condition. Such understanding commonly is of the type that spontaneously is generated and spontaneously communicated, the type that may be named commonsense. It is constitutive of the basic department of human knowledge, the department expressed in ordinary language. Like ordinary language it varies from place to place and from time to time. It enters into the intelligible form man communicates to the products of his ingenuity and his skill. It is part and parcel of human conduct. It is constitutive of the cognitional and the moral reality that makes man the 'symbolic animal' of the historians and the 'self-completing animal' of the sociologists.

Let us now revert to August Boeckh's definition of philology as the interpretative reconstruction of the constructions of the human spirit. The constructions of the human spirit are man and his world: for his world is a world mediated by meaning and motivated by value; and it is the human spirit that constructs the meanings and responds to the motivating values. But what man has constructed man can reconstruct. What man has responded to in thought and word and deed, he can respond to once more if only in thought and word and feeling. Such reconstructing and such responding-to-once-more are the interpretations of the scholar and the narratives of the historian.

We may conclude this section by noting that historical studies, so conceived, have all the marks of a distinct specialization. Like natural science history is empirical, but where the sciences seek universal principles, laws, structures, seriations, history would understand particular words, deeds, situations, movements. Where the several sciences each construct their own technical languages, historians as an ongoing group are confronted with the task of deciphering and learning all the languages of mankind whether still living or though long since dead. Where the sciences come to know parts or aspects of the universe that common sense never would discover, historians enlarge their own common sense to the point where it encapsulates something of the common sense of other places and times. Lastly, as other specializations, so the study of history leads to the formation of a professional group that develops its own proper procedures and traditions, enforces an initiation ritual of doctoral studies, meets in its own annual congresses, and stocks special libraries with its reference works, surveys, journals, and monographs.

4. DIALECTIC

As long as human studies copy the methods of the natural sciences, they obtain assured results, but they minimize or omit the human world mediated by meaning and motivated by value. On the other hand, when human studies attempt to deal bravely and boldly with the world mediated by meaning and motivated by value, they find themselves involved in philosophic, ethical, and religious issues. Philosophies oscillate between a world of immediacy and a world mediated by meaning. Individuals and groups esteem values, but they tend to maximize satisfactions, and they are ever tempted to the endless rationalizations that make their satisfactions into necessary incidents in the pursuit of values. Religions are many. They may differ very slightly, and they may diverge to the point of disparateness. And contradicting their multiplicity is the secularist rejection of all religion.

Such differences are radical. Philosophic differences affect the very meaning of meaning. Ethical differences affect all evaluations. Religious differences modify the meaning and value of one's world.

Such differences become traditional. None of us is an Adam living at the origin of human affairs, becoming all that he is by his own decisions, and learning all that he knows by personal experience, personal insight, personal discernment. We are products of a process that in its several aspects is named socialization, acculturation, education. By that process there is formed our initial mind-set, worldview, blik, horizon. On that basis and within its limitations we slowly begin to become our own masters, think for ourselves, make our own decisions, exercise our own freedom and responsibility.

Such radical and traditional differences put their stamp not only on the writings to be interpreted and the events to be narrated but also upon the mind-set, worldview, horizon of exegetes and historians. In utopia, no doubt, everyone in all his words and deeds would be operating with the authenticity generated by meeting the exigences of intelligence, reasonableness, responsibility. But our world is not utopia. Even if anyone manages to be perfectly authentic in all his own personal performance, still he cannot but carry within himself the ballast of his tradition. And down the millennia in which that tradition developed, one can hardly exclude the possibility that unauthenticity entered in and remained to ferment the mass through ages to come.

So we come to the end of the age of innocence, the age that assumed that human authenticity could be taken for granted. I do not mean that human wickedness was denied. But it was felt it could be evaded. Truth was supposed to consist in the necessary conclusions deduced from self-evident principles. Or it was thought that reality was already out there now, and that objectivity was the simple matter of taking a good look, seeing all that was there, and not seeing what was not there. Or there was admitted the real existence of a critical problem, but it was felt that a sound critical philosophy—such as Kant's or Comte's or some other—would solve it once for all.

difference in the observer effect what is seen?

The end of the age of innocence means that authenticity is never to be taken for granted. Mathematicians had to generalize their notion of number to include irrational and imaginary numbers. Physicists had to develop quantum theory because instruments of observation modified the data they were to observe. In similar fashion human studies have to cope with the complexity that recognizes both (1) that the data may be a mixed product of authenticity and of unauthenticity and (2) that the very investigation of the data may be affected by the personal or inherited unauthenticity of the investigators.

The objective aspect of the problem has come to light in Paul Ricoeur's distinction between a hermeneutic of recovery, that brings to light what is true and good, and a hermeneutic of suspicion, that joins Marx in impugning the rich, or Nietzsche in reviling the humble, or Freud in finding consciousness itself an unreliable witness to our motives. Again, it may be illustrated in my own account of "The Origins of Christian Realism," that distinguished the Christological and Trinitarian doctrines of Tertullian, Origen, and Athanasius on the basis of a philosophic dialectic. Tertullian under Stoic influence was oriented towards a world of immediacy. Origen under Middle Platonist influence was in a world mediated by meaning, where however meaning was the meaning of ideas. Athanasius finally was in the world mediated by meaning, where the meaning was the truth of the Christian kerygma.[5]

As dialectical analysis can be applied to problems of interpretation, so too it can be applied to historical issues; and the issues may be either such general issues as progress, decline, recovery, or the very specific issues that arise when historians are in radical disagreement.

On the general issue progress is analyzed as a cyclic and cumulative process. A situation gives rise to an insight. The insight generates policies, projects, plans, courses of action. The courses of action produce a new and improved situation. The new and improved situation gives rise to further insight, and so the cycle recommences.

Similarly, decline is cyclic and cumulative, but now unauthenticity distorts what authenticity would have improved. The policies, projects, plans, courses of action that come from creative insight into the existing situation have the misfortune of running counter not merely to vested interests but to any and every form of human unauthenticity. Doubts are raised, objections formulated, suspicions insinuated, compromises imposed. Policies, projects, plans, courses of action are modified to make the new situation not a progressive product of human authenticity but a mixed product partly of human authenticity and partly of human obtuseness, unreasonableness, irresponsibility. As this process continues, the objective situation will become to an ever greater extent an intractable problem. The only way to understand it correctly will be to acknowledge its source in human waywardness. The only way to deal with it will be to admonish the wayward. But such sophistication may be lacking, and then one can expect not repentance but rationalization. So decline continues unabashed. The intractable problem keeps growing. Rationalizations multiply, accumulate, are linked together into a stately system of thought that is praised by all who forget the adage: Whom the gods would destroy, they first make blind.

Can a people, a civilization, recover from such decline? To my mind the only solution is religious. What will sweep away the rationalizations? More reasoning will hardly do it effectively, for it will be suspected of being just so much more rationalizing. And when reasoning is ineffective, what is left but faith? What will smash the determinisms—economic, social, cultural, psychological—that egoism has constructed and exploited? What can be offered but the hoping beyond hope that religion inspires? When finally the human situation seethes with alienation, bitterness, resentment, recrimination, hatred, mounting violence, what can retributive justice bring about but a duplication of the evils that already exist? Then what is needed is not retributive justice but self-sacrificing love.[6]

Such is the general, schematic application of dialectic to historical issues. But there also is the specific application that deals with intractable problems in exegesis and in historiography. There problems are tractable when further research, new discoveries, increasing discernment bring solutions. But there are other problems that do not yield to such treatment. Rather they keep recurring in one guise or another no matter how much the context is changed by ongoing research, discovery, discernment. Their source does not lie in the data but in the investigators. The discovery to be made is not a better understanding of the data but a better understanding of the investigators.

Finally, besides the dialectic that is concerned with human subjects as objects, there is the dialectic in which human subjects are concerned with themselves and with one another. In that case dialectic becomes dialogue. It is particularly relevant when persons are authentic and know one another to be authentic yet belong to differing traditions and so find themselves in basic disagreement. It may be illustrated by the ecumenical movement among Christians and by the universalist movement set forth by R. E. Whitson in his *The Coming Convergence of World Religions,* by Raymond Panikkar's diacritical theology and by William Johnston's Christian monks frequenting Zen monasteries in Japan.[7]

5. PRAXIS

Experimental method reveals nature. Historical method reveals man, the self-completing animal, in the manifold variety of his concrete existing. Dialectic confronts us with the problem of the irrational in human life and, as well, provides a technique for distinguishing between authentic and unauthentic evaluations, decisions, actions. Praxis, finally, raises the final issue, What are you to do about it? What use are you to make of your knowledge of nature, of your knowledge of man, of your awareness of the radical conflict between man's aspiration to self-transcendence and, on the other hand, the waywardness that may distort his traditional heritage and even his own personal life.

It is only after the age of innocence that praxis becomes an academic subject. A faculty psychology will give intellect precedence over will and thereby it will liberate the academic world from concern with the irrational in human life. The speculative intellect of the Aristotelians, the pure reason of the rationalists, the automatic progress anticipated by the liberals, all provided shelter for academic serenity. But since the failure of the absolute idealists to encompass human history within the embrace of speculative reason, the issue of praxis has repeatedly come to the fore. Schopenhauer conceived the world in terms of will and representation. Kierkegaard insisted on faith. Newman toasted conscience. Marx was concerned not merely to know but principally to make history. Nietzsche proclaimed the will to power. Blondel strove for a philosophy of action. Paul Ricoeur has not yet completed his many-volumed philosophy of will, and Jürgen Habermas has set forth the involvement of human knowledge in human interests. Along with them have marched in varying ways pragmatists, personalists, existentialists, while phenomenologists have supplanted faculty psychology with an intentionality analysis in which cognitional process is sublated by deliberation, evaluation, decision, action.[8]

If I have referred to so many and so different thinkers, it has not been to agree with all of them but rather to discern despite their differences a common concern with what I have named praxis. On an older view contemplative intellect, or speculative reason, or rigorous science was supreme, and practical issues were secondary. But the older view grounded its hegemony on necessity. That claim no longer is made. If we are not simply to flounder, we have to take our stand on authenticity: on the authenticity with which intelligence takes us beyond the experimental infrastructure to enrich it, extend it, organize it, but never to slight it and much less to violate its primordial role; on the authenticity with which rational reflection goes beyond the constructions of intelligence and draws sharply the lines between astrology and astronomy, alchemy and chemistry, legend and history, magic and science, myth and philosophy; on the authenticity with which moral deliberation takes us beyond cognitional process into the realm of freedom and responsibility, evaluation and decision, not in any way to annul or slight experience or understanding or factual judgment, but to add the further and distinct truth of value judgments and the consequent decisions demanded by a situation in which authenticity cannot be taken for granted.

It follows that, while empirical method moves, so to speak, from below upwards, praxis moves from above downwards. Empirical method moves from below upwards, from experience to understanding, and from understanding to factual judgment. It can do so because it can presuppose that the data of experience are intelligible and so are objects that straightforward understanding can master. But praxis acknowledges the end of the age of innocence. It starts from the assumption that authenticity cannot be taken for granted. Its understanding, accordingly, will follow a hermeneutic of suspicion

as well as a hermeneutic of recovery. Its judgment will discern between products of human authenticity and products of human
unauthenticity. But the basic assumption, the twofold hermeneutic,
the discernment between the authentic and the unauthentic set up a
distinct method. This method is a compound of theoretical and practical judgments of value. The use of this method follows from a decision, a decision that is comparable to the claim of Blaise Pascal
that the heart has reasons which reason does not know.

6. RELIGION, THEOLOGY, RELIGIOUS STUDIES

While praxis is relevant to the whole of human studies, its relevance is particularly manifest in the sphere of religion. For that
sphere is the world as mediated by ultimate meaning and motivated
by ultimate value. But commonly the religions apprehend ultimate
meaning and ultimate value symbolically. The theologies endeavor
to discern whether there is any real fire behind the smoke of symbols
employed in this or that religion. Religious studies finally envisage
the totality of religions down the ages and over the expanse of the
globe.

The matter needs to be illustrated, illustration has to be particular, and so I shall speak in terms of Christian experience. There
occurs, then, a response to ultimate value in conversion from waywardness or in a call to holiness. The Christian message will
give that response a focus and an interpretation: the response will be
taken as God's love flooding our hearts through the Holy Spirit
given to us; the focus will be found in the objective expression of the
same love by the Father sending the Son to us and revealing his love
in the Son's crucifixion, death, and resurrection. From preaching the
message and from the gift of the Spirit, the Christian community is
born, spreads, passes on from generation to generation. It lives by its
discernment between the authenticity of a good conscience and the
unauthenticity of an unhappy conscience. It devotes its efforts to
overcoming unauthenticity and promoting authenticity. It is praxis
alive and active. But as yet it is not praxis questioned, scrutinized,
made explicit and thematic.

Theology comes out of such questioning, and three distinct
emergences must be distinguished. In the ancient Christian church

questions centered on such specific issues as Christology and Pela-gianism. In the medieval period there was a sustained effort to move from the symbolic expression of Christian thought to its literal mean-ing. But this effort's involvement in Aristotelian thought with its concern for proof, necessity, and eternal truth, not only fostered li-tigiousness and controversy but later led to its all but disruptive re-newal under the impact of modern science, modern exegetical and historical methods, and modern philosophies.

Sound renewal is not yet, in my opinion, a common achieve-ment. But the contemporary situation does seem favorable to an ire-nic and constructive use of dialectic and dialogue. The former ten-dency to controversy has greatly diminished, partly because modern science and human studies lay claim not to absolute truth but to no more than fuller understanding, partly because speculative intel-lect or pure reason has given way to the claims of praxis. There re-main differing Christian communions and each may be represented by more than one theology. But acceptance of dialectic, especially in the form of dialogue, is powerfully fostered by the ecumenical movement and by the promotion of union among the theologians of the same communion.

When I say that the contemporary situation favors an irenic and constructive use of dialectic, I must not be taken to imply that we can expect great and rapid results. For religious communions are histor-ical realities. Their authenticity is the resultant not only of the au-thenticity of their contemporary members but also of the heritage transmitted down the centuries. Whatever the defects of any such heritage, it comes to be accepted in good faith. Good faith is good not evil. It needs to be purified, but the purification will be the slow product of historical research into the screening memories and de-fense mechanisms and legitimations that betray an original way-wardness and a sinister turn.

Besides the Christian communions there are the manifold pre-literate religions and the great world religions. Religious studies takes as its field all religions. Its main thrust is the history of reli-gions, that is, the research that assembles and catalogues the relevant data, the interpretation that grasps their morphology, the history that locates them in place and time, studies their genesis, development, distribution, interaction.

But history itself is practised in varying manners. Its ideal can approximate the ideal of natural science, to minimize attention to meaning and values. In contrast, it can embrace the ideal of the German Historical School defined as the interpretative reconstruction of the constructions of the human spirit. Then meaning and values receive explicit attention. The need is felt and the desire expressed that one write of the religions of mankind in a manner that is recognizable by the respective groups that practise the religion. One can go further, as did Friedrich Heiler, and see the mission of the history of religions to lie in a preparation of the cooperation of religions;[9] and certainly such a purpose satisfies the cardinal point of method as praxis; for it discerns a radically distorted situation; it retreats from spontaneous to critical intelligence; it begins from above on the level of evaluations and decisions; and it moves from concord and cooperation towards the development of mutual understanding and more effective communication.

Finally, the more that the field of religious studies moves from the style of natural science to that of profounder historical study, the more it endeavors to understand the element of total commitment that characterizes religion, the more it is concerned to promote the cooperation of religions, then the more it finds itself involved in the radical oppositions of cognitional theory, of ethical practise, of religious and secularist man. At that point it too can undertake dialectic, a dialectic that will assemble all the dialectics that relate religions to organized secularism, religions to one another, and the differing theologies that interpret the same religious communion. At that point, again, it can invite to dialogue the representatives of related and ultimately of disparate religions.

7. CONCLUSION

I began by pointing out, this evening, that the issue, *Religious Studies and/or Theology,* if it is not to deal with static abstractions, has to plunge into the ongoing genesis of methods and has to view its terms as dynamic entities, as compounds of the actual and the potential, even as mixed products of human authenticity and unauthenticity.

I have distinguished different methods: experimental, foundational, historical, dialectical, critically practical.

My first conclusion is that the more religious studies and theology put to good use the whole battery of methods, the more they will move asymptotically towards an ideal situation in which they overlap and become easily interchangeable.

As a second conclusion I would say that such overlapping and interchangeability are ideal in the sense that they are desirable. Theology and religious studies need each other. Without theology religious studies may indeed discern when and where different religious symbols are equivalent;[10] but they are borrowing the techniques of theologians if they attempt to say what the equivalent symbols literally mean and what they literally imply. Conversely, without religious studies theologians are unacquainted with the religions of mankind; they may as theologians have a good grasp of the history of their own religion; but they are borrowing the techniques of the historian of religions, when they attempt to compare and relate other religions with their own.

Thirdly, if any agree that such an ultimate overlapping and interchangeability are desirable, their praxis will include a recognition of the obstacles that stand in its way and an effort to remove them. Now a discovery of the obstacles is not difficult. For we concluded to this end from the assumption that both theologians and students of religions would put to good use the whole battery of methods that have been devised. It follows that there are as many possible obstacles as there are plausible grounds for rejecting or hesitating about any of these methods. It follows, finally, if the methods really are sound, that the obstacles may be removed, at least for authentic subjects, by applying both the hermeneutic of suspicion and the hermeneutic of recovery: the hermeneutic of suspicion that pierces through mere plausibility to its real ground; the hermeneutic of recovery that discovers what is intelligent, true, and good in the obstruction and goes on to employ this discovery to qualify, complement, correct earlier formulations of the method.

This, the third in the Queen's University lectures of 1976, was previously published in *Studies in Religion*, Vol. VI (1976–1977), pp. 341–355; French translation, "La genèse des méthodes," in Bernard Lonergan, *Les voies d'une théologie méthodique . . .*, 1982.

Notes

1. Herbert Butterfield, *The Origins of Modern Science*, 1965, p. vii.

2. For a fuller statement, see B. Lonergan, "Aquinas Today," pp. 41–44, above.

3. *Ibid.*, pp. 36–40.

4. For references see my *Method in Theology*, 1972, pp. 208–212.

5. This dialectic I developed in "The Origins of Christian Realism," *Theology Digest*, Vol. XX (1972), pp. 292–305; reprinted in *A Second Collection*, 1974, pp. 239–261. The fuller version in my *De Deo Trino*, Vol. I, 1964, and *The Way to Nicea*, 1976.

6. This dialectic is developed at length in *Insight*, 1957, Chs. 7, 18, and 20.

7. R. Whitson, *The Coming Convergence of World Religions*, 1971. R. Panikkar, "Metatheology or Diacritical Theology as Fundamental Theology," *Concilium*, Vol. XLVI, pp. 43–55. W. Johnston, *The Mysticism of The Cloud of Unknowing*, 1967; *The Still Point*, 1970; *Christian Zen*, 1971; *Silent Music*, 1974. (See Ch. 5, notes 21, 28, 25, 26, 27 and 19, above.)

8. On sublation see *Method in Theology*, pp. 241, 316, 340.

9. F. Heiler, *op. cit.* (Ch. 8, note 2, above).

10. Eric Voegelin, "Equivalences of Experience and Symbolization in History," in *Eternità e Storia: I valori permanenti nel divenire storico*, a cura dell'Istituto Accademico di Roma (Florence: Vallecchi, 1970), pp. 215–234.

Part Three

Theory and Praxis

11

Natural Right
and Historical Mindedness

The notion of collective responsibility is not without its difficulty.
One may claim that, as men individually are responsible for the lives
they lead, so collectively they must be responsible for the resultant
situation. But that claim is too rapid to be convincing. No doubt, single elements in the resulting situation are identical with the actions
or the effects for which individuals are responsible. But the resulting
situation as a whole commonly was neither foreseen nor intended or,
when it does happen that it was, still such foresight and intention are
apt to reside not in the many but in the few and rather in secret
schemes and machinations than in public avowal.

It remains that if collective responsibility is not yet an established fact, it may be a possibility. Further, it may be a possibility
that we can realize. Finally, it may be a possibility that it is desirable
to realize.

Such is my topic. What I have in mind is the conjunction of two
elements already existing in our tradition. From the ancient Greeks
we have the notion of natural right. From nineteenth-century historical thought we have come to recognize that besides human nature
there also is human historicity. What we have to do, I feel, is to
bring these two elements together. We have so to develop the notion
of natural right as to make it no less relevant to human historicity
than it is to human nature.

1. HISTORICITY

A contemporary ontology would distinguish two components in concrete human reality: on the one hand, a constant, human nature; on the other hand, a variable, human historicity. Nature is given man at birth. Historicity is what man makes of man.

This making of man by man is perhaps most conspicuous in the educational process, in the difference between the child beginning kindergarten and the doctoral candidate writing his dissertation. Still this difference produced by the education of individuals is only a re-capitulation of the longer process of the education of mankind, of the evolution of social institutions and the development of cultures. Re-ligions and art-forms, languages and literatures, sciences, philoso-phies, the writing of history, all had their rude beginnings, slowly developed, reached their peak, perhaps went into decline yet later underwent a renaissance in another milieu. And what is true of cul-tural achievements, also, though less conspicuously, is true of social institutions. The family, the state, the law, the economy, are not fixed and immutable entities. They adapt to changing circumstance; they can be reconceived in the light of new ideas; they can be sub-jected to revolutionary change.

Moreover, and this is my present point, all such change is in its essence a change of meaning—a change of idea or concept, a change of judgment or evaluation, a change of the order or the request. The state can be changed by rewriting its constitution; more subtly but no less effectively it can be changed by reinterpreting its constitution or, again, by working on men's minds and hearts to change the ob-jects that command their respect, hold their allegiance, fire their loy-alty. More generally, human community is a matter of a common field of experience, a common mode of understanding, a common measure of judgment, and a common consent. Such community is the possibility, the source, the ground of common meaning; and it is this common meaning that is the form and act that finds expression in family and polity, in the legal and economic system, in customary morals and educational arrangements, in language and literature, art and religion, philosophy, science, and the writing of history.[1] Still, community itself is not a necessity of nature but an achievement of man. Without a common field of experience people get out of touch. Without a common mode of understanding, there arise misunderstanding, distrust, suspicion, fear, hostility, factions. Without a common measure of judgment people live in different worlds. Without common consent they operate at cross-purposes. Then common meaning is replaced by different and opposed meanings. A cohesion that once seemed automatic has to be bolstered by the pressures, the threats, the force that secure a passing semblance of unity but may prepare a lasting resentment and a smoldering rebellion.

As human nature differs from human historicity, so understanding human nature is one thing and understanding human historicity is another. To understand the constant, nature, one may study any individual. But to understand the variable, historicity, one has to study each instance in its singularity. So we come to what Alan Richardson has named 'historical mindedness.'[2] This means that to understand men and their institutions we have to study their history. For it is in history that man's making of man occurs, that it progresses and regresses, that through such changes there may be discerned a certain unity in an otherwise disconcerting multiplicity.

Indeed, historicity and history are related as object to be known and investigating subject. In a brilliant definition the aim of *Philologie* and later the aim of history was conceived as the interpretative reconstruction of the constructions of the human spirit.[3] The constructions of the human spirit were what we have termed man's making of man, the variable component in human ontology, historicity. The interpretative reconstruction of those constructions was the goal set itself by the German Historical School in its massive, ongoing effort to reveal, not man in the abstract, but mankind in its concrete self-realization.

2. NATURAL RIGHT IN HISTORICITY

It was the sheer multiplicity and diversity of the practises and beliefs of the peoples of the earth that led the ancient Greeks to contrast animals and men. The habits of each species of animal were uniform and so they could be attributed to nature. But the practises and beliefs of men differed from tribe to tribe, from city to city, from region to region: they had to be simply a matter of convention.

From that premise there followed a conclusion. What had been made by human convention, could be unmade by further convention. Underpinning human manners and customs there was no permanent and binding force.

The conclusion was scandalous, and in the notion of natural right was found its rebuttal. Underneath the manifold of human lifestyles, there existed a component or factor that possessed the claims to universality and permanence of nature itself.[4]

However, this component or factor admits two interpretations. It may be placed in universal propositions, self-evident truths, naturally known certitudes. On the other hand, it may be placed in nature itself, in nature not as abstractly conceived, but as concretely operating.[5] It is, I believe, the second alternative that has to be envisaged if we are to determine norms in historicity.

Now Aristotle defined a nature as an immanent principle of movement and of rest.[6] In man such a principle is the human spirit as raising and answering questions. As raising questions, it is an immanent principle of movement. As answering questions and doing so satisfactorily, it is an immanent principle of rest.

Specifically, questions are of three basic kinds: questions for intelligence, questions for reflection, questions for deliberation. In the first kind the immanent principle of movement is human intelligence. It thrusts us above the spontaneous flow of sensible presentations, images, feelings, conations, movements, and it does so by the wonder variously formulated by asking why, or how, or what for. With luck, either at once or eventually, there will follow on the question the satisfaction of having an insight or indeed a series of relevant insights. With the satisfactory answer the principle of movement becomes a principle of rest.

Still, intellectual satisfaction, however welcome, is not all that the human spirit seeks. Beyond satisfaction it is concerned with content and so the attainment of insight leads to the formulation of its content. We express a surmise, suggest a possibility, propose a project. But our surmise may awaken surprise, our suggested possibility give rise to doubts, our project meet with criticism. In this fashion intelligence gives way to reflection. The second type of question has emerged. As intelligence thrust us beyond the flow of sensitive spontaneity, so now reflection thrusts us beyond the more elementary concerns of both sense and intelligence. The formulated insight is greeted with such further and different questions as, Is that so? Are you sure? There is a demand for sufficient reason or sufficient evidence; and what is sufficient is nothing less than an unconditioned, though a virtually unconditioned (such as a syllogistic conclusion) will do.[7]

It remains that the successful negotiation of questions for intelligence and questions for reflection is not enough. They do justice to sensitive presentations and representations. But they are strangely dissociated from the feelings that constitute the mass and momentum of our lives. Knowing a world mediated by meaning is only a prelude to man's dealing with nature, to his interpersonal living and working with others, to his existential becoming what he is to make of himself by his own choices and deeds. So there emerge questions for deliberation. Gradually they reveal their scope in their practical, interpersonal, and existential dimensions. Slowly they mount the ladder of burgeoning morality. Asking what's in it for me gives way to asking what's in it for us. And both of these queries become tempered with the more searching, the wrenching question, Is it really worthwhile?

It is a searching question. The mere fact that we ask it points to a distinction between feelings that are self-regarding and feelings that are disinterested. Self-regarding feelings are pleasures and pains, desires and fears. But disinterested feelings recognize excellence: the vital value of health and strength; the communal value of a successfully functioning social order; the cultural value proclaimed as a life to be sustained not by bread alone but also by the word; the personal appropriation of these values by individuals; their historical extension in progress; deviation from them in decline; and their recovery by self-sacrificing love.[8]

I have called the question not only searching but also wrenching. Feelings reveal values to us. They dispose us to commitment. But they do not bring commitment about. For commitment is a personal act, a free and responsible act, a very open-eyed act in which we would settle what we are to become. It is open-eyed in the sense that it is consciously a decision about future decisions, aware that the best of plans cannot control the future, even aware that one's present commitment however firm cannot suspend the freedom that will be exercised in its future execution.

Yet all questioning heads into the unknown and all answering contributes to what we are to do. When I ask why or how or what for, I intend intelligibility, but the question would be otiose if already I knew what the intelligibility in question was. When I ask whether this or that is really so, I intend the true and the real, but as yet I do not know what is true or what will be truly meant. When I ask whether this or that project or undertaking really is worthwhile, I intend the good, but as yet I do not know what would be good and in that sense worthwhile.

Questioning heads into the unknown, yet answering has to satisfy the criterion set by the question itself. Otherwise the question returns in the same or in another form. Unless insight hits the bull's-eye, the question for intelligence returns. How about this? How does that fit in? A self-correcting process of learning has begun, and it continues until a complementary and qualifying set of insights have stilled the flow of further relevant questions for intelligence. In like manner questions for reflection require not just evidence but sufficient evidence; until it is forthcoming, we remain in doubt; and once it is had, doubting becomes unreasonable. Finally questions for deliberation have their criterion in what we no longer name consciousness but conscience. The nagging conscience is the recurrence of the original question that has not been met. The good conscience is the peace of mind that confirms the choice of something truly worthwhile.

I have been speaking of nature as a principle of movement and of rest, but I have come up with many such principles and so, it would seem, with many natures. There are different questions: for intelligence, for reflection, for deliberation. Each is a principle of movement. Each also is an immanent norm, a criterion, and thereby a principle of rest once the movement is complete.

It remains that the many form a series, each in turn taking over where its predecessor left off. What is complete under the aspect of intelligibility, is not yet complete under the aspect of factual truth; and what is complete under the aspect of factual truth, has not yet broached the question of the good.⁹ Further, if what the several principles attain are only aspects of something richer and fuller, must not the several principles themselves be but aspects of a deeper and more comprehensive principle? And is not that deeper and more comprehensive principle itself a nature, at once a principle of movement and of rest, a tidal movement that begins before consciousness, unfolds through sensitivity, intelligence, rational reflection, responsible deliberation, only to find its rest beyond all of these? I think so.[10]

The point beyond is being-in-love, a dynamic state that sublates all that goes before, a principle of movement at once purgative and illuminative, and a principle of rest in which union is fulfilled.

The whole movement is an ongoing process of self-transcendence. There is the not yet conscious self of deep sleep. There is the fragmentarily conscious self of the dream state. There is the awakened self aware of its environment, exerting its capacities, meeting its needs. There is the intelligent self, serializing and extrapolating and generalizing until by thought it has moved out of the environment of an animal and towards a universe of being. There is the reasonable self, discerning fact from fiction, history from legend, astronomy from astrology, chemistry from alchemy, science from magic, philosophy from myth. There is the moral self, advancing from individual satisfactions to group interests and, beyond these, to the overarching, unrelenting question, What would be really worthwhile?

Yet this great question commonly is more promise than fulfillment, more the fertile ground of an uneasy conscience than the vitality and vigor of achievement. For self-transcendence reaches its term not in righteousness but in love and, when we fall in love, then life begins anew. A new principle takes over and, as long as it lasts, we are lifted above ourselves and carried along as parts within an ever more intimate yet ever more liberating dynamic whole.

Such is the love of husband and wife, parents and children. Such again, less conspicuously but no less seriously, is the loyalty constitutive of civil community, where individual advantage yields to the advantage of the group, and individual safety may be sacrificed to the safety of the group. Such finally is God's gift of his own love flooding our hearts through the Holy Spirit he has given us (*Rom. 5: 5*). For it was by that divine gift that St. Paul could proclaim his conviction that ". . . there is nothing in death or life, in the realm of spirits or superhuman powers, in the world as it is or the world as it shall be, in the forces of the universe, in heights or depths—nothing in all creation that can separate us from the love of God in Christ Jesus our Lord" (*Rom. 8: 38–39*).

3. THE DIALECTIC OF HISTORY

I have said that people are responsible individually for the lives they lead and collectively for the world in which they live them. Now the normative source of meaning, of itself, reveals no more than individual responsibility. Only inasmuch as the immanent source becomes revealed in its effects, in the functioning order of society, in cultural vitality and achievement, in the unfolding of human history, does the manifold of isolated responsibilities coalesce into a single object that can gain collective attention.

Further, the normative source of meaning is not the only source, for the norms can be violated. Besides intelligence, there is obtuseness; besides truth there is falsity; besides what is worthwhile, there is what is worthless; besides love there is hatred. So from the total source of meaning we may have to anticipate not only social order but also disorder, not only cultural vitality and achievement but also lassitude and deterioration, not an ongoing and uninterrupted sequence of developments but rather a dialectic of radically opposed tendencies.

It remains that in such a dialectic one finds 'writ large' the very issues that individuals have to deal with in their own minds and hearts. But what before could be dismissed as, in each case, merely an infinitesimal in the total fabric of social and cultural history, now has taken on the dimensions of collective triumph or disaster. Indeed, in the dialectic there is to be discerned the experimental verification or refutation of the validity of a people's way of life, even though it is an experiment devised and conducted not by human choice but by history itself.

Finally, it is in the dialectic of history that one finds the link between natural right and historical mindedness. The source of natural right lies in the norms immanent in human intelligence, human judgment, human evaluation, human affectivity. The vindication of natural right lies in the dialectic of history and awesomely indeed in the experiment of history. Let us set forth briefly its elements under six headings.

First, human meaning develops in human collaboration. There is the expansion of technical meanings as human ingenuity advances from the spears of hunters and the nets of fishers to the industrial complexes of the twentieth century. There is the expansion of social meanings in the evolution of domestic, economic, and political arrangements. There is the expansion of cultural meanings as people reflect on their work, their interpersonal relationships, and the meaning of human life.

Secondly, such expansions occur on a succession of plateaus. The basic forward thrust has to do with doing, and it runs from primitive fruit gatherers to the wealth and power of the ancient high civilizations of Egypt, Mesopotamia, and other lands. Development then is mainly of practical intelligence, and its style is the spontaneous accumulation of insights into the ways of nature and the affairs of men. There also is awareness of the cosmos, of reality being more than nature and man, but this awareness has little more than symbolic expression in the compact style of undifferentiated consciousness.

An intermediate forward thrust has to do mainly with speech. Poets and orators, prophets and wise men, bring about a development of language and a specialization of attention that prepare the way for sophists and philosophers, mathematicians and scientists. There occurs a differentiation of consciousness, as writing makes language an object for the eye as well as the ear; grammarians organize the inflections of words and analyze the construction of sentences; orators learn and teach the art of persuasion; logicians go behind sentences to propositions and behind persuasion to proofs; and philosophers exploit this second-level use of language to the point where they develop technical terms for speaking compendiously about anything that can be spoken about; while the more modest mathematicians confine their technical utterances to relations of identity or equivalence between individuals and sets; and similarly the scientists have their several specialized languages for each of their various fields.

On a third plateau attention shifts beyond developments in doing and in speaking to developments generally. Its central concern is with human understanding where developments originate, with the methods in natural science and in critical history which chart the course of discovery, and more fundamentally with the generalized empirical method that underpins both scientific and historical method to supply philosophy with a basic cognitional theory, an epistemology, and by way of a corollary with a metaphysics of proportionate being.

On this plateau logic loses its key position to become but a modest part within method; and logical concern—with truth, with necessity, with demonstration, with universality—enjoys no more than marginal significance. Science and history become ongoing processes, asserting not necessity but verifiable possibility, claiming not certitude but probability. Where science, as conceived on the second plateau, ambitioned permanent validity but remained content with abstract universality, science and history on the third plateau offer no more than the best available opinion of the time, yet by sundry stratagems and devices endeavor to approximate ever more accurately to the manifold details and nuances of the concrete.

These differences in plateau are not without significance for the very notion of a dialectic of history. The notion of fate or destiny or again of divine providence pertains to the first plateau. It receives a more detailed formulation on the second plateau when an Augustine contrasts the city of God with the earthly city, or when a Hegel or a Marx set forth their idealistic or materialistic systems on what history has been or is to be. A reversal towards the style of the first plateau may be suspected in Spengler's biological analogy, while a preparation for the style of the third plateau may be discerned in Toynbee's *A Study of History*. For that study can be viewed, not as an exercise in empirical method, but as the prolegomena to such an exercise, as a formulation of ideal types that would stand to broad historical investigations as mathematics stands to physics.[11]

In any case the dialectic of history, as we are conceiving it, has its origin in the tensions of adult human consciousness, its unfolding in the actual course of events, its significance in the radical analysis it provides, its practical utility in the invitation it will present to collective consciousness to understand and repudiate the waywardness of its past and to enlighten its future with the intelligence, the reasonableness, the responsibility, the love demanded by natural right.

Our third topic is the ideal proper to the third plateau. Already in the eighteenth century it was anticipated in terms of enlightenment and emancipation. But then inevitably enough enlightenment was conceived in the well-worn concepts and techniques of the second plateau; and the notion of emancipation was, not a critique of tradition, but rather the project of replacing traditional backwardness by the rule of pure reason.

Subsequent centuries have brought forth the antitheses to the eighteenth-century thesis. The unique geometry of Euclid has yielded to the Riemannian manifold. Newtonian science has been pushed around by Maxwell, Einstein, Heisenberg to modify not merely physics but the very notion of modern science. Concomitant with this transformation has been the even more radical transformation in human studies. Man is to be known not only in his nature but also in his historicity, not only philosophically but also historically, not only abstractly but also concretely.

Such is the context within which we have to conceive enlightenment and emancipation, not indeed as if they were novelties for they have been known all along, but in the specific manner appropriate to what I have named the third plateau. As always enlightenment is a matter of the ancient precept, Know thyself. But in the contemporary context it aims to be such self-awareness, such self-understanding, such self-knowledge, as to grasp the similarities and the differences of common sense, science, and history, to grasp the foundations of these three in interiority which also founds natural right and, beyond all knowledge of knowledge, to give also knowledge of affectivity in its threefold manifestation of love in the family, loyalty in the community, and faith in God.

Again, as always, emancipation has its root in self-transcendence. But in the contemporary context it is such self-transcendence as includes an intellectual, a moral, and an affective conversion. As intellectual, this conversion draws a sharp distinction between the world of immediacy and the world mediated by meaning, between the criteria appropriate to operations in the former and, on the other hand, the criteria appropriate to operations in the latter.[12] Next, as moral, it acknowledges a distinction between satisfactions and values, and it is committed to values even where they conflict with satisfactions. Finally, as affective, it is commitment to love in the home, loyalty in the community, faith in the destiny of man.

We come to our fourth topic. It is the critique of our historicity, of what our past has made us. It will be an ongoing task, for the past is ever the present slipping away from us. It will be an empirical task but one within the orbit of human studies and so concerned with the operative meanings constitutive of our social arrangements and cultural intercourse. Accordingly, it will be a matter of the research that assembles the data, the interpretation that grasps their significance, the history that narrates what has been going forward.[13] It remains that all empirical inquiry that reaches scientific status proceeds within a heuristic structure. Just as mathematics provides the theoretical underpinning of the exact sciences, so there is a generalized empirical method or, if you prefer, a transcendental method that performs a similar role in human studies.[14] It sets forth (1) general critical principles, (2) a basic division of the materials, and (3) categories of analysis. On each of these something must be said.

The general critical principles are dialectical.[15] We have conceived emancipation on the third plateau to consist in a threefold conversion, intellectual, moral, and affective. But we do not postulate that all investigators will be emancipated. If some have been through the threefold conversion, others will have experienced only two, others only one, and some none at all. Hence we must be prepared for the fact that our researchers, our interpreters, our historians may exhibit an eightfold diversity of results, where the diversity does not arise from the data but rather from the horizon, the mindset, the blik, of those conducting the investigation.

A basic division of the materials is provided by the three plateaus already described. There will be meanings such as prove operative in men of action; further meanings that involve a familiarity with logical techniques; and a still further plateau of meanings that attain their proper significance and status within a methodical approach that has acknowledged its underpinnings in an intentionality analysis. It is to be noted, of course, that all three have their appropriate mode of development, and that their main developments differ chronologically; still, the proper locus of the distinction between the plateaus is not time but meaning.

Categories of analysis, finally, are differentiations of the historian's concern with "what was going forward." Now what was going forward may be either (1) development or (2) the handing on of development and each of these may be (3) complete or (4) incomplete. Development may be described, if a spatial metaphor is permitted, as "from below upwards": it begins from experience, is enriched by full understanding, is accepted by sound judgment, is directed not to satisfactions but to values, and the priority of values is comprehensive, not just of some but of all, to reveal affective conversion as well as moral and intellectual. But development is incomplete when it does not go the whole way upwards: it accepts some values but its evaluations are partial; or it is not concerned with values at all but only with satisfactions; or its understanding may be adequate but its factual judgments faulty; or finally its understanding may be more a compromise than a sound contribution.

Again, the handing on of development may be complete or incomplete. But it works from above downwards: it begins in the affectivity of the infant, the child, the son, the pupil, the follower. On affectivity rests the apprehension of values. On the apprehension of values rests belief. On belief follows the growth in understanding of one who has found a genuine teacher and has been initiated into the study of the masters of the past. Then to confirm one's growth in understanding comes experience made mature and perceptive by one's developed understanding. With experiential confirmation the inverse process may set in. One now is on one's own. One can appropriate all that one has learnt by proceeding as does the original thinker who moved from experience to understanding, to sound judgment, to generous evaluation, to commitment in love, loyalty, faith.

It remains that the process of handing on can be incomplete. There occur socialization, acculturation, education, but education fails to come to life. Or the teacher may at least be a believer. He can transmit enthusiasm. He can teach the accepted formulations. He can persuade. But he never really understood and he is not capable of giving others the understanding that he himself lacks. Then it will be only by accident that his pupils come to appropriate what was sound in their tradition, and it is only by such accidents, or divine graces, that a tradition that has decayed can be renewed.

Our fifth observation has to do with the ambiguity of completeness that arises when first-plateau minds live in a second-plateau context of meaning, or when first- and second-plateau minds find themselves in a third-plateau context. On the first plateau what has meaning is action; lack of completeness is lack of action; and so when the first-plateau mind examines a second- or third-plateau context, he diagnoses a lack of action, and insists on activism as the only meaningful course. On the second plateau there is the further range of meanings accessible to those familiar with classical culture. Second-plateau minds have no doubt that activists are just barbarians, but they criticize a third-plateau context for its neglect of Aristotle or Hegel.

However, such remarks as the foregoing should not be taken to imply that plateaus are uniform. For instance, the third plateau, characterized by method, also is marked by a whole series of methodological blocks. Linguistic analysts and Heideggerian pre-Socratics would confine philosophy to ordinary language. Offspring of the Enlightenment restrict knowledge to the exact sciences. Critical historians may praise human studies provided they are value-free. Humanists are open to values generally yet draw the line at such self-transcendence as is open to God.

Sixthly and finally, beyond dialectic there is dialogue. Dialectic describes concrete process in which intelligence and obtuseness, reasonableness and silliness, responsibility and sin, love and hatred commingle and conflict. But the very people that investigate the dialectic of history also are part of that dialectic and even in their investigating represent its contradictories. To their work too the dialectic is to be applied.

But it can be more helpful, especially when oppositions are less radical, for the investigators to move beyond dialectic to dialogue, to transpose issues from a conflict of statements to an encounter of persons. For every person is an embodiment of natural right. Every person can reveal to any other his natural propensity to seek understanding, to judge reasonably, to evaluate fairly, to be open to friendship. While the dialectic of history coldly relates our conflicts, dialogue adds the principle that prompts us to cure them, the natural right that is the inmost core of our being.

A lecture at the Fifty-first Annual Meeting of The American Catholic Philosophical Association, Detroit, April 16, 1977. Previously published in the *Proceedings* of that Association, Vol. LI (1977), pp. 132–143; French translation, "Le droit naturel et la mentalité historique," in Bernard Lonergan, *Les voies d'une théologie méthodique . . .* , 1982.

Notes

1. B. Lonergan, *Collection*, 1967, pp. 254–255.

2. A. Richardson, *History Sacred and Profane*, 1964, p. 32.

3. Peter Hünermann, *Der Durchbruch geschichtlichen Denkens im 19. Jahrhundert* (Freiburg: Herder, 1967), pp. 64–65, 106–108.

4. Leo Strauss, *Natural Right and History* (Chicago: University of Chicago Press, 1953), p. 90.

5. Cf. Eric Voegelin, "Reason: The Classic Experience," *The Southern Review,* Vol. X (1974), pp. 237–264.

6. Aristotle, *Physics,* II, 1, 195b 21–22.

7. B. Lonergan, *Insight,* 1957, Ch. 10.

8. *Ibid.,* pp. 207–242, 627–633, 696–703, 718–729.

9. On the human good, B. Lonergan, *Method in Theology,* Ch. 2.

10. On horizontal and vertical finality: Lonergan, *Collection,* 1967, pp. 18–22, 84–95; also Aristotle, *Nicomachean Ethics,* X, 7, 1177a 12–18.

11. Lonergan, *Method in Theology,* p. 228.

12. Lonergan, *Insight,* pp. 387–390.

13. Lonergan, *Method in Theology,* Chs. 6–9.

14. *Ibid.,* Ch. 1.

15. *Ibid.,* Ch. 10.

12

Theology and Praxis

If praxis is identified with practicality, then theology becomes an instance of praxis when it is converted into a tool for some distinct and praiseworthy end. So at the present time the conspicuous examples of theology as praxis would be the liberation theologies, whether geared to liberate Latin America from the fetters of capitalism, or to liberate black Americans from the injustice of racial discrimination, or to liberate women from the domination of patriarchal society.

It remains that there is an older connotation to the Greek word, and it is this older connotation that tends to justify the intrusion of ancient Greek into modern English.[1] For in Aristotle there is a contrast between *praxis* and *poiēsis* that may be paralleled by an English contrast between doing and making, conduct and product.[2] Moreover, it is precisely in the contrast that the connotation we desire is to be found. For products pass beyond the maker's control, and the ends to which they are used depend on the free decisions of others. But one's doing, one's conduct, results from the end which one has oneself chosen and, normally, chosen freely. Our making or producing, for ends we do not control, is guided simply by the know-how of technique. But our doing, our conduct, our praxis result from our own deliberation and choice under the guidance of the practical wisdom that Aristotle named *phronēsis* and Aquinas named *prudentia*.[3]

Now such attention to the responsible freedom of human conduct is very attractive to many at the present time. They are reacting against the behaviorists that deny scientific validity to explanations unable to reproduce human behavior in a robot or at least in a rat. They are reacting against the positivism that Jürgen Habermas has characterized as basically a refusal to reflect.[4] They are reacting against industry or again against government as managed by a face-less bureaucracy far too intricate ever to be brought to account.[5] Nor are they simply reacting, for they are adhering to a philosophic tend-ency that in the last two centuries has worked itself out in many di-verse forms. It appears in Kant's first and second critiques, in Schopenhauer's world as will and representation, in Kierkegaard's reliance on faith and Newman's reliance on conscience, in Nietzsche's will to power, in Blondel's philosophy of action, in Ri-coeur's philosophy of will, in Habermas's juxtaposition of knowl-edge and human interests.

Now to ask whether theology is a praxis in this second sense, is not to ask whether the views of Kant or Schopenhauer, Kierkegaard or Newman, Nietzsche or Blondel, Ricoeur or Habermas are to be made normative in theology. On the contrary, it is to ask a general question and a rather technical one. It is to ask whether there are basic theological questions whose solution depends on the personal development of theologians. Again, to use a distinction made by Paul Ricoeur, it is to ask whether issues on which theologians are badly divided call for the employment of both a hermeneutic of sus-picion and a hermeneutic of recovery, a hermeneutic of suspicion that diagnoses failures in personal development and a hermeneutic of recovery that generously recognizes the genuine personal devel-opment that did occur.[6]

1. BERNHARD WELTE'S QUESTION

Bernhard Welte is professor at Munich of interdisciplinary questions of concern to both theologians and philosophers. In the fifty-first volume of Herder's series entitled *Quaestiones Disputatae* he has asked whether the Nicene decree marks the invasion of the-ology by a Heideggerian forgetfulness of being.[7] In adverting to this question I must say at once that it is not my intention this morning to attempt to resolve it. My sole concern is to provide an instance that in my opinion illustrates a theological issue of some importance yet can be genuinely solved only inasmuch as individual theologians undergo an intellectual conversion.

The question, then, as proposed by Professor Welte, comes out of the history of philosophic and theological thought. In such history it is recognized that in different periods there emerge different approaches to reality and different apprehensions of it. An instance of such emergence and difference is found in a contrast of biblical and conciliar thought. The biblical approach to reality, by and large, is centered on events. Its concern is dynamic. In contrast, at Nicea and in subsequent councils there emerges the static approach of Greek metaphysics, an approach concerned with the present and permanent, and so an approach that Heidegger has criticized as a forgetfulness of being. There arises accordingly the question whether theologians today have on their hands the task of finding a different way of handling the issues that for centuries were thought to have been handled satisfactorily at Nicea.

Now I have no doubt that at different times, or at the same time among different individuals or groups, there exist different approaches to reality and different apprehensions of it. In fact I have argued for the possibility of some thirty-one distinct differentiations of consciousness;[8] and I have no hesitation in granting that in the Greek councils there comes into play a differentiation of consciousness that one hardly finds in the biblical authors.[9]

However, I do find a certain ambiguity in the use of the term, static. It may denote an actuality, or an ideal, or a mere possibility. Let me say a few words on each of these.

A doctrine clearly is actually static when it meets the requirements of the Aristotelian account of science (*epistēmē*) set forth in the *Posterior Analytics*. There science is described as knowing the cause, knowing that it is the cause, and knowing that the effect cannot be other than it is.[10] But the technical account of the expression of such knowledge is in terms of demonstration (*apodeixis*) which proceeds from first principles to conclusions in such a manner that every predicate pertains to its subject universally, necessarily, eternally.[11] Clearly if such a doctrine exists, it is static. But does such a doctrine exist? Aristotle acknowledged only one possibility: mathematics.[12]

Next there is a static ideal prescribed by a logic that aims at clarity in all its terms, coherence in all its propositions, rigor in all its arguments. Still such an ideal remains ineffective unless it is believed that clarity, coherence, and rigor have been attained or are about to be attained. Such a belief is canceled when the logical ideal is regarded as only part of a larger methodical ideal. So in the modern sciences the logical ideal is fully acknowledged. But this acknowledgment does not prevent the occurrence of new discoveries and the consequent correction of previous formulations. Similarly, in thirteenth-century theology the endless questions expressed the effort of reflection to attain clarity, coherence, and certain, or at least probable, reasons.[13] But the questions were only part of the method. There also was the reading of ancient authors, commentaries on their writings, compilations of the opinions of different authors, collations of these opinions with the questions that were being raised. Within that conjunction of research with reflection logic had free play but did not lead to fixity. On the contrary, it acted as a solvent, revealed the flaws in previously entertained views and, along with an ever fuller grasp of the sources, kept the questions on the move.[14] In contrast, in the fourteenth century, when logic and even the *Posterior Analytics* became dominant, criticism took over and headed theology into what really is static, into skepticism and decadence.[15]

Besides the static as actuality and the static as ideal there is the static as mere possibility. This possibility arises when one reaches the age of twelve years. For at that age, according to the educational psychology of Jean Piaget, one becomes capable of operating on propositions. It follows that one can define. For when one operates on propositions, one uses them as objects; when one uses them as objects, one can employ them to define the meaning of one's terms. Now once a meaning is defined, and as long as that definition is retained, the meaning remains the same. It is static. Moreover, the static meaning will yield a static apprehension of reality, provided the definition is not merely negative, not merely heuristic, not merely provisional, not merely partial, but positive, definitive, and complete. So a definition is merely negative, as when Aquinas asserts that we do not know what the divine essence is but only what it is not.[16] It is merely heuristic when it states what we are attempting to discover but as yet do not know.[17] It is merely provisional when it is proposed within a hypothesis. It is merely partial when it claims to be true as far as it goes but acknowledges that there is much more to be said.[18] It is positive, definitive, and complete, when it differs contradictorily from the preceding. The closest instance I recall occurs in the later stages of the Arian controversy. The Anomoean, Eunomius, is credited with the opinion that if one grasped the notion of the 'unbegotten' then one knew God just as well as God knew himself.[19]

Let us now ask how static was the approach to reality and the apprehension of it set forth in the Nicene decree. It will suffice to take the key term, *homoousios*. According to Athanasius this key term means that statements true of the Father also are true of the Son except that the Son is not the Father. Now is this meaning static or dynamic? Obviously we have to consider the statements that Athanasius had in mind. Nor is any difficulty involved, for Athanasius proceeds to quote a number of statements true both of the Father and of the Son. He finds them not in some text of Greek metaphysics but in the scriptures. As understood by Athanasius, then, the Nicene decree was just as static and just as dynamic as what Athanasius found in the Bible.[20]

Such continuity with biblical statement is not peculiar to Athanasius. A preface in the previous Roman missal, recited on a majority of Sundays throughout the year, employed the Athanasian formula in a prayer addressed to God the Father: "What because of your revelation we believe of your glory, the same of your Son, the same of the Holy Spirit we acknowledge without distinction or difference." There seems no disruptive departure from the scriptural mode of apprehension when one and the same Kabod Yahweh is acknowledged in Father, Son and Spirit.

2. ERIC VOEGELIN'S ALTERNATIVE

Even though it is granted that Nicea, rightly understood, is quite compatible with a biblical mode of apprehension, nonetheless Nicea does superpose upon the biblical mode a quite distinct doctrinal mode and, down the centuries, that doctrinal mode has come to dominate not only theological but to a great extent even religious thought.

It remains that this doctrinal mode cannot be combated coherently by setting up against it some antidoctrinal doctrine. Indeed, as Eric Voegelin has claimed, nothing can be achieved by pitting right doctrine against wrong doctrine,[21] for that only intensifies preoccupation with doctrine. What is needed, he urges, is the restoration of the search for the meaning of life, a search he would have us recognize no less in fourth-century Athens than in the Christian gospel.

A basic symbol for that search was phrased by Euripides when he exclaimed, ''Who knows if to live is to be dead and to be dead to live?'' The symbol was resumed by Plato in the *Gorgias* (492 E) and elaborated at the end of that dialogue in the Myth of the Judgment of the Dead. But its most effective setting occurs at the end of the *Apology* when Socrates concludes, ''But now the time has come to go. I go to die, and you to live. But who goes to the better lot is unknown to anyone but the God.''[22]

Obviously what Voegelin is raising is a question not just for philosophers but for everyman. So there is no occasion for surprise when the same symbol comes from the lips of Jesus in Matthew's Gospel, ''For whoever would save his life (*psychēn*) will lose it; and whoever loses his life for my sake will find it. What then will it profit a man, if he gains the whole world but has to suffer the destruction of his life'' (*Matt. 16:25–26*). Or again one may read in Paul, ''If you live according to the flesh, you are bound to die; but if by the spirit you put to death the deeds of the body, you will live'' (*Rom. 8: 15*).[23]

Variants can be multiplied but Voegelin finds particular satisfaction in the twelfth chapter of St. John's Gospel when it is Greeks that ask to see Jesus and their request evokes the reply, ''The hour has come for the Son of Man to be glorified. In truth, in very truth I tell you, a grain of wheat remains a solitary grain unless it falls into the ground and dies; but if it dies, it bears a rich harvest. The man who loves himself is lost, but he who hates himself in this world will be kept safe for eternal life'' (*John 12: 23–25*).[24]

I have been speaking of the double meaning of life and death as a symbol, and Voegelin would stress the point. For from the symbol one can either go backward to the engendering experience or forward to the doctrines Plato and Aristotle were later to formulate. The latter course obviously is contrary to Voegelin's intent, and so he directs our attention to the Parable of the Cave.

> There Plato lets the man who is fettered with his face to the wall be dragged up (*helkein*) by force to the light (Rep 515E). The accent lies on the violence suffered by the man in the Cave, on his passivity and even resistance to being turned round (*per-

iagōgē), so that the ascent to the light is less an action of seeking than a fate inflicted.[25]

In brief there are opposite principles at work, and to them Plato adverts. On the one hand, opinion may lead through reason (*logos*) to the best (*ariston*), and its power is called self-restraint (*sōphrosynē*); on the other hand, desire may drag us (*helkein*) towards pleasures and its rule is called excess (*hybris*).[26] Or as Voegelin illustrates the matter, a young man may be drawn to philosophy but by social pressure be diverted to a life of pleasure or to success in politics. But if he follows the second pull, the meaning of his life is not settled for him. The first pull remains and is still experienced as part of his living. Following the second pull does not transform his being into a question-free fact, but into a recognizably questionable course. He will sense that the life he leads is not his "own and true life" (495C).[27]

In brief there is a pull or attraction that, if followed, puts an end to questioning; and there are counterpulls that, when followed, leave questions unanswered and conscience ill at ease. The former alternative is what Voegelin means by a movement luminous with truth, or again by existing in the truth, or again by the truth of existence. The latter alternative is existence in untruth. As he contends, this luminosity of existence with the truth of reason precedes all opinions and decisions about the pull to be followed. Moreover, it remains alive as the judgment of truth in existence whatever opinions about it we may actually form.[28] In other words, there is an inner light that runs before the formulation of doctrines and that survives even despite opposing doctrines. To follow that inner light is life, even though to worldly eyes it is to die. To reject that inner light is to die, even though the world envies one's attainments and achievements.

For Voegelin, then, the classic experience of reason[29] in fourth-century Athens was something poles apart from the reason cultivated in late medieval metaphysics and theology,[30] from the reason of Descartes and the rationalists, from the reason of the French Enlightenment and the German absolute idealists. It took its stand not on logic but on inner experience. Its conflicts were not public disputations but inner trials. Its victory was the saving of one's life, keeping one's soul undefiled, holding ever to the upward way, pursuing righteousness with wisdom, so that we may be dear to ourselves and to the gods (*Rep.* 621BC).[31] This, of course, is Plato. But the sobriety of the *Nicomachean Ethics* does not imply that Aristotle holds a different view.

> If reason is divine, then, in comparison with man, the life according to it is divine in comparison with human life. But we must not follow those who advise us, being men, to think of human things, and, being mortal, of mortal things, but must, so far as we can, make ourselves immortal, and strain every nerve to live in accordance with the best thing in us; for even if it be small in bulk, much more does it in power and worth surpass everything.[32]
>
> If happiness is activity in accordance with virtue, it is reasonable that it should be in accordance with the highest virtue; and this will be that of the best thing in us. Whether it be reason (*nous*) or something else that is this element which is thought to be our natural ruler and guide and to take thought of things noble and divine, whether it be itself also divine or only the most divine element in us,[33] the activity of this in accordance with its proper virtue will be perfect happiness. That this activity is contemplative we have already said.[34]

It is not only classic philosophy but also the gospel that symbolizes existence as a field of pulls and counterpulls. Like Plato, the Gospel of John uses the word, draw, drag (*helkein*). Jesus on the eve of his passion can say, "And I shall draw all men to myself, when I am lifted up" (*John 12:32*). But the power of the crucified to draw men to himself is conditioned by the prior drawing by the Father. "No man can come to me unless he is drawn by the Father who sent me" (*John 6:44*). And that prior drawing is a listening and learning: "Everyone who has listened to the Father and learned from him comes to me" (*John 6:45*).[35]

On the basis of this drawing Voegelin distinguishes between revelation and information. To Peter's confession at Caesarea Philippi Jesus answered: "Simon son of Jonah, you are favoured indeed! You did not learn that from mortal man; it was revealed to you by my heavenly Father" (*Matt. 16:17*). Voegelin comments:

> The Matthean Jesus, thus, agrees with the Johannine (John 6:44) that nobody can recognize the movement of divine presence in the Son, unless he is prepared for such recognition by the pres-

ence of the divine Father in himself. The divine Sonship is not
revealed through information tendered by Jesus, but through a
man's response to the full presence in Jesus of the same Unknown God by whose presence he is inchoatively moved in his
own existence . . . In order to draw the distinction between revelation and information, as well as to avoid the derailment from
one to the other, the episode closes with the charge of Jesus to
the disciples "to tell no one that he was the Christ" (16:20).[36]

The distinction Voegelin finds in the revelation of Jesus as
Christ to Peter, he also finds in the communication by the apostles to
their converts. So Jesus prays: "O righteous Father . . . I know
thee, and these men know that thou didst send me. I made thy name
known to them, and will make it known, so that the love thou hadst
for me may be in them, and I may be in them" (*John 17: 25–26*). In
similar fashion we also read: "But it is not for these alone that I
pray, but for those also who through their words put their faith in me;
may they all be one: as thou, Father, art in me, and I in thee, so also
may they be in us, that the world may believe that thou didst send
me. The glory which thou gavest me I have given to them, that they
may be one, as we are one; I in them and thou in me, may they be
perfectly one. Then the world will learn that thou didst send me, that
thou didst love them as thou didst love me" (*John 17:20–23*).[37]

Let me conclude. Voegelin agrees with the estimate of Justin
Martyr that the gospel, so far from being opposed to the classic philosophy of Athens, is that philosophy brought to the state of perfection.[38] Both are responses to the question set by the twofold meaning
of life and death. Both take the issue with the full seriousness of the
death of Socrates or the fuller seriousness of the death and resurrection of Jesus. Both know of light and darkness, of pull and counterpull, of the need of free choice to support the gentle pull of the
golden cord, of the inner unrest that remains with those that turn
aside.[39] But the followers of Socrates speak of conversion (*peri-
agōgē*) and the followers of Jesus speak of repentance (*metanoia*).

3. THEOLOGY AS PRAXIS

I have drawn upon Bernhard Welte's question and Eric Voegelin's alternative because between them they raise a series of issues

that continuously crop up in doing theology yet are resolved far less by objective rules than by existential decisions.

Welte suspects the Nicene decree to have been forgetful of being because it speaks of *ousia* and so must mean *das beständig Anwesende, das beständig Vorliegende.*[40] In these expressions I would distinguish two elements. There is a perceptual element, the presence (*Anwesenheit*) of what lies before one (*Vorliegende*). There is a static logical element (*Beständigkeit*). Though both tie in with the massive problem Plato expressed symbolically in his Parable of the Cave, they do so in different manners and I shall speak of them separately.

Fourteenth-century Scholasticism discussed with considerable acumen the validity of an intuition of what exists and is present.[41] Now you may or may not hold that valid perception is what constitutes human knowledge as objective. But at least in all probability you did at one time take a perceptualism for granted. And if, by some lucky chance, you succeeded in freeing yourself completely from that assumption, then your experience would have been quite similar to that of the prisoner who struggled might and main against his release from the darkness of Plato's cave.

Is then perceptualism the same as Heidegger's forgetfulness of being? The question supposes Heidegger's meaning to be well known. Let me say very simply that perceptualism is forgetfulness of the inner light, the light that raises questions and, when answers are insufficient, keeps raising further questions. It is the inner light of intelligence that asks what and why and how and what for and, until insight hits the bull's-eye, keeps further questions popping up. It is the inner light of reasonableness that demands sufficient reason before assenting and, until sufficient reason is forthcoming, keeps in your mind the further questions of the doubter. It is the inner light of deliberation that brings you beyond the egoist's question—What's in it for me?—to the moralist's question—Is it really and truly worthwhile?—and if your living does not meet that standard, bathes you in the unrest of an uneasy conscience.

The ascent from the darkness of the cave to the light of day is a movement from a world of immediacy that is already out there now to a world mediated by the meaningfulness of intelligent, reasonable, responsible answers to questions.[42]

Are the dogmas caught in the forgetfulness of being? I should say that it all depends on the theologian interpreting the dogmas. When the dogmas are interpreted by one who habitually dwells in the world of the perceptualist there would be forgetfulness of the inner light and, as well, forgetfulness of being if by being is meant the world mediated by meaning and motivated by values. But if the dogmas are interpreted by one who habitually dwells in the world mediated by meaning and motivated by values, there is forgetfulness of the world of perceptualists but not of the world of those who have not seen but have believed (*John 20:29*).

Besides presence, the Greek word, *ousia*, is thought to connote permanence, to forget the dynamic, and point to the static.[43] I have expressed the opinion that static thinking has its source, not in Greek or other metaphysics, but in any thought or doctrine that gives one-sided attention to logic. The logical ideal of clarity, coherence, and rigor can be pursued with excellent results, provided the pursuit is only part of a larger ongoing investigation that has other resources and fuller goals than logic alone can attain. Admittedly there is to the *Posterior Analytics* a one-sidedness that concentrates on necessity and slights verifiable possibility; and it was by concentrating on verifiable possibility that modern science proved its superiority to Aristotelian logic. But that logic is so much less than the whole of Aristotle.

So, I should say, the same distinction is to be applied to metaphysics as was to dogma. For a metaphysics may be modeled on the dictates of the *Posterior Analytics* and then its doctrine will be static. But it may be conceived as the integration of the heuristic structures of such ongoing investigations as natural science, human studies, theology, and then it will be no more static than such ongoing investigations. Instead of being a dam that blocks the river's flow, it will be the bed within which the river does its flowing.[44]

If Welte and Voegelin hold contrasting views on the relevance of Greek philosophy to Christian truth, at least both insist upon events. Welte claims, rightly I believe, that by and large the Bible is a narrative of events. Voegelin also stresses events, but they are the inner events of pull and counterpull (*helkein, anthelkein*) that invite to life and seduce to death.

There also is a further point on which, I think, their agreement may be discerned. For if I argued that Nicea can be taken in a properly biblical manner, I also granted that it has become down the ages the fountainhead of a proliferating doctrinal mode of thought. Now such a mode of thought, in a mind more inclined to logic than to understanding, is a real source of static thinking. Nor may one suppose such minds to be rare, for the easier course is the commoner, and it is far easier to draw conclusions from what one already holds than to deepen one's understanding of what one's convictions mean.

I believe, then, that Welte has a real point insofar as he associates doctrine with a grave risk of congealed minds. But Voegelin makes a similar point though in a quite different manner. He is aware of the self-transcending dynamism of truly human living, of its mythical and symbolic expression, of its philosophic expression, and of its expression in the prophets of the Old Testament and in the writers of the New.[45] He is aware that only through one's own experience of that dynamism can one advert to its working in others. By a brilliant extension he moves on to his distinction between revelation and information. Items of information are all about us: they are the stock in trade of the media. But revelation is not just one more item of information. In its essential moment it is a twofold pull: being drawn by the Father, listening to him, learning from him; and being drawn by the Son, crucified, dead, and risen. Again, it is a twofold grace: an inner operative grace that plucks out hearts of stone and replaces them with hearts of flesh; and the outer grace of the Christian tradition that brings the gospel to our ears.

Now I think Voegelin's criticism of doctrines and doctrinization to be exaggerated.[46] But everyone will expect this of me, so there is no point in my repeating here what I have already said rather abundantly. What I do believe to be important on the present occasion is to insist how right I consider Voegelin to be in what he does say. For what he does say is foundational. It is the kind of knowledge by which people live their lives. It is the kind of knowledge that scientists and scholars, philosophers and theologians, presuppose when they perform their specialized tasks. It is the knowledge of which Newman wrote in his *Grammar of Assent,* Polanyi wrote in his *Personal Knowledge,* Gadamer in his *Truth and Method.* It is the kind of knowledge thematized by ascetical and mystical writers when they speak of the discernment of spirits and set forth rules for distinguishing between pull and counterpull, between being drawn by the Father to be drawn to the Son and, on the other hand, the myriad other attractions that distract the human spirit.[47]

Indeed it is in this long history of spiritual writing that one finds the confirmation of Voegelin's "In-Between" and his "Beyond." For being drawn by the Father is neither merely human nor strictly divine but "In-Between." As movement is from the mover but in what is moved, so the drawing is from the Father but in the suppliant. Again, because the drawing is from the Father, it bears the stamp of unworldliness; it is not just me but from the "Beyond." Finally, because there are not only pulls but also counterpulls, because the first can dignify the second, and the second can distort the first, there is need for discernment and, no less, difficulty in attaining it.[48]

Now such thematization pertains to experiential or ascetical or mystical theology and Voegelin regrets its separation from school theology.[49] But separation is one thing and distinction is another. I believe a distinction is to be made between the spiritual life of a theologian and his professional activities: the former is religion in act; the latter is concerned with the interdependence of a religion and a culture.[50] But separation arises from the controversialist's need to claim total detachment. It arises from criteria of objectivity such as necessity and self-evidence that seem to imply that our minds should work with an automatic infallibility. It arises from an unawareness that the interpretation of texts and the investigation of history are conditioned by the personal horizon of the interpreter or the historian.[51] It arises from an inadvertence to the dominant role of value judgments in much of theology as in much of human life. Finally, because I consider such grounds for a separation to be no longer tenable, I have assigned in my *Method in Theology* a key role to two functional specialties, *Dialectic* and *Foundations*. Now *Dialectic* stands to theology, as pull and counterpull stand to the spiritual life. And *Foundations* stands to theology as discernment stands to the spiritual life where it sorts out pull and counterpull and does not permit counterpull to distort the pull or pull to let seep some of its dignity and worth on to counterpull.

So we arrive at a conception of theology as basically a praxis. In conclusion three points seem to be in order: (1) the structure of individual development, (2) the occurrence of identity crises in the Christian community, and (3) the necessity of a certain doctrinal pluralism.

The structure of individual development is twofold. The chronologically prior phase is from above downwards. Children are born into a cradling environment of love. By a long and slow process of socialization, acculturation, education they are transferred from their initial world of immediacy into the local variety of the world mediated by meaning and motivated by values. Basically this process rests on trust and belief. But as it proceeds, more and more there develops the capacity to raise questions and to be satisfied or dissatisfied with answers. Such is the spontaneous and fundamental process of teaching and learning common to all. It is at once intelligent and reasonable and responsible. But while it is consciously intelligent, consciously reasonable, consciously responsible, still these properties attain no more than a symbolic objectification and representation. Even when subjected to higher education, one does well to attain some clear and precise understanding of one's own activities in this or that field of specialization. Few indeed attempt the philosophic task of coming to grasp the similarities and the differences of the many ways in which basic operations are variously modified and variously combined to yield the appropriate procedures in different fields. And of the few that attempt this, even fewer succeed in mapping the interior of the "black box" in which the input is sensations and the output is talk.

What holds in general for self-understanding in our world mediated by meaning and motivated by values, also holds when that world is transfigured by God's self-revelation in Christ Jesus. The one revelation was made to many and thereby brought about a new type of community. For that community Christ prayed to his Father that "they all be one: as thou, Father, art in me, and I in thee, so also may they be in us, that the world may believe that thou didst send me" (*John 17:21*). It remains that a community is one not only by God's grace but also by a consequent union of minds and of hearts. Again, it remains that that consequent union can be troubled, disturbed, undergo an identity crisis; and then the solution to that crisis will be a common confession of faith. It is such confessions of faith that have been given the name, dogmas. In the older liturgies they often were enshrined in various manners, but in the recently devised Roman liturgy such confessions tend to be reduced to their scriptural basis.

So there emerges the question of doctrinal pluralism. Its real basis, I believe, is the multiple differentiation of consciousness possible at the present time and often needed to master issues in theology. But the development that may be expected of a theologian is not to be required generally, nor is it easy to defend the mere repetition of formulas that are not understood. Personally I should urge that in each case one inquire whether the old issue still has a real import and, if it has, a suitable expression for that import be found. For example, at Nicea the real import was whether Christ, the mediator of our salvation, was a creature. Today many perhaps will be little moved by the question whether we have been saved by a creature or by God himself. But the issue may be put differently. One can ask whether God revealed his love for us by having a man die the death of scourging and crucifixion? Or was it his own Son, a divine person, who became flesh to suffer and die and thereby touch our hard hearts and lead us to eternal life?

A lecture at the Thirty-second Annual Convention of The Catholic Theological Society of America, Toronto, June 16, 1977. Previously published in the *Proceedings* of that Society, Vol. XXXII (1977), pp. 1–16; French translation; ''Théologie et praxis,'' in Bernard Lonergan, *Les voies d'une théologie méthodique* . . . , 1982.

Notes

1. Richard J. Bernstein, *Praxis and Action: Contemporary Philosophies of Human Activity* (Philadelphia: University of Pennsylvania Press, 1971).

2. In the *Nicomachean Ethics* one reads that praxis is shared neither by animals (VI, 2, 1139a 19–20) nor by the gods (X, 8, 1178b 7–22). It differs from *poiēsis* and so from *technē* (VI, 4, 1140a 1–23). As is *phronēsis* (VI, 7, 1141b 16), it is concerned with particulars (III, 1, 1110b 6–7). Desire and the *logos* of the end are the principle of *proairesis,* and *proairesis* is the efficient principle of praxis (VI, 2, 1139a 31–33). As the hypothesis is the principle in mathematics, so the end is the principle in praxis (VII, 9, 1151a 16–17).

3. St. Thomas Aquinas, *Sum. Theol.,* II–II, qq. 47–56.

4. Jürgen Habermas, *Knowledge and Human Interests,* tr. by Jeremy J. Shapiro (Boston: Beacon Press, 1971), pp. 67–69.

5. R. N. Goodwin, *The American Condition,* 1974, pp. 197 ff.

6. A basic presentation is by Don Ihde, *Hermeneutic Phenomenology: The Philosophy of Paul Ricoeur* (Evanston: Northwestern University Press, 1971), pp. 140–143.

7. B. Welte, "Die Lehrformel von Nikaia," *op. cit.* (above, Ch. 6, note 20).

8. A succinct presentation of the pieces that may be combined in various ways may be found in my *Method in Theology*, 1972, p. 302–305.

9. The movement has been sketched in B. Lonergan, *The Way to Nicea*, 1976 (above, Ch. 6, note 33).

10. Aristotle, *Posterior Analytics*, I, 2, 71b, 9–12.

11. *Ibid.*, I, 4; 6; 8.

12. So Sir David Ross, *Aristotle's Prior and Posterior Analytics*, 1949, p. 14.

13. Abelard's *Sic et Non* is thought to have inspired the *Videtur quod non* and *Sed contra* of the medieval *quaestio*. The relevance of probable as well as certain arguments is attested by Aquinas, *Contra Gentiles*, I, 9.

14. I became vividly aware of this in studying Aquinas on *gratia operans*. See my *Grace and Freedom*, 1971 (above, Ch. 3, note 3).

15. The seminal work is Konstanty Michalski, *La philosophie au XIVᵉ siècle: Six études*, ed. and intro. by Kurt Flasch (Frankfurt: Minerva, 1969).

16. *Contra Gentiles*, I, 14.

17. As when Augustine explains what he means by the term, person, as "what there are three of in the Trinity," *De Trinitate*, VII, iv, 7 (*Patrologia Latina*, Vol. XLII, 939); see also B. Lonergan, *A Second Collection*, p. 199.

18. Hence the rule: *Abstrahentium non est mendacium*.

19. J. Liébaert, "Eunomios," *Lexikon für Theologie und Kirche*, 2nd ed., Vol. III (Freiburg: Herder, 1959), cols. 1182–1183.

20. See B. Lonergan, *The Way to Nicea*, 1976, p. 91.

21. Eric Voegelin, "The Gospel and Culture," in *Jesus and Man's Hope*, ed. by Donald G. Miller and Dikran Y. Hadidian, Vol. II (Pittsburgh: Pittsburgh Theological Seminary, 1971), pp. 59–101; see p. 66.

22. *Ibid.*, p. 67.

23. *Ibid.*, pp. 66–67.

24. *Ibid.*, p. 68.

25. *Ibid.*, p. 72.

26. *Phaedrus*, 237E–238A.

27. Voegelin, "Gospel and Culture," p. 71.

28. *Ibid.*, pp. 71–76.

29. E. Voegelin, "Reason: The Classic Experience," *The Southern Review*, 1974, pp. 237–264.

30. Cf. "Gospel and Culture," p. 66.

31. *Ibid.*, p. 67.

32. *Nicomachean Ethics*, X, 7, 1177b 30–1178a 2, *The Basic Works*

of Aristotle, the Oxford translation ed. by Richard McKeon (New York: Random House, 1941), p. 1105.

33. The passage suggests that Aristotle did not take faculty psychology with the rigidity it acquired in Scholasticism.

34. *Nicomachean Ethics,* X, 7, 1177a 12–18.

35. "Gospel and Culture," p. 77.

36. *Ibid.,* p. 91.

37. *Ibid.,* p. 78.

38. *Ibid.,* p. 60.

39. *Ibid.,* p. 73.

40. Welte, "Die Lehrformel von Nikaia," p. 112: "Als das Ständige ist der Gegenstand oder das Seiende nun für das Denken der neuen Zeit in der Weise zeitlich, dass es, in der Zeit stehend, zugleich wie gar nicht von ihr berührt ist. So steht es dem Geschehen oder dem Ereignis als ein Statisches gegenüber. Es wird mit Vorzug Usia genannt. Diesen Ausdruck versteht Heidegger als das beständig Anwesende."

Fùrther, p. 113: "Vielmehr entsteht jetzt die ganz anders gestimmte Frage als Leitfrage, was ist? Und diese Frage hat einen offensichtlich statischen Sinn. Sie schliesst die andere, was geschehen ist und was geschieht, nicht aus, aber sie läuft in einer anderen Richtung. Sie frägt doch, was ist in Jesus das beständig Vorliegende?"

41. The extreme views of Nicholas of Autrecourt are listed in Denzinger-Schönmetzer, *Enchiridion* (above, Ch. 6, note 41), nos. 1028–1049. The distinction between divine power itself and divine power as ordered by divine wisdom opened the way to advancing that divine power itself could do anything that did not involve a contradiction. There followed questions of the type, Is there any contradiction in supposing that one can have an intuition of X as existing and present although X neither is present nor even exists?

42. Again, it is a movement from the horizon of ocular vision to the horizon of being, where the horizon of being is the horizon that is enlarged when one discovers and follows up a significant question, and the horizon that is contracted when one brushes aside a significant question.

43. See note 40 above.

44. See the definition of metaphysics in my *Insight,* pp. 390–396.

45. Voegelin's sweep is breathtaking: in his "The Gospel and Culture" he pulls together Myth, Philosophy, Prophecy and Gospel.

"Myth is not a primitive symbolic form, peculiar to early societies and progressively to be overcome by positive science, but the language in which the experiences of human-divine participation in the In-Between become articulate" (p. 76).

"The Amon Hymns (to the god above the gods and unknown by the gods) are the representative document of the movement at the stage where the splendor of the cosmological gods has become derivative, though the gods themselves have not become false. Seven hundred years later, in the Deutero-Isaianic equivalent to the Amon Hymns (Is 40: 12–25), the gods have become man-made idols who no longer partake of divine reality, while the unknown god has acquired the monopoly of divinity'' (p. 85).

''The noetic core, thus, is the same in both Classic Philosophy and the Gospel movement'' (p. 80).

''In the historical drama of revelation, the Unknown God ultimately becomes the God known through his presence in Christ'' (p. 88).

46. His statements (e. g., pp. 74–76) seem to me to go well beyond a repudiation of a doctrinaire *carabiniere*. (Editor: For a reliable account of Voegelin's attitude to doctrines, Fr. Lonergan would now refer to Eugene Webb, *Eric Voegelin: Philosopher of History* [Seattle: University of Washington Press, 1981]; see the Index, s. v., Dogmatism.—Oral communication, June 19, 1982.)

47. On this topic for a brief account, Karl Vladimir Truhlar, "Discernment of Spirits," *Sacramentum mundi: An Encyclopedia of Theology,* Vol. II (Montreal: Palm; New York: Herder and Herder; etc., 1968), pp. 89–91. For a fuller treatment, *Dictionnaire de spiritualité ascétique et mystique,* articles on "Consolation spirituelle" (II, cols. 1617–1634), "Démon" (III, cols. 141–238), "Direction spirituelle" (III, cols. 1002–1214), "Discernement des esprits" (III, cols. 1222–1291).

48. On the key discriminant in the Ignatian *Spiritual Exercises,* consolation without a previous cause, a notable study recommended with a preface by Karl Rahner is Harvey D. Egan, *The Spiritual Exercises and the Ignatian Mystical Horizon* (St. Louis: The Institute of Jesuit Sources, 1976).

49. "The Gospel and Culture," p. 88.

50. Lonergan, *Method in Theology,* p. xi.

51. *Ibid.,* p. 195.

13

A Post-Hegelian Philosophy
of Religion

Hegel's philosophy included both a philosophy of history and a philosophy of religion. As the whole philosophy, so also its parts on history and religion were worked out *a priori* as the necessary implications of Hegel's dialectical logic.

This position was acceptable neither to the German Historical School nor to its offshoot the History of Religions School. To both it was plain that the study of history and the study of religion had to begin with research and that they reached conclusions only when their respective accounts were verified empirically. For this reason it seemed incumbent upon me, in offering a philosophy of religion to members of the International Association for the History of Religions, to present such a philosophy in post-Hegelian terms.

But if I withdraw entirely from the necessity attributed by Hegel to dialectical logic, I would find it difficult to be philosophic about religion if it were not possible to retain something of his comprehensiveness. And such a possibility I find in shifting attention from Hegel's dialectical logic to a philosophic account of empirical method.

Such a shift I find recommended both on grounds of familiarity and on the authority of R. G. Collingwood who was not only a philosopher but also an archeologist and a historian.

First, on grounds of familiarity, for most scientists will find the notion of a dialectical logic not only puzzling but also mysterious. On the other hand, all scientists have personal knowledge of scientific method, practical knowledge of what scientists in their field do and, if not a formulated, at least a tacit understanding of methodical procedure. Many, I fancy, would be surprised to hear that such a personal, practical, tacit attainment may be named a philosophy. But not a few, I suspect, would be relieved to discover that philosophy is not so alien to their attainments as they may have been told.

So much for familiarity. Besides that, there is authority, and I quote Collingwood's *The Idea of History*:

> Philosophy cannot interfere with history according to the Hegelian formula of superimposing a philosophical history on the top of ordinary history. . . . Ordinary history is already philosophical history. . . . . . . within the concrete whole which is historical knowledge, philosophical knowledge is a component part. . . .[1]
> . . . (history is necessary) relatively to philosophy as the concrete thought of which philosophy is only the methodological moment. . . .[2]
> . . . (history is) the consciousness of one's own activity as one actually performs it. . . . For even when the events which the historian studies are events that happened in the distant past, the condition of their being historically known is that . . . the evidence for them should be here and now before him and intelligible to him. For history . . . lives only, as a present interest and pursuit, in the mind of the historian when he criticizes and interprets . . . documents, and by so doing relives for himself the states of mind into which he inquires.[3]

Now in these phrases Collingwood is following Croce and breaking from Hegel. He wants the philosophy of history to be, not a distinct history superimposed on ordinary history, but the methodological component present in the consciousness that a scientific historian has of his own performance. Moreover, since Collingwood attributed to history a key role in all science, he considered the methodological component within history to be, not just a "philosophy of . . . ," but philosophy pure and simple.

Such a position suggests that other sciences are endowed with "philosophy of . . ." inasmuch as historians of science thematize their conscious grasp of scientific developments. While I would not urge that this is impossible, I do find it cumbrous. It seems more expeditious to discover that the consciousness of every scientist in-

cludes a consciousness of the proper method of his subject. Just as
the historian needs such a consciousness of historical method, so too
do physicists, chemists, biologists, psychologists, exegetes, and so
on, need to be effectively aware of the methodical exigences of their
respective fields. In this fashion we are led to recognizing as many
"philosophies of . . . ," as there are distinct sciences with appropriately differentiated methods.

Moreover, this multitude of "philosophies of . . ." will not be
a mere pile or heap of unrelated procedures. For methods and procedures are dynamic, and all share a common dynamism that is
proper to our common humanity. It is this common dynamism that
grounds the real unity and common philosophy of scientists and, as
well, enables them to appeal to men of common sense.[4]

Such in bare outline is my proposal. It will be worked out in
two main parts. A first part will treat both the common dynamics
discernible in methods generally and the different dynamics in distinct fields of inquiry. The second part will deal with the divergence
and the possible unity of results that arise when different methods
are employed in the same field, as in religious studies.

1. METHOD AS GENERAL DYNAMICS:
PART ONE

Method is not to be confused with anything as pedestrian as a
recipe, a prescription, a set of directions. For recipes, and the like,
lead only to single results. They may be repeated as often as you
please, but the repetition yields no more than another instance of the
original product. What may be advertised as the New Method Laundry may clean anyone's clothing, but it will never do anything else.

The key instance to method, I feel, lies in the relation between
questioning and answering. The questioner, while he does not know
the answer, at least intends it. Moreover, the question itself sets a
standard that leads to the rejection of insufficient answers; and insufficient answers need not be useless: they may help the questioner
to pin down more accurately the precise issue he wished to raise.
Further, such clarification may bring to light the existence of intermediate questions that have to be resolved before the initially intended question can be met. There is then an ongoing dynamism in

questioning and answering. It heads through insufficient answers to the clarification and, as well, to the distinction of questions; and while this prepares the way to the eventual discovery of relevant answers, those very answers in turn can provide the source and stimulus to a fresh wave of questions

I have been speaking of this ongoing process as though it occurred between a pair of individuals. But, far more importantly, it can be the common concern of associations of scientists. The members of such associations will have passed successfully through the initiatory ritual of attaining a Ph.D. They will be at home in the technical language which they alone understand and speak. That language will provide the repository of the novel conceptual systems introduced by the pioneers and the renovators in their field. It provides the instrument through which are handed on the ideals that should govern their thinking and the procedures to be followed in their investigations. It is kept alive and up-to-date through congresses, through journals and books, through school libraries, and interdisciplinary undertakings. In this fashion questions raised anywhere can be known elsewhere; they can give rise to an array of insufficient answers that successively beg for a clarification of the issue or issues; and the clarifications will hasten, as far as is possible at the time, the new answers which initial questions may have done more to intimate than to formulate.

I have been stressing what I have noted elsewhere, that a method is not a set of rules to be followed meticulously by a dolt but a framework for collaborative creativity.[5] But now I have to add that (1) questions are of different kinds, (2) each kind has its own immanent objective and criterion, and (3) the objectives stand in an ascending order with each completing what its predecessor had attained.

The first of the kinds is the question for understanding. It arises when one is intelligent enough to experience a lack: one lacks an understanding of some aspect or aspects of the data. As long as that lack continues to be experienced, answers that are proposed and considered will have to be rejected simply because the lack remains. So the objective of the first kind of question is the attainment of an understanding of specified data. The criterion of the attainment of a proper understanding is that answers are proving sufficient, that questions no longer need further clarification, that the initial lack of understanding has been replaced by an insight that grasps why things are so.

The second kind of question is for reflection. Aristotle remarked that we think we understand when we know the cause, know that it is the cause, and know that the effect cannot be other than it is.[6] Now the open point in this affirmation is the meaning of "necessity." From the beginning of the fourteenth century, by and large, it seems to have been tacitly assumed that necessary knowledge results from the necessary implication of one concept in another. But such a view cannot, I believe, be foisted on Aristotle or Aquinas. For them the primary object of understanding was the representative image, the example, the instance, in which intelligence grasped the intelligibility of what the image represents. Such a grasp is a conscious intellectual event that, at times, is resoundingly satisfactory. Its formulation in concepts is a further process, equally conscious, and intelligently resting on the content of the insight.[7]

It follows that over and above the abstract necessity that may be elicited from the implication of one abstract concept in another, there is the more concrete necessity that may be intelligently grasped in representative images and, under due provisos, in sensible data. For example, one can ask abstractly what an eclipse is. But one may also refer to a concrete situation in which a man, pointing to the darkening of the moon, asks why the moon is darkened in this manner.[8] The abstract question demands an abstract answer, and to proceed from the abstract definition to an actual necessity no number of further abstract necessities are enough. There also is needed an understanding of an existing situation into which the abstractions fit. But if the question is put with regard to a concrete situation in which an eclipse actually is taking place, then an understanding of that situation will grasp not only the cause of the darkening of the moon but also the necessity of that effect.

The third type of question regards responsibility. There are responsibilities intrinsic to natural science, others intrinsic to human science, others to religious studies. Our observations, for the moment, must be confined to natural science. In such science there is a responsibility to the data: it is violated when the data are fraudulently produced. There is a responsibility to intelligence or reasonableness, and it is neglected when one overlooks the inadequacy of answers and, no less, when one withholds a qualified assent when further relevant questions are not made available. Finally, there is responsibility regarding the possible products of scientific advance. Because knowing is good, advance in knowing is good. Because the products of science can be turned to evil use by evil will, one's own will becomes evil in approving the evil use.

Such are the three questions, and I have said that their objectives stand in an ascending order. For the second question has its origin in an incompleteness of the first question and answer, and the third question has its origin in an incompleteness of the second question and answer. So our hypotheses and theories remedy our previous lack of understanding; but are they just bright ideas, or do they represent the best available opinion of the day? Still, even a consensus in favor of high probability would not preclude a still further question. New knowledge opens up new possibilities, and possibilities may be put to good or evil use; and so the question of responsibility arises out of the question for reflection and the answer to it.

It remains that this triad of questions and answers are only part of the ascensional structure of our intentional activity. Its hidden root is the unconscious, and it is not only the dark abode of primordial desires and fears but also the obscure home of the drive that makes man not merely the symbolic animal but also the self-completing animal. In all animals it is the store of the cognitypes and the dynatypes[9] that release and guide instinctive activity. But in man's sleep there are not only the dreams of the night that correspond to biological tensions but also the dreams of the morning in which the human subject before waking is already taking a stance towards his coming day. Beyond dreams, there is the daytime unfolding of this process that has been studied from different viewpoints by Jean Piaget, Erik Erikson, and Lawrence Kohlberg. Piaget examined operational development and placed its key in a repeated *decentering* that keeps shifting the center of the subject's activity from himself to his ever enlarging universe. Erikson's approach is from depth psychology and his eight developmental stages are successive and cumulative shifts in what one's *identity* becomes. Kohlberg, finally, attends to morals, distinguishes preconventional, conventional, and postconventional morality, divides each into two stages, and reveals the defects of each earlier stage as compared with its successor. It happens, however, that the ideas of all three writers have been brought together in a unitary view in terms of *self-transcendence*. The author of this work is Prof. Walter Conn, and I have had the privilege of reading it in galleys. The benefit I must leave to the reader to reap for himself, since a brief reproduction is impossible, and a summary cannot be just.[10]

But before closing this first part of my first section, I feel I should indicate roughly, not yet the stages, but perhaps the successive degrees of self-transcendence. The *first* is the emergence of consciousness in the fragmentary form of the dream, where human substance yields place to the human subject. The *second* is waking when our senses and feelings come to life, where our memories recall pleasures and our imaginations anticipate fears, but our vitality envisages courses of action. The *third* is inquiry which enables us to move out of the mere habitat of an animal and into our human world of relatives, friends, acquaintances, associates, projects, accomplishments, ambitions, fears. The *fourth* is the discovery of a truth, which is not the idle repetition of a "good look" but the grasp in a manifold of data of the sufficiency of the evidence for our affirmation or negation. The *fifth* is the successive negotiation of the stages of morality and/or identity till we reach the point where we discover that it is up to ourselves to decide for ourselves what we are to make of ourselves, where we decisively meet the challenge of that discovery, where we set ourselves apart from the drifters. For drifters have not yet found themselves. They have not yet found their own deed and so are content to do what everyone else is doing. They have not yet found a will of their own, and so they are content to choose what everyone else is choosing. They have not yet developed minds of their own, and so they are content to think and say what everyone else is thinking and saying. And everyone else, it happens, can be doing and choosing and thinking and saying what others are doing and choosing and thinking and saying.

But this fifth stage in self-transcendence becomes a successful way of life only when we really are pulled out of ourselves as, for example, when we fall in love, whether our love be the domestic love that unites husband and wife and children, or the love of our fellows whose well-being we promote and defend, or the love of God above all in whom we love our neighbor as ourselves.

2. METHOD AS GENERAL DYNAMICS:
PART TWO

The first part of our consideration of method as dynamics was very general. It included questions for intelligence, questions for reflection, questions for responsibility. But no attempt was made to say precisely what questions were to be asked. Such an attempt must now be made, and so we turn from the core of methods generally to the differentiation of that core.

Such differentiation is a difficult task and one, I am inclined to feel, that has not been squarely met. Aristotle's deductivist view of science could be verified only in mathematics and, indeed in the mathematics of the ancient world; it followed that subjects other than the mathematical could be given the name of science only by courtesy.[11] In the modern period, the success of Newtonian mechanics gave the key role to empirical science and, in the course of time, mechanics came to share its prestige with physics, while extending its mantle over physical chemistry, chemistry, and a statistical reformulation of Darwin's chance variations and survival of the fittest.

Such are the natural sciences. They have been extremely successful. But it is important for us to understand the root of that success and the reason why it does not transfer in any thoroughgoing fashion to human studies.

Very simply, the natural sciences, in the measure they are subject to quantitative relations, are in close dependence on mathematics. In turn, modern mathematics has vastly purified mathematical thinking by an insistence on clarity, generality, and precision; and it has handed over to physics notions of space, time, and indeterminacy, that profoundly liberate the scientific mind. There is a liberation from the domination of Euclidean imagination and, as well, a liberation from the domination of the mechanist determinism that reigned from the heydey of Newton's triumph through the first quarter of this century. As the mathematician, so too the natural scientist can now avail himself of freely constructed yet internally coherent systems.

But a parallel liberation can be bestowed on human studies. One way to this goal is the quantification of statements about human beings. An alternative way is to have philosophy do for human studies what mathematics does for natural science. I may presume that you are familiar with the former procedure, and so I may be content to indicate what the latter entails. In 1923 George Santayana published a book entitled *Skepticism and Animal Faith*. The pair were considered opposites with skepticism the lot of an elite and animal faith the lot of the masses. But neither animal faith nor skepticism is compatible with the general dynamics of method: animal faith asks no questions, and skepticism answers none. For me the real alternatives are animal faith and critical philosophy. On the one hand, animal faith is the fate of everyone who learns in childhood to speak his mother tongue, may entertain no doubt about all he believes he knows, but never has found out for himself and in himself just what are the events that come together to constitute human knowledge. On the other hand, in the measure that one finds out for oneself and in oneself just what these events are, one not merely is a critical philosopher but also one successful enough to be liberated, especially from animal faith in some unknowable thing-in-itself.

I may be asked just what events do come together to constitute human knowing. Very schematically, there are three: first, the givenness of the data, which is the objective of research; secondly, a cumulative series of insights into the data, which respond to the question for intelligence and yield a hypothesis; thirdly, a probable judgment on the adequacy of the insights.

At this point there may return the notion that human knowing is not a threefold compound but a single simple act at least in the field of our own consciousness. Certainly many have thought of consciousness as an inward look, an instance of what they may name introspection, and it is by such a look (they might claim) that we are aware of the givenness of the data, the occurrence of insights, the sufficiency of the evidence. But to my mind this is just a fresh avatar of the intuitions attributed to animal faith. For I believe that the data of sense and the data of consciousness are parallel. The data of sense do not constitute human knowledge but only a first step to such knowledge. Similarly the data of consciousness are not an instance of self-knowledge but only a first step towards attaining such knowledge. All our intentional acts also are conscious acts. But to advert to them as conscious, we have to deemphasize the intentional and heighten the conscious side of the act. Only when that is achieved can we proceed to gain insight into the relations that unify our conscious acts and then to pass judgment on the validity of the relations.

We have been speaking of the structure of human knowing and the nature of human consciousness only as a preliminary to indicating our main point, namely, that man's world is a world mediated by meaning and motivated by value, and so a world that includes all mathematics but is not to be mastered within their scope. After all, mathematics embraces only one of the many different fields of meanings.

To this end we propose to speak of the four basic functions of meaning: it is cognitive, efficient, constitutive, communicative. It is cognitive. Human knowledge is discursive, a matter of questions and answers, and so one's knowledge is no better (and no worse) than the questions one can raise and the answers one can give. The world of the infant is no bigger than the nursery, but the world of the adult extends from the present back to its past and forward to its future. It includes not only the factual but also the possible, the ideal, the normative. It expresses not only what one has found out for oneself but also what we have managed to learn from the memories of other men, from the common sense of the community, from the pages of literature, from the labors of scholars, from the investigations of scientists, from the experience of saints, from the meditations of philosophers and theologians. It is within this larger world that we live out our lives. To it we refer when we speak of the real world. But because it is mediated by meaning and motivated by value, because meaning can go astray and evaluation become corrupt, because there is myth as well as science, fiction as well as fact, deceit as well as honesty, error as well as truth, that larger world is insecure.

Besides being cognitive, meaning is efficient. We work but our work is not mindless. We imagine, we plan, we investigate possibilities, we weigh pros and cons, we enter into contracts, we have countless orders given and executed. Over the world given us by nature, there is an artificial, man-made world; it is the cumulative, now planned, now chaotic, product of human acts of meaning.

A third function of meaning is constitutive. Just as language is constituted by articulate sound and meaning, so social institutions and human cultures have meanings as intrinsic components. Religions and art-forms, languages and literatures, sciences, philosophies, histories, all are inextricably involved in acts of meaning. What is true of cultural achievements, no less is true of social institutions. The family, the state, the law, the economy are not fixed and immutable entities. They adapt to changing circumstances; they can be reconceived in the light of new ideas; they can be subjected to revolutionary change. But all such change involves change of meaning—a change of idea or concept, a change of judgment or evaluation, a change of the order or the request. The state can be changed by rewriting its constitution. More subtly but no less effectively it can be changed by reinterpreting the constitution or, again, by working on men's minds and hearts to change the objects that command their respect, hold their allegiance, fire their loyalty.

A fourth function of meaning is communicative. What one man means can be communicated to another in many ways: intersubjectively, symbolically, linguistically, incarnately. But a rich store of common meaning is not the work of isolated individuals or even of single generations. Common meanings have histories. They originate in single minds, but they become common only through successful and widespread communication. They are transmitted to successive generations only through training and education. Slowly and gradually they are clarified, expressed, formulated, defined, only to be enriched and deepened and transformed, and no less often to be impoverished, emptied out, deformed.

The conjunction of both the constitutive and communicative functions of meaning yield the three key notions of community, existence in the sense of *Existenz*, and history.

Community is not just a by-product of a geographical frontier but the achievement of common meaning. Such common meaning has four degrees. It is potential when there is a common field of experience, and to withdraw from that common field is to get out of touch. Common meaning is formal when there is common understanding, and one withdraws from that common understanding as misunderstanding and incomprehension supervene. Common meaning is actual inasmuch as there are common judgments, areas in which all affirm and deny in the same manner; but common meaning is diluted as consensus fails. Common meaning is realized by decisions and especially by permanent dedication, in the love that makes families, in the loyalty that makes states, in the faith that makes religions.

As it is only within communities that men are conceived and born and reared, so too it is only with respect to the available common meanings that the individual grows in experience, understanding, judgment, responsibility, and so comes to find out for himself that he has to decide for himself what to make of himself. Such is the existential moment.

It is momentous, for it can be authentic or unauthentic, and this can happen in two distinct ways. There is the minor authenticity or unauthenticity of the subject with respect to the tradition in which he was raised. There is the major authenticity or unauthenticity that justifies or condemns the tradition itself. As Kierkegaard asked whether he was a Christian, so divers men can ask themselves whether they are authentically religious, authentically philosophers, authentically scientists. They may answer that they are, and they may be right. But they may answer affirmatively and still be mistaken. On a series of points they will realize what the ideals of the tradition demand; but on another series their lives diverge from those ideals. Such divergence may be overlooked from a selective inattention, a failure to understand, an undetected rationalization. What I am is one thing; what an authentic Christian or Buddhist is, is another, and I am unaware of the difference. My unawareness is unexpressed. I have no language to express what I am, so I use the language of the tradition that I unauthentically appropriate, and thereby I devaluate, distort, water down, corrupt that language.

Such devaluation, distortion, dilution, corruption may occur only in scattered individuals. But it may occur on a more massive scale, and then the words are repeated but the meaning is gone. The chair remains the chair of Moses, but occupied by scribes and Pharisees. The theology is still Scholastic, but the Scholasticism is decadent. The name of science may be invoked but, as Edmund Husserl has argued, all significant scientific ideals can vanish to be replaced by the conventions of a clique. So the unauthenticity of individuals becomes the unauthenticity infecting a tradition. For a subject to take the tradition uncritically is for him to realize what objectively is unauthentic but for him subjectively is thought authentic.

So we come to history in its radical difference from nature. Nature unfolds in accord with classical and statistical laws. But history is an expression of meaning, and meaning is open both to enduring stationary states, to development, the fruit of authenticity, and to aberration that matches the unauthenticity of its source.

A sound development calls for heightened attention, a new insight into the situation, a workable proposal for a changed course of action, and a responsible decision on the matter. Such a sound development not only is an improvement on the previous situation but also a change. Change is apt to awaken further attention, open the way to fuller insight, to a still no less workable proposal, to another responsible decision. As the former change, so this change invites still further change. Progress has begun and it may continue. So Arnold Toynbee in his *A Study of History*—which I have found less a narrative of events than a repertory of ideal types—has depicted a series of challenges and responses with a creative minority taking the lead and the rank and file only too happily accepting that leadership.

But Toynbee also depicted the creative minority ceasing to be creative and becoming merely dominant. He has listed a series of manners in which this shift may come about. But I wish to suggest that our present analysis also throws light on the matter. For it should seem that the creative minority was creative because it hit upon a cumulative sequence of relevant insights. But in such a sequence the point can be reached when immediate benefits (or advantages) are small and the long-term benefits, though great, not only are distant but also difficult to depict and communicate. Then wise counsel does not easily prevail, compromise proposals are highly attractive, responsible decisions fail to win acceptance. The creative minority wishes to remain in the saddle; it can choose to become a merely dominant minority; to go along with the apologists that praise such practical wisdom; to be lulled into the easy security of philosophies that stand on the unreasoning and so irrefutable basis of animal faith. The shift may occur gradually enough to pass unnoticed, but once it has occurred, consistency becomes a force working for its perpetuity.

Such a change in the leadership involves a change in the social situation. As long as creativity was in charge, the situation was becoming increasingly intelligible. The implementation of insights in a situation not only modifies the situation but also suggests still further insights and still further complementary changes. In contrast, when intelligent proposals are mangled by compromise, their implementation results in an objective surd. It does not make sense. It calls not for further insights but for further compromises. Only with great difficulty can that call be resisted by a leadership that already has preferred dominance to creativity.

In brief, besides progress there also is decline. As progress rests on authenticity, on the self-transcendence of men and women ready to be attentive, to grow in intelligence, reasonableness, responsibility, so decline rests on unauthenticity. Basic decisions are shirked. Judgments lean towards superficiality. Difficult insights are ignored. Problems are referred to committees.

I once remarked that the wheel of progress not only turns but also rolls along. But the wheel of decline has a similar but opposite momentum, and a far greater power of acceleration—until things just fall apart.

3. PHILOSOPHY OF RELIGION

Up to now I have been attempting to elucidate what might be meant by the phrase, philosophy of . . . , and I have been doing so by speaking of "method of . . ."; first I spoke of methods in general as an ongoing dynamic, secondly of the possibility of matching the liberation of natural science through mathematics by using not mathematics but philosophy for a liberation of human studies. What has made natural science successful has been the Galilean proposal to mathematicize nature; what can make human studies no less penetrating seems to be, not the mathematicization of man's world, but the discovery that it is a world mediated by meaning and motivated by value. For it is through meanings that we come to know man's world. It is through meanings that we communicate concerning man's world. It is through meanings that we transform the world of nature into either a more excellent or a more deficient human world. It is through the meanings we accept and the values we embrace that we constitute both ourselves and our communities, our authentic and unauthentic traditions, our heady bursts of progress and our headlong periods of decline, of breakdown, of dissolution and decay.

In all this our aim has been an account of a philosophy of religion, and so we have now to compare the respective relevance of divers methods to the study of religions. Historically, then, the methods of natural science have been applied in this field; the methods of history also have been applied; and if any problems remain after viewing such work, we have to ask whether an appeal to philosophy would be of avail.

First, with regard to the relevance in religious studies of the methods of the natural sciences, I cannot do better than recall the opening remarks of Professor Wilfred Cantwell Smith at a public lecture in the University of Toronto in January 1968. He acknowledged that much fruitful energy had been devoted to exploring man's many religious traditions and to reconstructing the history of the overt data on man's religious living. Both in detail and in wide compass the observable forms had been observed and the observations had been recorded. But he went on to claim that a further, a more important, and a more difficult question must be raised. To live religiously is not merely to live in the presence of certain symbols but, he urged, it is to be involved with them or through them in a quite special way—a way that may lead far beyond the symbols, that may demand the totality of a person's response, that may affect his relation not only to the symbols but to everything else, to himself, to his neighbor, to the stars.

This special involvement, commitment, engagement, Professor Smith claimed, pleads to be elucidated. If it both inspires and is inspired by religious traditions, religious beliefs, religious imperatives, religious rituals, still it is distinct from them. Members of the same religion are not all equally committed to their religion. The same man may be at one time indifferent to religion, at another profoundly concerned, at a third vehemently hostile. The question is, then, what makes religion come alive? What has happened when it withers and dies?[12]

In brief, the methods of natural science have contributed much to religious studies, but their contribution is incomplete. What is wanting is an account of the meaningfulness of religious tradition, belief, imperatives, rituals: not indeed of the meaningfulness that would meet the requirements of a logical positivist or linguistic analyst, but of the meaningfulness that can demand the totality of a person's response. Again, it is the meaningfulness that is expressed by a historian of religion, read by those for whom the religion has come to life, and by them recognized as an account of their own commitment.

But what is that meaningfulness? How is it reached? How is it investigated?

It is, I should say, the meaningfulness of striving to become self-transcendent and of making progress on the way. It is the emergence of the self not only from the consciousness of the dream into waking consciousness but into intelligent consciousness that gradually promotes us from being animals in a habitat to becoming human beings in a universe, into the reasonable consciousness that judges in accord with the evidence, into the responsible consciousness that makes its way from individual and group egoism beyond the bias of omnicompetent common sense to the consciousness of one in love—in love with the family, in love with fellow citizens in this world, in love with God above all.

How is it reached? The process begins with socialization, acculturation, education. Its culmination is within religion. Both the Judaic tradition (*Deut. 6:4*; *Lev. 19:18*) and the Christian command followers to ". . . love the Lord your God with all your heart, with all your soul, with all your mind, and with all your strength," and to love your neighbor as yourself (*Mark 12:29–31*).

Nor are the Judaic and Christian traditions singu in this respect. Friedrich Heiler has listed seven principal areas of unity to be discerned in all the world religions: in Judaism, Christianity, Islam, Zoroastrian Mazdaism, in Hinduism, Buddhism, Taoism. But what he devoted eleven pages to narrating, I must compress under seven brief headings with apologies for the omission of many a nuance and qualification.[13] There is the reality, then, of the transcendent, the divine, the holy, the Other. Next, the divine while transcendent also is immanent in human hearts. Thirdly, this reality, transcendent and immanent, is for man the highest good, the highest truth, righteousness, goodness, beauty. Fourthly, the reality of the divine is ultimate love, mercy, compassion. Fifthly, the way of man to God is universally the way of sacrifice, repentance, discipline, prayer. Sixthly, as these religions seek God, so too they seek their neighbor's well-being, even the well-being of their enemies. Finally, while religious experience is endlessly manifold, the superior way to God is love.

A special fruitfulness seems to reside in the study of ascetics and mystics. Not only did Prof. Heiler write a fundamental work on prayer,[14] but Raymond Panikkar in a volume of *Concilium*, devoted to fundamental theology, advocated a turn in the same direction. If we wish a theology, he wrote, that has its ground free from the influence of particular places and times, particular cultures and viewpoints, we have to have recourse to the wordless prayer of the mystics representing the world religions. We have to ask them to dialogue, not to clarify their differences from one another, but to let shine forth the interrelatedness constituted by the peace they experience as distinct from any words they may silently or vocally utter.[15]

In somewhat similar fashion the foundations envisaged in my own *Method in Theology* are simply religious conversion in the sense of a total commitment to religious self-transcendence.

There remains a crucial issue on which, I feel, something must be said, for sooner or later it is bound to confront anyone who investigates the history of religions on the basis of his personal self-transcendence. I shall attempt to state it as briefly as possible in terms of three currently accessible views: materialism, immanentism, critical realism.

My starting point was our questions and answers, and it probably has not escaped you that such a basis fits in very neatly with Feuerbach's contention that man's notion of God is a projection on the sky of idealized human qualities. We seek understanding, and God is all-intelligent; we seek sufficient evidence for our judgments and God is all-knowing; we seek moral excellence and God is goodness and love.

I must be content with two observations. First, such seeking is not mere quality but potentiality and finality; and it is potentiality and finality not confined to some category but, on the contrary, scorning any arbitrary burking of questions.

Secondly, I note that the word, projection, recalls the cinematic projector and before it the magic lantern. But the slide or film does not experience, does not inquire intelligently, does not judge on the basis of sufficient reason, does not decide freely and responsibly. In brief, a projection does not differ from George Santayana's animal faith.

So much for a materialist option. Next, I propose to consider both the immanentist and the critical realist options simultaneously, not because the two do not differ, but because one can say much about religious experience without opting for either side of a philosophic difference.

Dr. Eric Voegelin has explained that he got into problems of religious understanding one winter when, at an adult education institute in Vienna where he grew up, he followed weekly lectures by Deussen, the philosopher who translated the Upanishads.[16] Dr. Voegelin is author of a work in many volumes on *Order and History;* but his parerga include incisive essays on Greek philosophy and the New Testament. He has set aside the common but strange assumption that reason, for Plato and Aristotle, was much the same as the deductivism of late medieval Scholasticism, seventeenth-century rationalism, nineteenth-century idealism. His contention has been that reason in the Greek classic experience was moral and religious; in Athens the appeal to reason was the appeal of men in an age of social and cultural decay seeking a way to recall their fellows from darkness and lead them towards the light.[17] His account of religious experience centers on the struggle in the soul and it draws freely on both Plato and the New Testament.[18] He acknowledges pulls and counterpulls. To follow the former puts an end to questioning. To opt for the latter leaves questions unanswered and conscience ill at ease. The former alternative is what Voegelin means by a movement luminous with truth, or again by existing in the truth, or again by the truth of existence. The latter alternative is existence in untruth. As he contends, this luminosity of existence with the truth of reason precedes all opinions and decisions about the pull to be followed. Moreover, it remains alive as the judgment of truth in existence whatever opinions about it we may actually form. In other words, there is an inner light that runs before the formulation of doctrines and that survives even despite opposing doctrines. To follow that inner light is life, even though to worldly eyes it is to die. To reject that inner light is to die, even though the world envies one's attainments and achievements.[19]

Voegelin holds that such experiences, while valid symbols and legitimately made the basis of a "Saving Tale" to guide our lives, are not to be handed over to hypostatizing and dogmatizing.

> There is no In-Between other than the *metaxy* experienced in a man's existential tension toward the divine ground of being; there is no question of life and death other than the question aroused by pull and counter-pull; there is no Saving Tale other

than the tale of the divine pull to be followed by man; and there
is no cognitive articulation of existence other than the noetic
consciousness in which the movement becomes luminous to itself.[20]

A little later we read:

Myth is not a primitive symbolic form, peculiar to early societies and progressively to be overcome by positive science, but
the language in which the experiences of divine-human participation in the In-Between become articulate. The symbolization
of participating existence, it is true, evolves historically from
the more compact form of the cosmological myth to the more
differentiated forms of Philosophy, Prophecy, and the Gospel,
but the differentiating insight, far from abolishing the *metaxy* of
existence, brings it to fully articulate knowledge. When existence becomes noetically luminous as the field of pull and
counter-pull, of the question of life and death, and of the tension
between human and divine reality, it also becomes luminous for
divine reality as the Beyond of the *metaxy* which reaches into the
metaxy in the participatory event of the movement. There is no
In-Between of existence as a self-contained object but only existence experienced as part of a reality which extends beyond the
In-Between.[21]

Let me now attempt to say what I make of this. First, I shall
quote and comment. I quote: ". . . there is no Saving Tale other
than the tale of the divine pull to be followed by man." What is this
divine pull? We have explicit references to *John 6:44:* "No man can
come to me unless he is drawn by the Father who sent me," and to
John 12:32: "And I shall draw all men to myself, when I am lifted
up from the earth."[22] The context then is not only biblical but Joan-
nine.
    Next, I quote: ". . . there is no cognitive articulation of exist-
ence other than the noetic consciousness in which the movement becomes luminous to itself." I ask: What is the movement of noetic
consciousness and when does it become luminous to itself? For Voegelin "nous," whence the adjective, noetic, is in the classic experience moral and religious. But in the present context the religious
component becomes far more emphatic. For in this movement of

consciousness there is ". . . a mutual participation (*methexis, metalepsis*) of human and divine; and the language symbols expressing the movement are not invented by an observer who does not participate in the movement but are engendered in the event of participation itself. The ontological status of the symbols is both human and divine." So Voegelin appeals both to Plato who claimed that his myth of the puppet player was "an *alethes logos,* a true story," whether "received from a God, or from a man who knows" (*Laws* 645B) and, as well, to the prophets promulgating their sayings as the "word" of Yahweh.[23] In brief, we are offered an account of revelation or, perhaps, inspiration.

It is, however, an account of revelation or inspiration that can meet the needs of a philosophy of religion. For as Voegelin further remarked, "The symbolization of participating existence . . . evolves historically from the more compact form of the cosmological myth (the reference is to ancient Egypt and Mesopotamia) to the more differentiated forms of Philosophy, Prophecy, and the Gospel, but the differentiating insight, far from abolishing the *metaxy* of existence, brings it to fully articulate knowledge."

One may ask whether one is not to confuse this differentiating insight with its fully articulate knowledge and, on the other hand, the repudiated dogmatizing and doctrinization. There are grounds for such an interpretation for later Voegelin speaks of ". . . the loss of experimental reality through doctrinization."[24] Now the luminous experience of existing in the truth is indeed an instance of experimental reality, and a doctrinization that abolishes the one also is the loss of the other. In that case doctrinization seems associated with what Newman would have named merely notional apprehension and merely notional assent, which do imply an exclusion of real apprehension and assent.[25]

There remains the repudiation of "hypostatization." It seems to me fully justified if applied to Gnostic constitutions of the pleroma through the designation of abstract names, or even, if anyone wishes, applied to the Hegelian dialectical deduction of the universe through an interplay of opposed *Begriffe.* But behind such applications there is a far deeper issue, and on it I can now do no more than invite you to an examination of Giovanni Sala's comparison of my cognitional theory with Kant's,[26] and of William Ryan's comparison of my intentionality analysis with that of Edmund Husserl.[27] The seminal work seems to me to be Le Blond's *Logique et méthode chez Aristote*.[28]

A lecture at the XIVth Congress of The International Association for the History of Religions, Winnipeg, Aug. 18, 1980. Also given at Boston College, June, 1980, during the seventh annual Lonergan Workshop. Previously published in Fred Lawrence (ed.), *Lonergan Workshop*, Vol. III (Chico, Cal.: Scholars Press, 1983), pp. 179–199.

Notes

1. R. G. Collingwood, *The Idea of History* (Oxford: At the Clarendon Press, 1946), p. 201.

2. *Ibid.*

3. *Ibid.*, p. 202.

4. Cf. B. Lonergan, "The Ongoing Genesis of Methods" (Ch. 10 of this volume).

5. B. Lonergan, *Method in Theology*, 1972, p. xi.

6. Aristotle, *Posterior Analytics*, I, 2, 71b 9–16.

7. B. Lonergan, *Verbum*, 1967, pp. 25–45.

8. Aristotle, *Metaphysics*, VII (Z), 17, 1041a 16. (Editor: although Fr. Lonergan refers here to the *Metaphysics*, elsewhere he has referred to the much fuller account Aristotle gives in the *Posterior Analytics*, II, 1–2, 89b 23–90a 34.)

9. Ira Progoff, *Depth Psychology and Modern Man* (New York: McGraw-Hill Paperbacks, 1973; first published, 1959), pp. 182–188.

10. Walter E. Conn, *Conscience: Development and Self-Transcendence* (Birmingham, Alabama: Religious Education Press, 1981).

11. Sir David Ross, *Aristotle's Prior and Posterior Analytics*, 1949, p. 14.

12. B. Lonergan, "Religious Commitment," in *The Pilgrim People: A Vision with Hope*, ed. by Joseph Papin (Villanova, Pa.: The Villanova University Press, c1970—for the symposium of 1971), pp. 45–69; see p. 45.

13. Friedrich Heiler, "The History of Religions as a Preparation for the Co-operation of Religions," *op. cit.* (above, Ch. 8, note 2), pp. 142–153.

14. P. Misner, "Heiler, Friedrich," *New Catholic Encyclopedia*, Vol XVI: Supplement 1967–1974 (Washington, D. C.: The Catholic University of America, 1974), pp. 203–204.

15. R. Panikkar, "Metatheology or Diacritical Theology as Fundamental Theology," *Concilium*, 1969, pp. 43–55.

16. *Conversations with Eric Voegelin*, ed. R. Eric O'Connor (Thomas More Institute Papers/76; Montreal: Thomas More Institute, 1980), pp. 153–154.

17. E. Voegelin, "Reason: The Classic Experience," *The Southern Review*, 1974, pp. 237–264.

18. E. Voegelin, "The Gospel and Culture," *op. cit.* (above, Ch. 12, note 21).

19. B. Lonergan, "Theology and Praxis," above, p. 190.

20. E. Voegelin, "The Gospel and Culture," p. 75.

21. *Ibid.*, p. 76.

22. *Ibid.*, p. 77.

23. *Ibid.*, p. 75.

24. *Ibid.*, p. 88.

25. John Henry Cardinal Newman, *An Essay in Aid of a Grammar of Assent* (London, etc.: Longmans, Green and Co., 1930); see especially Ch. 1, no. 2, "Modes of Apprehending Propositions," pp. 9–12, and Ch. 4. "Notional and Real Assent," pp. 36–97. (Editor: Newman allows for combining real and notional apprehension [pp. 10–11], but then the notional is not *merely* notional.)

26. Giovanni Sala, *Das Apriori in der menschlichen Erkenntnis: Eine Studie über Kants Kritik der reinen Vernunft und Lonergans Insight*, Monographien zur philosophischen Forschung, Band 97 (Meisenheim am Glan: Verlag Anton Hain, 1971).

27. William F. J. Ryan, "Intentionality in Edmund Husserl and Bernard Lonergan," *International Philosophical Quarterly*, Vol. XIII (1973), pp. 173–190.

28. J. M. Le Blond, *Logique et méthode chez Aristotle: Etude sur la recherche des principes dans la Physique aristotélicienne* (Paris: Vrin, 1939).

14

Pope John's Intention

In this series of four lectures Boston College is celebrating the tenth anniversary of its Institute of Religious Education and Pastoral Ministry. So ten years ago, and only six years after the end of the second Vatican council, sufficient staff had been assembled and money collected to make the Institute possible. Such proximity suggests that the council itself provided the inspiration for this venture and, in turn, the council points to the inaugural address in which Pope John XXIII explained to the bishops his reasons for calling them to Rome.

So we begin from Pope John's intention. He wanted a council that differed from previous councils, one that was specifically "pastoral." That fact will be our first topic.

Our second will be a clarification of the meaning, the precise significance, of that fact.

Our third will be the relevance of the pastoral council to the Institute, and our fourth will be the authenticity, the genuineness, of the Christian spirit that the Institute is to promote.

1. PASTORAL

A simple drama in the unfolding of the second Vatican council provides, I believe, an effective means of communicating what was meant by the word, pastoral. The first element was the declaration by Pope John XXIII of the purpose he had in mind in summoning the council. A second element was the view, put forward by His Eminence, the Cardinal Archbishop of Genoa, that all the councils of the church had been pastoral. The final element was a paper in which the

Dominican theologian, M.-D. Chenu, explained the difference between the doctrinal teaching of councils and, on the other hand, the pastoral preaching of our Lord, of the apostles and, down the ages, of all those entrusted with the care of souls.

First, the intention of Pope John XXIII. At the solemn inauguration of the second Vatican council, the Pope explained to the assembled bishops both what was his purpose in summoning them to the council and what was not his purpose. There was no point, he said, in their gathering together merely to repeat what anyone could find in familiar theological handbooks. Equally, there was no point in going over ancient decrees and clearing up this or that obscurity to satisfy the curiosity of antiquarians. What was desired was advertence to the distinction between the unchanging deposit of faith and the changing modes of its presentation to meet the needs of different times. What was required now was a fresh presentation, one that met current needs, one that fitted in with the teaching office of the church, a teaching office that in the main was pastoral.[1]

During the first session of the council there came to light divergent views on the precise meaning of the word, pastoral. Pope John had no intention of entering into these debates. His interventions were incidental, rare, pragmatic, strategic, and readily understood by the majority of the bishops. Still, a few weeks after the first session had come to an end, in responding to the Christmas greetings of the curial cardinals and prelates, the Pope harked back to his inaugural address. The inspiration he had had in calling the council was hope for a widespread and more fervent renewal in the life of the church. It was for a new and more vigorous spread of the gospel in the whole world. He wanted our contemporaries to be made aware of the church's striving for the spiritual and, no less, for the material betterment of the whole of mankind. He begged leave to repeat the point he had endeavored to make in his inaugural address on October 11. Undoubtedly a first duty of the council was fidelity to the basic truths of the deposit of faith and of the church's teaching. But this duty was not to be fulfilled by any wrapping of one's talent in a napkin and burying it in the ground. It called for a prompt and fearless will to draw upon ancient doctrine and to apply it under the conditions of our day. The business of the council, he had then insisted, was not the discussion of this or that topic in the fundamental doctrines of the church. It was not any elaboration of the teaching of the fathers or of ancient or of modern theologians. That sort of thing can be done very well without holding a council. What was expected was a leap forward (*un balzo innanzi*) that would set forth the faith in the mental forms and literary style of modern thought, while satisfying the requirements of the teaching office—an office that predominantly was pastoral.[2]

John XXIII died before the second session met. But in the first session His Eminence, Giovanni Cardinal Montini, had shown that he understood the meaning of a pastoral council and, when he became Paul VI, he had the council continue its work for three more years. It can be maintained, I feel sure, that the further sessions revealed how well the vast majority of the assembled bishops understood the scope and spirit of the council. But for present purposes it will suffice to recall the longest of the documents, *Gaudium et Spes,* which was entitled *A Pastoral Constitution on the Church in the Modern World.* It began with an expression of worldwide solidarity. The joy and hope, the sorrow and anguish of men today are also the joy and hope, the sorrow and anguish, of the disciples of Christ. So the statements of the decree were addressed not only to those that invoke the name of Christ but to the whole of mankind. Its aim was to present its conception of the role of the church in the world of today. That role included no earthly ambition. It was to be led by the Paraclete and it was to continue the work of Christ, who came into the world not to judge but to save, not to be served but to serve.[3]

2. A PASTORAL COUNCIL

It remains that the expression, a pastoral council, involved a certain novelty. In ecumenical councils from Nicea on, there had been a custom of distinguishing between doctrinal decrees that expounded truths, and disciplinary decrees that sought remedies for current defects and abuses. But Pope John's pastoral council seems to evade these categories. It expounded truths but hurled no anathemas. It was concerned with concrete living, but its thrust was positive rather than remedial.

The issue came to a head with an acute observation made by Giuseppe Cardinal Siri, Archbishop of Genoa. For him the word, pastoral, did not mean merely smiles and condescension. First and foremost it meant presenting the truths revealed by our Lord. Further, since every council had conceived its aim to be the presentation of revealed truths, the term, pastoral, could not be the distinguishing mark of any council.

While one must grant that such a contention was apt to be found startling in the context of what officially was styled a pastoral council, one should add that it rested on a centuries-old tradition of concern for technically formulated truths. In any case the very contrast could be illuminating. For the leap forward that Pope John desired in the church might well be the enrichment of the technical formulation by the vital, the personal, the existential.

It is in this direction that points the response, written by Fr. Chenu shortly after the end of the first session of Vatican II, published the following April in the review, *Parole et Mission,* and a year later included in a two-volume collection of Fr. Chenu's writings.[4]

Fr. Chenu recognized that Cardinal Siri's position was in accord with the work of the preconciliar committees. Theirs had been the task of putting together the suggestions, the requests, the plaints of the bishops, and of presenting the initial drafts, named *schemata,* for the council to approve, modify, or reject. In fact, however, the council had rejected more than one of these *schemata,* pronouncing them to be abstract, and scholastic, but neither biblical, nor pastoral, nor ecumenical.

What then does "pastoral" mean? For Fr. Chenu one gets into difficulty when one puts the cart before the horse. The words of the Good Shepherd preceded conciliar decrees. But if first one clarifies the meaning of "doctrine" and then sets about explaining the meaning of "pastoral," one tends to reduce "pastoral" to the application of "doctrine" and to reduce the application of "doctrine" to the devices and dodges, the simplifications and elaborations of classical oratory. But what comes first is the word of God. The task of the church is the kerygma, announcing the good news, preaching the gospel. That preaching is pastoral. It is the concrete reality. From it one may abstract doctrines, and theologians may work the doctrines into conceptual systems. But the doctrines and systems, however valuable and true, are but the skeleton of the original message. A word is the word of a person, but doctrine objectifies and depersonalizes. The word of God comes to us through the God-man. The church has to mediate to the world not just a doctrine but the living Christ.

God spoke to us in the prophets, he spoke in his Son, he still speaks today in scripture and tradition, in the biblical movement, the liturgical movement, the catechetical movement, the ecumenical movement. First and foremost he speaks to the poor, to the poor in the underdeveloped nations, to the poor in the slums of industrialized nations. And if the word of God is not preached to the poor, then the church has failed. So it was in the word of God preached to the poor—a theme so lucidly and powerfully set forth by, among others, Cardinal Lercaro—that the bishops assembled in council, together discovered and collectively responded to the momentous meaning of the phrase, a pastoral council.

Alive, personal, communal, the word of God also is historic. As the old covenant, so also the new names a dispensation, an economy, an ongoing disposition of divine providence both emergent in human history and carrying it forward to an ultimate, an eschatological goal. With its origins in the distant past and its term in an unknown future, its scope extends to the ends of the earth and its mission to all men. Once more there comes to light the complete inadequacy of attempting to begin from doctrines and then attempting to flesh them out into living speech, when it is living speech that, from the start, alone can be at once concrete and alive, interpersonal and communal, historical and ecumenical.

Let me add just one more point from Fr. Chenu's account. An ideology can be expressed in the propositions of a doctrine, in the premises and multitudinous conclusions of a system. But the words of a pastor, of a shepherd of souls, are far more than an ideology. They are words spoken in faith and awakening faith. They are words of salvation, a salvation that is God's gift of himself, of his peace and joy, of his eternal hope.

3. THE RELEVANCE OF THE PASTORAL COUNCIL

I have been dwelling on the meaning and function of a pastoral council because I felt these topics especially relevant to our current celebration—the tenth anniversary of our Institute of Religious Education and Pastoral Ministry. Just as Vatican II, while remaining faithful to the basic tenets of our faith, aimed at evoking a fresh vitality, an *aggiornamento,* an updating of apostolic activity in the church, so too both religious education and pastoral ministry call for a similar fidelity to the truths of faith and a bold leap forward into contemporary significance and relevance. Religious education is not just indoctrination in an ideology; it would realize each person's religious potential; and that realization would reenact in our own day what St. Paul named putting off the old man and putting on the new. Pastoral ministry may consist in words or in deeds from a twofold action of the Holy Spirit. There is the grace the Spirit brings to the minister. There is the grace given those that hear his words and are touched by his deeds.

On this point St. Augustine composed a dialogue with the title, *The Teacher,* in which his main point was the existence of two teachers: the teacher outside us whose words we hear; and the teacher within us: God the Father, his Son, and their Spirit. The teacher outside utters sounds. If we are familiar with the language, the sounds will be recognized as words; memory will recall their meanings; intelligence combines them into sentences; and sentences coalesce into discourse which we can understand. But if we go further and ask whether the discourse is true or false, wise or foolish, we may have recourse to the common sense or the wisdom we have acquired over the years. Still we must bear in mind that, while common sense and human wisdom may suffice in human affairs, they are unequal to the affairs of God. As St. Paul wrote to the Corinthians, " 'Things beyond our seeing, things beyond our hearing, things beyond our imagining, all prepared by God for those who love him,' these it is that God has revealed to us through the Spirit" (*I Cor. 2:9–10*). And in contrast with that revelation he shortly added, "A man who is unspiritual refuses what belongs to the Spirit of God; it is folly to him; he cannot grasp it, because it needs to be judged in the light of the Spirit" (*I Cor. 2:14*).

Now if to acquire knowledge that lies within human reach we listen to many teachers and devote years of serious study, we can readily infer that no less time and effort are needed to learn what lies beyond our seeing, our hearing, our imagining. But in divine affairs as in human the first requirement is the transition from drifting to commitment. Drifters lack a mind of their own. They do and say and think what everyone else is doing and saying and thinking, and the people they imitate are drifters too. There are countless sheep and among them there is no shepherd.

Still their condition is not hopeless. To each may come the existential moment when they discover in themselves and for themselves that it is up to themselves to settle what they are to be. Whether their tradition be Jewish or Christian, Muslim or Hindu, Buddhist or Taoist, there are things to be done and things to be left undone, things to be said and things to be passed over, thoughts to be entertained and thoughts to be dismissed. As a life spent in mere drifting lacks meaning, so a lifetime of commitment to a selected style or pattern of thinking, saying, doing is an incarnation of a meaning and makes one's living meaningful. Again, the greater the commitment, the more meaningful the life; and the less the commitment, the obscurer and the more dubious is the meaning.

There is a further aspect to the matter. For attention to the meaning of one's life leads to the further question of the meaning of death. Is death the end of living or is it the entry into another world? The question comes easily to man. The Greek tragedian, Euripides, could exclaim, ''Who knows if to live is to be dead, and to be dead to live?'' Plato at the end of the *Apology* has Socrates say to his judges, ''But now the time has come to go. I go to die, and you to live. But who goes to the better lot is unknown to anyone but the God.''⁵ Four centuries later in the fourth gospel, in the chapter that precedes the Last Supper, Jesus says to the apostles, Philip and Andrew,

> In truth, in very truth I tell you, a grain of wheat remains a solitary grain unless it falls into the ground and dies; but if it dies, it bears a rich harvest. The man who loves himself is lost, but he who hates himself in this world will be kept safe for eternal life. If anyone serves me, he must follow me; where I am, my servant will be. Whoever serves me will be honoured by my Father (*John 12: 24–26*).

For Christians, then, the meaning of life is momentous. The twofold meaning of life and the twofold meaning of death that occurs in the Greek classics also occurs in a far sharper form in the words of our Lord. He who loves himself is lost. He who hates himself in this world will be kept safe for life eternal.

This is strong doctrine and it is put into practise only through the grace of God. It is the grace of being drawn by the Father. In the sixth chapter (*vv. 41–45*) of St. John's Gospel we read:

> At this the Jews began to murmur disapprovingly because he said, 'I am the bread which came down from heaven.' They said, 'Surely this is Jesus son of Joseph; we know his father and mother. How can he now say, "I have come down from heaven"?' Jesus answered, 'Stop murmuring among yourselves. No man can come to me unless he is drawn by the Father who sent me . . . Everyone who has listened to the Father and learned from him comes to me.'

Not only does the Father draw us to Christ, but Christ himself also draws us by his passion and death. For he himself said, "And I shall draw all men to myself, when I am lifted up from the earth." And the evangelist comments immediately, "This he said to indicate the kind of death he was to die" (*John 12: 32–33*). Drawn by the Father and drawn by the Son, the Holy Spirit brings God's own love to us. So St. Paul could write, ". . . God's love has flooded our inmost heart through the Holy Spirit he has given us" (*Rom. 5:5*).

St. Paul's estimate of the magnitude of this gift of the Holy Spirit is known to all with his chapter on love.

> I may speak in tongues of men or of angels, but if I am without love, I am a sounding gong or a clanging cymbal. I may have the gift of prophecy, and know every hidden truth; I may have faith strong enough to move mountains; but if I have no love, I am nothing. I may dole out all I possess, or even give my body to be burnt, but if I have no love, I am none the better.
>
> Love is patient; love is kind and envies no one. Love is never boastful, nor conceited, nor rude; never selfish, not quick to take offense. Love keeps no score of wrongs; does not gloat over other men's sins, but delights in the truth. There is nothing love cannot face; there is no limit to its faith, its hope, and its endurance.
>
> Love will never come to an end. Are there prophets? their work will be over. Are there tongues of ecstasy? they will cease.

Is there knowledge? it will vanish away; for our knowledge and our prophecy alike are partial, and the partial vanishes when wholeness comes. When I was a child, my speech, my outlook, and my thoughts were all childish. When I grew up, I had finished with childish things. Now we see only puzzling reflections in a mirror, but then we shall see face to face. My knowledge now is partial; then it will be whole, like God's knowledge of me. In a word, there are three things that last forever: faith, hope, and love; but the greatest of them all is love (*I Cor. 13*).

The only admissible comment on these words of St. Paul involves a transition from written words to the memory of deeds. That memory was reawakened for me by Rosemary Haughton in her recent book on *The Passionate God*, where she recalls the thoughtfulness for others that Jesus exhibited repeatedly during the passion that ended in his death. She wrote:

There is a quality about the behaviour of Jesus during his passion which sets it apart from any other kind of heroism. In a sense, it is not heroism at all, because a hero is intent on *being* a hero, on making clear to everyone his moral superiority and his indifference to the worst that his enemies can do. Jesus did not behave in a heroic way. His attention was, at every point on which we are informed, not on himself but on others, ready to respond in whatever way was needed. There is a detailed attentiveness, an extremity of compassionate awareness of the nature of others' reactions and needs, which we easily overlook because we have heard it all so often. From his concern in Gethsemane for the wounded servant and for the fate of his own followers, to his plea for the men who nailed him to the cross and the assurance of salvation to his fellow sufferer, the impulse of his whole being is a love poured out in detailed, personal care as it was poured out in the gift of his body to destruction. He did not merely surrender to death; he gave himself away, body and mind and human heart, all one gift.[6]

Jesus' thoughtfulness of others from the garden of Gethsemane to his death on Calvary illustrates what St. Paul was later to write: "There is nothing love cannot face; there is no limit to its faith, its hope, and its endurance."

4. AUTHENTICITY

The question of authenticity is twofold: there is the minor authenticity of the subject with respect to the tradition that has nourished him; there is the major authenticity that justifies or condemns the tradition itself. The first passes a human judgment on persons; the second is the judgment of history and ultimately the judgment of divine providence upon traditions.

As Kierkegaard asked himself whether he was a Christian, so divers men can ask themselves whether or not they are genuine Catholics or Protestants, Muslims or Buddhists, Platonists or Aristotelians, and so on. They may answer that they are, and be correct in their answers. But they also may answer affirmatively and still be mistaken. In this case there will exist a series of points in which what they are coincides with what the ideals of the tradition demand, but there will be another series in which there is a greater or less divergence. These points of difference are overlooked, whether from a selective inattention, or a failure to understand, or an undetected rationalization. What I am is one thing, what a genuine Christian or Buddhist is, is another, and I am unaware of the difference. My unawareness is unexpressed; I have no language to express what I really am, so I use the language of the tradition I unauthentically appropriate, and thereby I devaluate, distort, water down, corrupt that language.

Such devaluation, distortion, corruption may occur only in scattered individuals. But it may occur on a more massive scale, and then the words are repeated but the meaning is gone. The chair is still the chair of Moses, but it is occupied by scribes and Pharisees. Traditional doctrine is still taught, but it is no longer convincing. The religious order still reads out the rules, but one may doubt that the home fires are still burning. The sacred name of science is still invoked, but when each field is divided into more and more specialties and these specialties cultivated by ever smaller groups, one may be led to ask with Edmund Husserl to what extent any significant ideal of science actually functions, indeed to what extent the ideals of science are being replaced by the conventions of a clique. If, in such eventualities, anyone were to accept a tradition as it stands, he could hardly do more than authentically realize unauthenticity.

Truly enough, the modern world is in advance of its predecessors in its mathematics, its natural science, its human science, and the wealth and variety of its literary potentialities. But it was on the basis of his trust in God that modern man had erected his states and cultures, yet more and more he has opted to sustain them by an appeal to man's complete autonomy. He would acknowledge man's intelligence, his rationality, his responsibility, but he would not acknowledge more. For the consistent secularist to speak of God is, at best, irrelevant; to turn to God—except by way of a political gesture or an emotional outlet—is to sacrifice the good that man both knows and, by his own resources, can attain.

Such has been the mounting challenge to religion and, since it provides a paradigm for its many parallels, it seems worthwhile to analyze its elements. I shall first indicate ambiguities that arise when a people, sharing a common language, divides into this-worldly secularists and other-worldly believers. For the two groups will differ both in the realities and in the values they acknowledge. The other-worldly believers hold that God exists and is operative in religious living; the this-worldly secularists do not. Again, the other-worldly believers acknowledge other-worldly values, and this acknowledgment influences in varying degrees their this-worldly valuations; but the this-worldly secularists avoid such a complication for they acknowledge no other-worldly values and so are free to concentrate on the values of this world.

Next, a person's horizon is the boundary of what he knows and values. There follows a notable difference in the horizons of this-worldly secularists and other-worldly believers. For what we know and how we arrange our scale of values determines our horizons, and our horizons determine the range of our attention, our consideration, our valuations, our conduct.

Further, there are two main components in a person's horizon. There is the main stem: what we know and what we value. There are extensions through the persons we know and care for, since knowing them and caring for them involve us in what they know and care for.

Moreover, such extensions may be mutual, and then the horizon of each is an extension of the horizon of the other. They may interrelate all the members of a group, and as such a cohesive group increases in size, there is a need for organizing—for distinguishing, within the whole, smaller groups comparable to the organs of a living body.

Horizons develop both in their main stem of knowing and caring and in their extensions through involvement in the knowing and caring of others. Development in the main stem increases the depth and range of the consequent horizon; and this increase leads to a development in the extensions, since our knowing others and our concern for them involve some sharing in the objects they know and care for. Moreover, inasmuch as among such objects there will be persons that know and care for their own circle, there will result a mediation of involvement at a second remove. Finally, developing horizons open the way to reciprocity on the part of those with whom one has become involved.

There are many ways, familiar and perhaps unfamiliar, in which people come to know and care for others. But I think it best to omit the familiar and to avoid the obscurity of the unfamiliar. What seems more pressing is to turn to three things: barriers, breakthroughs, and breakdowns. Barriers block development. Breakthroughs overcome barriers. Breakdowns undo past achievement.[7]

We have already illustrated the notion of a barrier in contrasting this-worldly secularists and other-worldly believers. The realities they acknowledge and the values they esteem diverge, and for St. Paul that divergence is extremely grave:

> . . . only the Spirit of God knows what God is. This is the Spirit
> that we have received from God, and not the spirit of the world,
> so that we may know all that God of his own grace gives us. . . .
> A man who is unspiritual refuses what belongs to the Spirit of
> God; it is folly to him; he cannot grasp it, because it needs to be
> judged in the light of the Spirit (*I Cor. 2:11–14*).

Such was the message of St. Paul to the Corinthians almost two millennia ago. While I think it relevant to an account of the barrier between secularists and believers, I must recall what I have already said tonight, that people may accept in good faith mistaken views that have become traditional, and that even the original mistake would hardly have occurred without the scandal given by other-worldly believers.

But from this particular instance of a barrier, we must turn to their multiplicity. Christian development is over a long series of barriers, barriers to purification, barriers to enlightenment, barriers to loving God above all and our neighbor as ourselves. The first barrier to purification is habitual mortal sin. There may be only one; there may be many; but one by one they all have to be overcome; and once that victory has been won, we have to watch and pray lest we relapse. The second barrier to purification is the occasional mortal sin; we have to study the occasions that give rise to temptations, to ferret out the feelings that give the temptation its attraction for us, to plan how we can evade the occasions and encourage countervailing feelings. There remain the barriers that are habitual venial sins; but now the struggle is on a new front; the campaign is essentially the same as before, for there are bad habits to be broken; but it is not so urgent; as the evil, so the risk is less. But the very slackening of urgency can give place to tepidity, and when that danger appears, we have to proceed against the barriers to enlightenment.

In this campaign one does well to turn to John Henry Cardinal Newman's *Grammar of Assent* and, specifically, to the passages in which he distinguishes notional apprehension from real apprehension, and notional assent from real assent. For the barriers to enlightenment are merely notional apprehension and merely notional assent, when we are content with understanding the general idea and give no more than an esthetic response that it is indeed a fine idea. On the other hand, the attainment of enlightenment is the attainment of real apprehension, real assent, and the motivation to live out what we have learnt. It is brought about through regular and sustained meditation on what it really means to be a Christian, a real meaning to be grasped not through definitions and systems but through the living words and deeds of our Lord, our Lady, and the saints, a meaning to be brought home to me in the measure that I come to realize how much of such meaning I have overlooked, how much I have greeted with selective inattention, how much I have been unwilling to recognize as a genuine element in Christian living. So gradually we replace shallowness and superficiality, weakness and self-indulgence, with the imagination and the feelings, with the solid knowledge and heartfelt willingness of a true follower of Christ.

Both in the process of purification and in the process of enlightenment there are times when we resemble the two disciples on the road to Emmaus before the stranger joined them on their journey, when they recalled with dismay how high had been their hopes before Jesus was scourged, condemned, and crucified; and there are other times when we resemble the disciples as they listened to the stranger's account of all that the scriptures had foretold and, as they later remarked, "Did we not feel our hearts on fire as he talked with us on the road . . .?" (*Luke 24:32*). Such times of spiritual dismay and spiritual elation have been interpreted as the language used by the inner teacher in his converse with our hearts. And if the elation is accompanied by a willingness to do good that hitherto we were unwilling to do, then it is the sign of a grace that Aquinas named operative,[8] a grace foretold by Ezekiel with the words: "I will . . . put a new spirit into them; I will take the heart of stone out of their bodies and give them a heart of flesh. Then they will conform to my statutes and keep my laws. They will become my people, and I will become their God" (*Ezek. 11:19–20*).

Both in the Old Testament and in the New there are given the two commandments.

> Then one of the lawyers . . . asked him, 'Which commandment is first of all?' Jesus answered, 'The first is, "Hear, O Israel: The Lord your God is the only Lord; love the Lord your God with all your heart, with all your soul, with all your mind, and with all your strength." The second is this: "Love your neighbour as yourself." There is no other commandment greater than these' (*Mark 12:28–31*; cf. *Deut.6:4–5, Lev.19:18*).

A real apprehension of these commandments and a real assent to their binding force for each of us are given us by sanctifying grace, for then "God's love has flooded our inmost heart through the Holy Spirit he has given us" (*Rom.5:5*). But even then we must watch and pray that we enter not into temptation, for beyond sanctifying grace we also need actual graces, even operative actual graces, that take us through the processes of purification and enlightenment towards the state of union with God.

I began by recalling how Pope John XXIII desired the church to leap forward in its apostolic mission by preaching to mankind the living Christ. I spoke in turn of the meaning, the function, and the relevance of a pastoral council. I ended by speaking of authenticity, of the genuine fruit of religious education and of pastoral ministry. Since that fruit fundamentally comes through God's grace, since that grace is given in answer to prayer, I would conclude by begging you one and all to pray that this Institute of Religious Education and Pastoral Ministry, and all similar undertakings, prove to be instruments that bountifully promote the realization of Pope John's intentions. It is a prayer that the members of Christ's body on earth bring forth fruit thirtyfold, sixtyfold, a hundredfold.

A lecture given twice at Boston College, 1981, first in June, during the eighth annual Lonergan Workshop, then in July, during the tenth-anniversary celebration of The Institute of Religious Education and Pastoral Ministry. To be published in the proceedings of that celebration and in a future volume of *Lonergan Workshop*.

Notes

1. *Acta Apostolicae Sedis*, Vol. LIV (1962), pp. 791–792.

2. *Ibid.*, Vol. LV (1963), pp. 43–45.

3. *Gaudium et Spes*, nos. 1–3; see *The Documents of Vatican II*, ed. by Walter M. Abbott and Joseph Gallagher (New York: The America Press, 1966), pp. 199–201.

4. M. D. Chenu, "Un Concile 'Pastoral'," in *La Parole de Dieu*. Vol. II: *L'Evangile dans le temps* (Paris: Cerf, 1964), pp. 655–672; originally published in *Parole et mission*, no. 21 (15 avril, 1963), pp. 182–202.

5. See above, p. 189.

6. Rosemary Haughton, *The Passionate God* (London: Darton, Longman & Todd, and New York: Paulist, 1981), pp. 147–148.

7. "Barriers" and "breakthroughs" are among the basic concepts in Rosemary Haughton's *The Passionate God*.

15

Unity and Plurality:
The Coherence of Christian Truth

This paper falls into three parts: (1) Differentiations of Consciousness; (2) Pluralism and Theological Doctrines; and (3) Pluralism and Conversion.

I. DIFFERENTIATIONS OF CONSCIOUSNESS

For centuries theologians were divided into diverse schools. The schools differed from one another on most points in systematic theology. But all shared a common origin in medieval Scholasticism and so they were able to understand one another and could attempt, if not dialogue, at least refutation. But with the breakdown of Scholasticism, that common ancestry is no longer a bond. Wide divergences in doctrine are being expressed by Catholic theologians. If each abounds in his wisdom, he also tends to be mystified by the existence of views other than his own.

If one is to understand such diversity, one must, I believe, advert to the sundry differentiations of human consciousness. A first differentiation arises in the process of growing up. The infant lives in a world of immediacy. The child moves towards a world mediated by meaning. For the adult the real world is the world mediated by meaning, and his philosophic doubts about the reality of that world arise from the fact that he has failed to advert to the difference between the criteria for a world of immediacy and, on the other hand, the criteria for a world mediated by meaning.

239

Such inadvertence seems to be the root of the confusion concerning objects and objectivity that has obtained in Western thought
since Kant published his *Critique of Pure Reason.*[1] In the world of
immediacy the only objects are objects of immediate experience,
where "experience" is understood in the narrow sense and denotes
either the outer experience of our senses or the inner experience of
our consciousness. But in the world mediated by meaning—i.e.,
mediated by experiencing, understanding, and judging—objects are
what are intended by questions and known by intelligent, correct,
conscientious answers. It is by his questions for intelligence (*quid
sit, cur ita sit*), for reflection (*an sit*), for moral deliberation (*an ho-
nestum sit*), that man intends without yet knowing the intelligible,
the true, the real, and the good. By that intending man is immediately related to the objects that he will come to know when he elicits
correct acts of meaning. Accordingly, naive realism arises from the
assumption that the world mediated by meaning is known by taking
a look. Empiricism arises when the world mediated by meaning is
emptied of everything except what can be sensed. Idealism retains
the empiricist notion of reality, insists that human knowledge is constituted by raising and answering questions, and concludes that human knowledge is not of the real but of the ideal. A critical realism
finally claims that human knowledge consists not in experiencing
alone but in the threefold compound that embraces experiencing and
understanding and judging.

Besides the differentiation of consciousness involved in growing up, further differentiations occur with respect to the world mediated by meaning. Here the best known is the eventual separation of
scientific from commonsense meaning.

Its origins are celebrated in Plato's early dialogues in which
Socrates explains what he means by a definition that applies *omni et
soli,* seeks such definitions of courage, sobriety, justice, and the
like, shows the inadequacy of every proposed solution, and admits
that he himself is unable to answer his own questions. But a generation or so later in Aristotle's *Nicomachean Ethics* we find not only
general definitions of virtue and vice but also definitions of an array
of specific virtues each one flanked by a pair of vices that sin by excess or by defect. But Aristotle was not content merely to answer
Socrates' question. By his example he showed how it can be done;
he scrutinized linguistic usage; selected the precise meanings that

suited his purpose; constructed sets of interrelated terms; and employed such sets to systematize whole regions of inquiry.

In this fashion was effected the differentiation of commonsense meaning and scientific meaning. Socrates and his friends knew perfectly well what they meant by courage, sobriety, justice. But such knowledge does not consist in universal definitions. It consists simply in understanding when a term may be used appropriately; and such understanding is developed by adverting to the response others give to our statements. As common sense does not define, so it does not enounce universal principles; it offers proverbs, i.e., bits of advice it may be well to bear in mind when the occasion arises; hence "Strike the iron while it is hot" and "He who hesitates is lost" are not so much contradicted as complemented by "Look before you leap." Finally, common sense does not syllogize; it argues from analogy; but its analogies resemble, not those constructed by logicians in which the analogue is partly similar and partly dissimilar, but rather Piaget's adaptations which consist of two parts: an assimilation that calls on the insights relevant to somewhat similar situations; and an adjustment that adds insights relevant to the peculiarities of the present situation.

But besides the world mediated by commonsense meanings, there is another world mediated by scientific meanings, where terms are defined, systematic relationships are sought, and procedures are governed by logic and methods. This second world was approximated by Plato's distinction between the flux of phenomena and the immutable forms. It was affirmed more soberly in Aristotle's distinction between what is first for us and what is first in itself. It has reappeared in Eddington's two tables: one brown, solid, heavy; the other colorless, mostly empty space, with here and there an unimaginable wavicle. So it is that scientists live in two worlds: at one moment they are with the rest of us in the world of common sense; at another they are apart from us and by themselves with a technical and controlled language of their own with reflectively constructed and controlled procedures.

Besides the scientific there is a religious differentiation of consciousness. It begins with asceticism and culminates in mysticism. Both asceticism and mysticism, when genuine, have a common ground that was described by St. Paul when he exclaimed: ". . . God's love has flooded our inmost heart through the Holy Spirit he has given us'' (*Rom. 5:5*). That ground can bear fruit in a consciousness that lives in a world mediated by meaning. But it can also set up a different type of consciousness by withdrawing one from the world mediated by meaning into a cloud of unknowing.[2] Then one is for God, belongs to him, gives oneself to him, not by using words, images, concepts, but in a silent, joyous, peaceful surrender to his initiative.

Ordinarily the scientific and the religious differentiations of consciousness occur in different individuals. But they can be found in the same individual as was the case with Thomas of Aquin. At the end of his life his prayer became so intense that it interfered with his theological activity. But earlier there could have been an alternation between religious and theological differentiation, while later still further differentiation might have enabled him to combine prayer and theology as Teresa of Avila combined prayer and business.

Besides the scientific and the religious there is the scholarly differentiation of consciousness. It combines the common sense of one's own place and time with a detailed understanding of the common sense of another place and time. It is a specifically modern achievement and it results from nothing less than a lifetime of study.

Besides the scientific, the religious, and the scholarly, there is the modern philosophic differentiation. Ancient and medieval philosophers were concerned principally with objects. What differentiation they attained, did not differ from the scientific. But in modern philosophy there has been a sustained tendency to begin, not from objects mediated by 'ordinary' meaning, but from the immediate data of consciousness. In a first phase from Descartes to Kant, the primary focus of attention was cognitional activity. But after the transition, operated by absolute idealism, there was a notable shift in emphasis. Schopenhauer wrote on *Die Welt als Wille und Vorstellung;* Kierkegaard took his stand on faith; Newman took his on conscience; Nietzsche extolled the will to power; Dilthey aimed at a *Lebensphilosophie;* Blondel at a philosophy of action; Scheler was abundant on feeling; and similar tendencies, reminiscent of Kant's emphasis on practical reason, have been maintained by pragmatists, existentialists, personalists.

We have distinguished four differentiations of consciousness: the scientific, the religious, the scholarly, and the modern philosophic. We have noted the possibility of one compound differentiation in which the scientific and the religious were combined in a single individual. But there are five other possibilities of a twofold differentiation,[3] and there are four possibilities of a threefold differentiation.[4] In addition there is one case in which a fourfold differentiation may occur by combining scientific, religious, scholarly, and the modern philosophic differentiation. Similarly, there is a single case of simply undifferentiated consciousness which is at home only in the realm of common sense.

2. PLURALISM AND THEOLOGICAL DOCTRINES

By far the most common type of consciousness is undifferentiated. It is unimpressed by the subtleties of science, the oracles of religion, the oddity of scholarship, the alleged profundity of the current philosophic differentiation.

To teach it or to preach to it, one must use its own language, its own procedures, its own resources. These are not uniform. What is common to common sense is not what it knows but the untaught spontaneity of its manner in coming to know. So there are as many brands of common sense as there are languages, sociocultural differences, almost differences of place or time. The stranger acts strangely because his common sense is not our own.

Hence to preach the gospel to all nations calls for almost as many apostles as there are distinct places and times, and it requires each of them to get to know the people to whom they have been sent, and to catch on to the manner and style and way of their thought and speech. There follows a manifold pluralism, but primarily it is a pluralism not of doctrine but of communications. It remains that within the realm of undifferentiated consciousness there is no communication of doctrine except through the available rituals, narratives, titles, parables, metaphors, modes of praise and blame, of command and prohibition, of promise and threat.

An exception to this last statement must be noted. The educated classes in a society, such as was the Hellenistic, normally are instances of undifferentiated consciousness. But their education had among its sources works of genuine philosophers, so that they could be familiar with logical operations and take propositions as objects on which they reflected and from which they inferred. In this fashion the meaning of *homoousion* for Athanasius was contained in a rule concerning propositions about the Father and the Son: What is true of the Father also is true of the Son, except that the Son is not Father.[5]

Similarly, the meaning of the one person and two natures mentioned in the second paragraph of the decree of Chalcedon, stands forth in the repeated affirmation of the first paragraph, namely, it is one and the same Son our Lord Jesus Christ that is perfect in divinity and the same perfect in humanity, truly God and the same truly man, consubstantial with the Father in his divinity and the same consubstantial with us in his humanity, born of the Father before all ages in his divinity and these last days the same . . . born of the Virgin Mary in his humanity.[6] Now the meaning of this first paragraph can be communicated without the addition of any new technical terms. But it can give rise to reflection and to questions. Only after someone asks whether the divinity is the same as the humanity and, if not, then how can the same be both God and man, is it relevant to explain that a distinction can be drawn between person and nature, that divinity and humanity refer to two natures, that it is one and the same person that is both God and man. Such logical clarification is within the meaning of the decree. But if one goes on to raise the metaphysical question whether person and nature can be really distinct or the anthropological question whether there can be any real distinction between subject and subjectivity,[7] then the issue is being transported from the fifth century to the thirteenth on the metaphysical issue, and to the twentieth on the anthropological issue. One not only steps beyond the context of Chalcedon but also beyond the capacity of undifferentiated consciousness to discover any possible solution.[8]

Turning now to religiously differentiated consciousness, we observe that it can be content with the negations of an apophatic theology. For it is in love, and on its love there are not any reservations or conditions or qualifications. It is with one's whole heart and whole soul and all one's mind and all one's strength. By such love one is oriented positively to what is transcendent in lovableness. Such a positive orientation and the consequent self-surrender, as long as they are operative, enable one to dispense with any intellectual analogy or concept;[9] and when they cease to be operative, the memory of them enables one to be content with enumerations of what God is not.

The Christian however knows God not only through the grace of God in his heart but also through the revelation of God's love in Christ Jesus and the witness to that revelation down the ages through the church. Essential to Christianity is the Christian community which is the carrier of its constitutive meaning and values. So there emerges the function of church doctrines and theological doctrines: the function of explaining and defending the authenticity of the church's witness to the revelation in Christ Jesus.

As already indicated, there was a slight tincture of theoretically differentiated consciousness in the Greek councils. But principally it was in the medieval period that there was undertaken the systematic and collaborative task of reconciling all that had been handed down by the church from the past. A first step was Abelard's *Sic et Non,* in which one hundred and fifty-eight propositions were both proved and disproved by arguments drawn from scripture, the fathers, the councils, and reason.[10] In a second step Gilbert of Porreta used Abelard to define the existence of a question; in this fashion Abelard's *Non* became *Videtur quod non* and his *Sic* became *Sed contra est.* To these were added a general response, in which principles of solution were set forth, and then particular responses to the arguments advanced on either side. A third step was the composition of books of sentences that collected and classified relevant passages from scripture and tradition. A fourth step was the commentaries on books of sentences, in which the technique of the question was employed to reconcile or eliminate contrary views. A fifth step was to obtain a conceptual system that would enable theologians to give coherent solutions to all the questions they raised; and this coherence was sought partly by adopting and partly by adapting the Aristotelian corpus.

Scholastic theology was a monumental achievement. Its influence on the church has been profound and enduring. Up to Vatican II, which preferred a more biblical turn of speech, it has provided much of the background whence proceeded pontifical documents and conciliar decrees. Yet today by and large it is abandoned, and that abandonment leaves the documents and decrees that relied on it almost mute and ineffectual. Such is the contemporary crisis in Catholicism. It is important to indicate why it exists and how it can be overcome.

The Scholastic aim of reconciling differences in statements of

Catholic tradition had one grave defect: it was content with a logically and metaphysically satisfying reconciliation; it did not realize how much of the multiplicity in its inheritance constituted not a logical or a metaphysical but basically a historical problem.

Secondly, the Aristotelian corpus, on which Scholasticism drew for the framework of its solutions, suffers from a number of defects. The *Posterior Analytics* set forth an ideal of science in which the key element is the notion of necessity. On this basis science is said to be of the necessary, while opinion regards the contingent; similarly, wisdom is said to be of the necessary, while prudence regards contingent human affairs. There follows the supremacy of speculative intellect, and this can be buttressed with a verbalism that attributes to common terms the properties of scientific terms. Finally, while man is acknowledged to be a political animal, the historicity of the meanings that inform human living is not grasped, and much less is there understood the possibility of history being scientific.

In contrast, modern mathematics is fully aware that its axioms are not necessary truths but freely chosen and no more than probably consistent postulates.[11] The modern sciences ascertain, not what must be so, but only what is in itself hypothetical and so in need of verification. First principles in philosophy are not just verbal propositions but the *de facto* invariants of human conscious intentionality. What was named speculative intellect now turns out to be merely the operations of experiencing, understanding, and judging, performed under the guidance of the moral deliberation, evaluation, decision, that selects an appropriate method and sees to it that the method is observed. The primacy now belongs to praxis and the task of philosophy is to foster the emergence of authentic human beings. Finally, it is only on the basis of intentionality analysis that it is possible to understand human historicity or to set forth the foundations and criticize the practise of contemporary hermeneutics and critical history.

The defects of Scholasticism, then, were the defects of its time. It could not inspect the methods of modern history and thereby learn the importance of history in theology. It could not inspect modern science and thereby correct the mistakes in Aristotle's conceptual system. But if we cannot blame the Scholastics for their shortcomings, we must undertake the task of remedying them. A theology is the product not only of faith but also of a culture. It is cultural change that has made Scholasticism no longer relevant and demands the development of a new theological method and style, continuous indeed with the old, yet meeting all the genuine exigences both of Christian religion and of up-to-date philosophy, science, and scholarship.

Until that need is met, pluralism will not be exorcized. Undifferentiated consciousness will always want a commonsense theology. Scientifically differentiated consciousness will drift towards secularism. Religiously differentiated consciousness will continue to wobble between empiricism and idealism. But the worthy successor to thirteenth-century achievement will be the fruit of a fivefold differentiated consciousness, in which the workings of common sense, science, scholarship, intentionality analysis, and the life of prayer have been integrated.[12]

3. PLURALISM AND CONVERSION

Conversion involves a new understanding of oneself because, more fundamentally, it brings about a new self to be understood. It is putting off the old man and putting on the new. It is not just a development but the beginning of a new mode of developing. Hence besides the beginning there is to be considered the consequent development. This may be great or average or small. It may be marred by few or by many relapses. The relapses may have been fully corrected, or they may still leave their traces in a bias that may be venial or grave.

Conversion is three-dimensional. It is intellectual inasmuch as it regards our orientation to the intelligible and the true. It is moral inasmuch as it regards our orientation to the good. It is religious inasmuch as it regards our orientation to God. The three dimensions are distinct, so that conversion can occur in one dimension without occurring in the other two, or in two dimensions without occurring in the other one. At the same time the three dimensions are solidary. Conversion in one leads to conversion in the others, and relapse from one prepares for relapse in the others.

By intellectual conversion a person frees himself from confusing the criteria for knowledge of the world of immediacy with the criteria for knowledge of the world mediated by meaning. By moral conversion he becomes motivated primarily not by satisfactions but by values. By religious conversion he comes to love God with his whole heart and his whole soul and all his mind and all his strength; and in consequence he will love his neighbor as himself.

The authentic Christian strives for the fulness of intellectual, moral, and religious conversion. Without intellectual conversion he tends to misapprehend not only the world mediated by meaning but also the word God has spoken within that world. Without moral conversion he tends to pursue not what truly is good but what only apparently is good. Without religious conversion he is radically desolate: in the world without hope and without God (*Eph. 2:12*).

While the importance of moral and religious conversion may readily be granted, hesitation will be felt by many when it comes to intellectual conversion. They will feel it is a philosophic issue and that it is not up to theologians to solve it. But while these contentions are true, they are not decisive. The issue is also existential and methodical. Theologians have minds. They have always used them. They may use them properly and they may use them improperly. Unless they find out the difference for themselves or learn about it from someone else, they will be countenancing a greater pluralism than can be tolerated.

Indeed in my opinion intellectual conversion is essentially simple. It occurs spontaneously when one reaches the age of reason, implicitly drops earlier criteria of reality (Are you awake? Do you see it? Is it heavy? etc.), and proceeds to operate on the criteria of sufficient evidence or sufficient reason. But this spontaneous conversion is insecure. The use of the earlier criteria can recur. It is particularly likely to recur when one gets involved in philosophic issues. For then the objectification of what is meant by sufficient evidence or sufficient reason may become exceedingly complex, while the objectification of taking a good look is simplicity itself. So one becomes a naive realist; if one takes that seriously, one becomes an empiricist; if that proves uncomfortable, one can move on to idealism; then to pragmatism; then to phenomenology. But far less laborious than traveling round that circuit is the task of finding out just what sufficient evidence is. I grant that facing that issue calls for some concentration. But enormously more concentration is needed to explore the philosophies that either neglect sufficient evidence or, on the other hand, propose excessive criteria.

4. THE COHERENCE OF CHRISTIAN TRUTH

Any incoherence in what Christians believe by faith in God is due, not to God, but to their own unauthenticity.

Unauthenticity is overcome by full conversion, that is, not just the initial stages of religious, moral, and intellectual conversion but also the ongoing course of development to which conversion commits one.

That commitment is great indeed. In the second gospel we read:

Then one of the lawyers . . . came forward and asked him, 'Which commandment is first of all?' Jesus answered, 'The first is, "Hear, O Israel: the Lord your God is the only Lord; love the Lord your God with all your heart, with all your soul, with all your mind, and with all your strength." The second is this: "Love your neighbour as yourself." There is no other commandment greater than these, (*Mark 12: 28–31*).

A lecture at the ninth annual Lonergan Workshop, Boston College, June 17, 1982. Published in Italian translation, ''Unità e pluralità: La coerenza della verità cristiana,'' in Karl H. Neufeld, ed., *Problemi e prospettive di teologia dogmatica* (Brescia: Queriniana, 1983), pp. 121–131.

Notes

1. On the Kantian notion of object: very briefly, Lonergan, *Collection,* 1967, p. 208 (in ''Metaphysics as Horizon,'' pp. 202–220); very thoroughly, G. B. Sala, *Das Apriori,* 1971 (above, Ch. 13, note 26).

2. See W. Johnston, *The Mysticism of the Cloud of Unknowing* (above, Ch. 5, note 25); Karl Rahner, *The Dynamic Element in the Church,* tr. by W. J. O'Hara (Quaestiones Disputatae, 12, Freiburg: Herder; Montreal: Palm, 1964), pp. 129–156 (in Ch. 3: ''The Logic of Concrete Individual Knowledge in Ignatius Loyola,'' pp. 84–170).

3. The five are: scientific and scholarly; religious and scholarly; religious and philosophic; scholarly and philosophic; philosophic and scientific.

4. The four are: scientific, religious, and scholarly; scientific, religious and philosophic; scientific, scholarly, and philosophic; religious, scholarly, and philosophic.

5. Athanasius, *Oratio III contra Arianos*, 4: *Patrologia Graeca*, Vol. XXVI, 329A.

6. Denzinger-Schönmetzer, *Enchiridion* (above, Ch. 6, note 41), nos. 381–382.

7. As ontologically Christ is one person in two natures, so psychologically he is one subject with two subjectivities, one divine, one human. See my "Christology Today," above, pp. 90–94.

8. Differentiations of consciousness justify or lead to the discovery of previously unnoticed implications in the sources of revelation.

9. God's gift of his love is the cause of our knowledge of God by connaturality. See Aquinas, *Sum. Theol.*, II-II, q. 45, a. 2 c.

10. *Patrologia Latina*, Vol. CLXXVIII, 1339–1610.

11. Cf. Jean Ladrière, *Les limitations internes des formalismes: Etude sur la signification du théorème de Gödel et des théorèmes apparentés dans la théorie des fondements des mathématiques* (Louvain: E. Nauwelaerts, and Paris: Gauthier-Villars, 1957).

12. Our listing of differentiations of consciousness is not intended to go beyond the needs of this paper.

Index of Biblical References

Index of Names